Praise for *My Body, Their Baby*

"This book provides an expansive Christian vision for surrogacy that bravely probes complex social ethics questions surrounding it. Kao's accessibly articulated and social-justice-oriented guidelines offer a roadmap for decision-making that contributes fresh, thought-provoking analysis to feminist reproductive ethics."

—TRACI C. WEST, Drew University Theological School,
author of *Solidarity and Defiant Spirituality: Africana Lessons
on Religion, Racism, and Ending Gender Violence*

"The world needs more scholars like Grace Kao. With thoughtful rigor and deeply human tenderness, she provides a faithful framework for understanding surrogacy. Her cogent, compassionate arguments illuminate a practice that is often consigned to the shadows, and her work shines with creativity, empathy, and care."

—JEFF CHU, author of *Does Jesus Really Love Me? A Gay
Christian's Pilgrimage in Search of God in America*

"Kao masterfully weaves together personal narrative, exploration of data, and engagement with scholarly sources in an accessible theology of surrogacy that is responsive to its complexities and generous to her interlocutors."

—KENDRA G. HOTZ, Rhodes College, author of *Dust and Breath:
Faith, Health, and Why the Church Should Care about Both*

"Kao's descriptions of her experience as a surrogate succeed in bringing the moral arguments for and against surrogacy into sharper focus. This insightful book shows us how narratives shape our moral visions."

—ALINE KALBIAN, Florida State University, author of *Sex,
Violence, and Justice: Contraception and the Catholic Church*

"This book breaks the ice on Christian feminist reluctance to think about surrogacy. Painstakingly researched and accessibly written, it will not only inspire needed attention to surrogacy but also influence the whole landscape of Christian ethics of reproduction."

—CRISTINA TRAINA, Fordham University, author of *Erotic Attunement: Parenthood and the Ethics of Sensuality between Unequals*

"Drawing on her own experience both as a surrogate and a Christian theologian, Kao makes a powerful and rigorously argued Christian ethical case for surrogacy. An invaluable resource for parents, pastors, and all concerned with reproduction and its ethical implications."

—SUSAN A. ROSS, Loyola University Chicago, author of *Anthropology: Seeking Light and Beauty*

MY BODY, THEIR BABY

ENCOUNTERING TRADITIONS

Rumee Ahmed, Randi Rashkover, and Jonathan Tran, Editors

MY BODY, THEIR BABY

A Progressive Christian Vision for Surrogacy

GRACE Y. KAO

STANFORD UNIVERSITY PRESS
Stanford, California

Stanford University Press
Stanford, California

Printed in the United States of America on acid-free, archival-quality paper

Library of Congress Cataloging-in-Publication Data
Names: Kao, Grace (Grace Y.), author.
Title: My body, their baby : a progressive Christian vision for surrogacy / Grace Y. Kao.
Other titles: Encountering traditions.
Description: Stanford, California : Stanford University Press, 2023. | Series: Encountering traditions | Includes bibliographical references and index.
Identifiers: LCCN 2022045427 (print) | LCCN 2022045428 (ebook) | ISBN 9781503610262 (cloth) | ISBN 9781503635975 (paperback) | ISBN 9781503635982 (ebook)
Subjects: LCSH: Surrogate motherhood—Religious aspects—Christianity. | Surrogate motherhood—Moral and ethical aspects. | Christian ethics. | Feminist ethics.
Classification: LCC HQ759.5 (print) | LCC HQ759.5 (ebook) | DDC 176/.2—dc23/eng/20230503
LC record available at https://lccn.loc.gov/2022045427
LC ebook record available at https://lccn.loc.gov/2022045428

Cover design: Daniel Benneworth-Gray
Cover photograph: Matthew Wiebe on Unsplash
Typeset by Elliott Beard in Minion Pro 10/14

CONTENTS

ACKNOWLEDGMENTS

Much has been made of the analogy that publishing a book is like giving birth to a baby. I'm unclear whether this comparison is more apt or problematic when the book in question is principally about the ethics of giving birth to a baby intended for someone else.

To the extent a finished book requires moving from conception to birth, credit must go to others for the idea of even committing my impromptu reflections about surrogate motherhood to writing. My dear friend and colleague, Jonathan Tran, not only encouraged me to this end, but he went further than others who similarly did by putting me in touch with a publisher, Emily-Jane Cohen, the then-executive editor at Stanford University Press. I'm most grateful to Jonathan for that initial nudge, which occurred when he asked me what was up after seeing my breast pump peeking out of my conference bag, and also for his strategic interventions at critical times after I took his advice.

Special thanks to Emily-Jane Cohen for recognizing this book's potential by signing me to publish in SUP's Encountering Traditions series and for helping me think through how to engage both specialists and a broad readership. When Erica Wetter took up the mantle as executive editor, she graciously read drafts of several chapters and made recommendations on how I might rearrange different parts for maximum impact. Thanks also to former associate editor Faith Wilson Stein who allowed me to take several lengthy extensions after my transition from working in one institutional context to another during the height of the Covid-19 pandemic while helping my school-aged children manage their own pandemic-related disruptions impeded my ability to meet deadlines. Finally, I'm grateful for the ways associate editor Caroline McKusick gave me concrete suggestions about writing style by marking up one draft chapter in particular and then efficiently and judiciously attending to all final things in the last stages of production.

To the extent "it takes a village," including institutional support, to produce both books and babies, there are others beyond the staff at Stanford University Press to whom I owe a debt of gratitude. My home institution, Claremont School of Theology, granted me research leave to make progress on my writing. The anonymous reviewers at the book proposal and manuscript stage gave me helpful feedback; I have no doubt this book in its final form is all the better for it and hope they will see their influence on the revisions I made. I have also had the good fortune of presenting earlier portions of this book to several audiences.

My firsthand reflections on surrogate motherhood and constructive framework of ethical principles for surrogacy is something I first sketched out as a trial balloon in a paper at the Society of Christian Ethics. I thank my many attendees there for their keen interest and thoughtful questions—something I honestly did not know if I would receive given the controversial nature of this topic. Thanks also to the JSCE for permission here to expand upon my ideas first published there: Grace Y. Kao, "Toward a Feminist Christian Vision of Gestational Surrogacy," *Journal of the Society of Christian Ethics* Volume 39, Issue 1 (2019):161–179, https://doi.org/10.5840/jsce20194228.

My faculty colleagues and graduate students in the Department of Theological Studies at Loyola Marymount University in my first year as visiting professor also thoughtfully attended yet another meeting on Zoom in the first year of the pandemic when nearly everything was virtual and offered constructive feedback when I presented an earlier version of material that is now split across chapters 4 and 5. I thank Roberto Dell'Oro who issued a challenging critique in his role as respondent and both Eric Haruki Swanson and Anna Harrison for convening our theology colloquium.

Rita Nakashima Brock and Benny Liew invited me to contribute to a *festschrift* for Kwok Pui Lan and later present it at a session at the 2021 American Academy of Religion. I took the occasion to apply Pui Lan's earlier suggestions for methodology in Asian American Christian ethics when she earlier served on a panel for my co-edited, eponymously titled anthology (*Asian*

American Christian Ethics). Her counsel to draw more from the most creative and subversive voices in the literature beyond Western canonical classics, to take inspiration from the distinctive methodological choices and ethical insights from other racial-ethnic minoritized scholars and communities, and to start more self-consciously with lived experiences (not theory) not only shaped the chapter I wrote in her honor, but key choices I have made in this book. Thanks also to Claremont Press for permission to build upon that publication here: Grace Y. Kao, "Rethinking Surrogacy from an Asian American Christian Ethical Perspective," *Theologies of the Multitude for the Multitudes: The Legacy of Kwok Pui-lan*, eds. Rita Nakashima Brock and Tat-siong Benny Liew, 271–292 (Claremont, CA: Claremont Press, 2021).

Finally, the participants of the Political Theology Network's Summer Virtual Workshops also put aside a portion of their summer vacation to review an earlier version of my reflections on commercial, transnational, and traditional surrogacy. I give thanks to my respondent, Sam Shuman, for helping to kickstart a lively discussion about feminist ethics, queerness, gendered language about pregnancy, and the ways surrogacy both reinforces traditional notions of the family and subverts them. Thanks especially to workshop facilitators Mary Nickel and Kathy Chow who warmly invited me to present as a way for us to reflect on the use of autoethnography as method.

Many other friends and colleagues helped me in informal ways to develop lines of argumentation in this book. Longtime activist Toni Bond first introduced me to the reproductive justice framework, and my approach to reproductive issues has not been the same since. Christian Iosso who was formerly the coordinator of the Advisory Committee on Social Witness Policy (ACSWP) of the Presbyterian Church (U.S.A.) supplied me with documents and resolutions from our denomination that has grounded my progressive Christian vision of surrogacy. Kate Ott provided suggestions for how best to discuss and disclose what surrogacy involves to young kids. My understanding of and thinking about adoption has been greatly aided by several generative exchanges I have had with Darlene Fozard Weaver. One extended late night conversation with John Berkman years ago not only influenced my thinking about surrogacy in light of other possibilities, real or science fiction (e.g., the use of artificial wombs), but also showed me how kind fellow Christian ethicists can be even when their commitments and baseline assumptions lead them to draw totally opposite conclusions. I also turned to Cristie Traina for advice about the risks of publishing on surrogacy while working at Christian institutions and to both Toddie Peters and Scott Paeth on how I might move from a stand-alone article to a book on the topic.

Finally, since my book's argument draws heavily from my personal experience as a surro-mom, I especially want to thank a host of friends for their support and friendship throughout my surrogacy journey: Irene Oh, Elizabeth Bucar, Toddie Peters, Anna Jackson, Jack Jackson, Duane Bidwell, Karee Galloway, Monica A. Coleman, Najeeba Syeed, Susan Lai, and Stephen Williams. Because of them, I had people in my life to confide in and process my feelings about different aspects of the long and uncertain surrogacy process both before we were public with the news and well after journey's end. They also supported me in meaningful and practical ways during my longer than anticipated postpartum recovery period.

I dedicate this book to my spouse, Nathaniel Walker, for all the ways he did those things and makes possible the abundant life we share together; my children—PJ and KC Walker—in whom I take sheer delight as their mother; and my two good friends whose child we collaboratively brought to life. May their daughter continue to flourish and may her very existence bear witness to the truth that all things are possible with God.

MY BODY, THEIR BABY

INTRODUCTION

IN THE WANING WEEKS OF my third pregnancy, when my shape even under billowy summer dresses served as a telltale sign of my condition, I could no longer run into an acquaintance, colleague, or student without having an exchange that would go something like this:

"Wow, Grace [or Dr. Kao]—I didn't know you were expecting! When are you due?"

"October 1."

"Congrats! Do you know what you're having?"

"Thanks! Yes, it's a girl. But here's the thing—I'm actually carrying my friends' baby, not my own."

The eyes of whomever I was talking to would usually then widen with shock. After all, I was forty years old at that time and a married, middle-class Taiwanese American tenured professor with two kids—hardly the stereotype of someone who bears children for others. How my conversation partners would then respond would vary.

Most would pay me some sort of compliment: "How generous of you!" "That's amazing!" "What a gift!" Others would struggle to process what they'd just heard—"You mean you're a surrogate?" Through their indirect questions, I could tell most were also curious whether the baby was genetically mine or how my unusual arrangement with my friends even came to be.

Many of my women interlocutors would first register surprise like the others and then imaginatively place themselves in a parallel situation. They would blurt out "Wow, I could never do *that*" before narrating how difficult their pregnancy, labor and delivery, or postpartum experiences had been or why they couldn't imagine undergoing all that it takes to bring a child into the world for someone else.

Through these exchanges, I even came to learn something I hadn't known previously—how surrogacy had been a live option for others. Four women took the occasion of my pregnancy to disclose to me that they, too, had once contemplated carrying a child for a loved one, but ultimately didn't go through with it for one reason or another. Two others reacted in a way suggesting they had at least considered surrogacy in their long road to parenthood. A good friend with a school-aged child and a sad history of miscarriages reacted to my news in partial jest: "Grace, I didn't know you were available!" One of my oldest son's coaches exclaimed "Why couldn't we have met four years ago when we needed you?" before recounting the ordeal his wife and he had endured of several rounds of in vitro fertilization (IVF) and several miscarriages before adopting their daughter overseas.

My visibly pregnant body and one-sentence mention of my carrying a baby for my friends had been enough to induct me into a society I had scarcely known existed. It was a world where fertility problems were freely told and shared and where people found themselves strangely moved—even flooded with tears—upon hearing scant details about our story. Years later while researching this book, I came to understand that these reactions were par for the course. In the words of Elizabeth Kane, America's first contractually paid surrogate mother: "Infertility isn't exactly cocktail party talk, but as soon as anyone finds out the details of my pregnancy, they feel free to tell me the most intimate . . . details of their lives."[1]

———

I know from personal experience and my work as an ethicist that surrogacy as a way of bringing children into the world is not something the public feels indifferent about. Some people marvel at what modern medicine makes possible while others are aghast at this use of science to "play God." Some people lavish praise on persons like me who become pregnant for others out of a desire to help them while other people feel pity and revulsion for anyone who would perform such metaphorical and literal labor for money. Some people sympathize with couples who cannot bear children of their own while others judge them for hiring surrogates to endure significant health risks on their behalf, when in those critics' minds, such couples should "just adopt."

While statistically the least common and most contested method of family expansion,[2] surrogacy is nonetheless on the rise. Singles and couples who are involuntarily childless, facing secondary infertility (i.e., they cannot become pregnant or carry to term after previously giving birth), or in a same-sex relationship are increasingly commissioning others to bear children for them while many nations across the world are clamping down on the practice. But what explains this escalating usage and why are opponents agitating for tougher regulations or even total prohibitions on what critics have derisively called "outsourcing" pregnancy? How do surrogates like me actually feel about birthing babies for others and how do they and the children they bear ultimately fare?

With *My Body, Their Baby*, I help readers sort through these and other questions while advancing the moral permissibility—even moral good—of this reproductive technique when conducted under certain parameters. I intersperse reflections on the time I spent carrying and delivering a child for my friends, Katie and Steven,[3] with the research amassed on other families expanded by "collaborative reproduction"[4] to offer readers something more than an academic treatise on a contested topic. In the following pages, I offer my firsthand account and scholarly assessment of surrogate motherhood for anyone who has ever struggled with infertility, pondered what it would be like to hand over a baby to someone else to raise, or attempted to sort out the moral parameters of this "brave new world" of reproductive medicine.

As someone who identifies as a feminist and progressive Christian, I have also written *My Body, Their Baby* in a way that especially engages those who are feminist but not necessarily Christian, those who are Christian but not necessarily feminist, and those who, like me, claim both sets of identities and commitments.

Feminists have long been divided on surrogacy. Some welcome it and other assisted reproductive technology (ART) for allowing individuals to exert more control over their own fertility and thus exercise greater bodily autonomy. Others oppose the practice for exploiting, commodifying, and objectifying women's bodies and/or children: they liken paying women to bear children for others to reproductive prostitution, human trafficking, or both. Some feminists also worry about surrogacy's implications for the abortion debate and potential to exacerbate tensions between and among persons of different races or social classes. Other feminists believe these dangers to be exaggerated and resent the paternalism they detect in critics' assumptions that women cannot—or should not—be trusted to make their own informed decisions about their own reproductive lives, be it to terminate a pregnancy or to undertake one for someone else. What is clearly in dispute is whether surrogacy as a social practice is good or bad for women (and others capable of pregnancy) overall and is therein compatible with, or contrary to, the central aims of the feminist movement.

Christians likewise do not hold one unified position on surrogacy, just as they differ among themselves on many other social issues. Catholics in conformity with the *Magisterium*, the teaching authority of the Catholic Church, condemn all practices separating the unitive from the procreative ends of marriage (i.e., that detach sex from reproduction) in contravention of the natural law. Many conservative evangelical Protestants and Orthodox Christians appeal more to the Bible than to reason or nature to ground similar protests against surrogacy for the all-too-common destruction of embryos during the IVF process typically involved and for deviating too far from their understanding of the biblical ideal of a heterosexual married couple bearing children together as the fruit of conjugal love. Progressive mainline Protestants, however, generally respond more favorably to advancements in reproductive medicine for providing an additional pathway beyond adoption for infertile married couples to still realize one of the three traditional goods of marriage: offspring (*bonum prolis*). To wit: several mainline Protestant denominations, including my ecclesial home—the Presbyterian Church (U.S.A.)—have endorsed the responsible use of IVF and other ART while urging caution and further study on surrogacy.

The central argument of *My Body, Their Baby* is that surrogacy need not betray core feminist or progressive Christian ideals when pursued under certain conditions. Against opponents of ART who extol the moral superiority of adoption or lament surrogacy's division of motherhood into its component parts, I show how collaborative reproduction can be an ethically justified way of bringing children into the world if the members of any arrangement proceed justly with great care. But beyond simply parrying popular objections, I offer a positive vision where surrogacy could be a thing of beauty and advance certain commitments progressive Christians already profess as holding, including a view of children as a traditional good or end of marriage for those who have discerned a vocation to parenthood, the removal of barriers for same-sex couples to head families as per the logic of "marriage equality," and respect for the conscientious decisions persons capable of pregnancy make about reproductive matters affecting their own bodies and families.

As a work of Christian ethics, this book offers a positive vision and framework of seven principles for surrogacy to protect the well-being of all members involved that are grounded upon the four traditional sources of Christian ethics: Scripture, tradition, reason or secular sources of knowledge, and experience. More specifically, my account builds upon selected *biblical* themes and concepts, including covenant, vocation, and fidelity, and from *traditions* of progressive Christianity, including several mainline Protestant denominational positions on sex, marriage, family, and science and technology. The *reason* or secular sources of knowledge I turn to include international human rights; professional medical societies' ethics committee opinions on assisted reproduction; and the reproductive justice framework which was founded by Black activists in the mid-1990s and developed further by a broader coalition of women of color when they judged the reigning "pro-choice" platform insufficiently attentive to their realities. Finally, the *experiences* I draw upon include my having jointly brought a baby girl to life with my friends and the reproductive journeys of other "surrogacy triads" as documented in the ethnographic and social scientific literature: other persons who have become pregnant for others, other parents who have opted for this method of ART after considering all possible avenues to parenthood, and the surrogate-born children themselves.

This fourth source of moral wisdom—experience—is a connecting point between Christian ethics and feminist methodology. I argue for certain kinds of lived experiences, namely those of former surrogates like me and of others who have had at least one pregnancy resulting in a live birth (a common prerequisite for surrogate motherhood), to be regarded as "epistemically transformative"[5] and thus carry greater normative weight in applied ethical debates involving pregnancy, including any pregnancies undertaken for others. The point in surfacing my and other surrogates' experiences as studied in the social scientific research is to call upon anyone ambivalent about or opposed to the practice to actually listen to the stories of those who have entered into these reproductive agreements with others. I also mine the perspectives of persons not always at the forefront of discussions about family formation— same-sex couples—with an eye for showing why surrogacy for an increasing number is their first choice (in contrast to it nearly always being the last resort for infertile heterosexual couples) and how queer families have always had to involve someone outside of their marriage or committed partnership to become parents: a known or unidentified gamete donor, a surrogate, or a birth mother in an adoption scenario. It is my hope the witness of queer families will give readers a more expansive—and thus accurate—understanding of surrogacy while simultaneously being of special interest to all couples exploring alternative paths to parenthood when natural conception is foreclosed to them. May my friends' and my experiences and those of others disrupt persistent myths about the practice, including widespread fears that any given surrogate's post-birth handover of the child will be emotionally distressing because all pregnant women via the maternal instinct will have grown attached to the life developing inside of them.

Today, many persons among the general public beyond self-identified feminists or Christians are grappling with what to make of the social practice of prospective parents commissioning a third party to bear their child. When I ask my students what comes to mind when they think of surrogacy, just as many rattle off celebrities who have proudly announced the birth of their surrogate-born babies—singer Elton John! model Tyra Banks! actress Nicole Kidman! reality TV star Kim Kardashian! broadcast journalist Anderson Cooper!—as they describe dystopian nightmares of an underclass of "breeders" gestating the offspring of the elite, such as in novelist Margaret Atwood's *The Handmaid's Tale* (1985) and the book's adaptation into an award-winning TV show on a popular streaming service. Decades ago in the 1980s, the public struggled with the then-new reality of "test-tube babies," though in vitro fertilization has long since been medically, if not socially, normalized in many quarters as the estimated eight million people in the world born through IVF since the first IVF-conceived baby, Louise Joy Brown, was born on July 25, 1978, in Great Britain attests. Will surrogacy, which requires IVF in the preponderance of cases, follow a similar trajectory of moving from widespread controversy to measured acceptance and increased usage? While *that* is an empirical question, the more pertinent one for ethics is whether it *should*. In *My Body, Their Baby*, I respond with a conditional "yes."

Outline of the Book

The argument of my book proceeds in steps. To assist readers, I begin with a primer: I explain surrogacy's logistics in chapter 1 while contextualizing my own surrogate motherhood in California against the wider landscape of surrogacy customs, trends, and laws across the globe. To clear the conceptual underbrush for my constructive vision and framework for the practice, I discuss in the next two chapters what about surrogacy most troubles three discrete but overlapping sets of commentators—feminists, Christians, and members of the general public—while also connecting their concerns to my loved ones' reservations about my carrying and delivering my friends' baby girl. I also fold in key findings from the scholarly literature on families expanded by collaborative reproduction so readers can better grasp what surrogacy is like and thus judge for themselves which of those fears are substantiated by the data—and which are not. Where relevant, I also compare surrogacy through-out this book to other morally laden social practices: I show how premedita-tively birthing babies for others is both similar to and different from placing children for adoption, having an abortion, donating or selling body parts (namely, gametes, live organs, hair, blood, plasma, breastmilk), negotiating and signing a prenuptial agreement, or partaking in other labor involving physical and psychosocial risks, including sex work.

The constructive heart of *My Body, Their Baby* lies in the next section of the book. In chapter 4, I argue for the practice's moral permissibility—and even beauty—when willing persons extend reproductive hospitality to cou-ples who long for a child but lack a suitable uterus between them to birth one into the world. Because there are different types of surrogacy arrangements, I first clarify the conditions surrounding the type initially under consider-ation, including the surrogacy being gestational (not traditional), altruistic (not commercial), and intrastate (not cross-border). I spend the remainder of the chapter describing how the four traditional sources of Christian ethics bear upon my argument and then connect my vision with extant progressive Christian ideals. Finally, I provide in chapter 5 a framework of seven norms and principles to guide members of surrogacy triads in their discernment and relationships with one another *and* the general public in their posture toward the arrangements of others. These are (1) discernment without haste, (2) cov-enant before contract, (3) empathy, care, and stewardship, (4) medical self-determination, (5) disclosure, not secrecy, (6) "trust women," and (7) social justice.

In my final chapter, I critically assess different kinds of surrogacies where not all of these simplifying conditions obtain, such as when there is financial payment above expenses (profit), the interaction of two or more sets of laws due to the surrogate and intended parents residing in different jurisdictions, and/or the involvement of a surrogate's genetic (not just gestational) contri-bution. I then describe the challenges these more ethically and sometimes logistically complex arrangements raise before recommending ways to structure them to meet the moral baseline. Both in this chapter and in my opening primer, I seek to correct popular, but overly simplistic, characterizations about the practice, such as fears that surrogacy when racially understood is mostly a matter of white intended parents hiring women of color or from the Global South or that transnational surrogacy is mostly a matter of "reproductive tourists" looking to save money by traveling overseas to cheaper destinations.

A Few Disclaimers

Five disclaimers are now in order about how I will proceed in the remainder of the book.

First, when discussing a couple's possible use of the sperm or eggs of an unknown genetic parent to create embryo(s) to be transferred into their surrogate, I will use the terminology of "non-identified" donation or "non-identified" donors. Though it is much more common for ordinary people to speak and write about "anonymous" sperm or egg donation and "anonymous" sperm or egg donors, several medical societies have encouraged this "transition in language" to reflect our emerging global reality of a decrease in anonymity. There has not only been a rise of direct-to-consumer DNA testing and their large ancestry databases exposing long-held family secrets, but also an uptick in bans on anonymous gamete donation across the world, including in one state in the U.S. starting in 2025—Colorado.[6]

Second, I will commonly refer to persons who can undergo a pregnancy or donate eggs as "women," follow convention in calling such persons gestational or genetic "mothers," and use "she/her/hers" pronouns when describing them. I do so because at the time of this writing, there are no published cases of surrogates who have not identified as women and because popular and scholarly objections to surrogacy are often couched in the language of protecting vulnerable *women* and children from harm. Still, readers should know that some persons who can either become pregnant or donate their eggs (apart from surrogacy) do not identify as women but as men or transgender men and thus use different pronouns (he/him/his/they/their/theirs) and different referents (father or parent).[7] Because there is wisdom in beginning to alter our gendered ways of thinking, talking, or writing about surrogates in advance of the reality of trans or nonbinary persons bearing children for others, I will also vary my usage and make references to pregnant *persons* (not just women) as well.

Third, I mostly write about intended parents (IPs) in the plural while acknowledging that a minority who commission others to bear their children are not coupled but single. I remember watching news coverage about Latin popstar Ricky Martin becoming a father for the first time to his surrogate-born twin boys while he was reportedly single. Someone my nephew looks up to, the soccer superstar Cristiano Ronaldo, also became a father for the first time to his surrogate-born son and years later to his surrogate-born twins while he was reportedly single before later having more children with his girlfriend.[8] Still, my reference to plural, not singular, IPs is connected to the empirical reality that the majority of persons who turn to surrogates are romantically partnered with an intention to co-parent. It is also supported by my assumption in my progressive Christian vision and framework for surrogacy that the parents-to-be are in a marital or otherwise committed relationship.

Fourth, I will regard the terms "surrogate mother" or "surrogate" to mean anyone who agrees in advance to carry and deliver a baby for someone else to raise, regardless of their genetic relation (or lack thereof) to that child. I do so not only to follow social convention, but also because those who perform these maternal functions for others frequently self-identify as surrogates, surrogate mothers, or more colloquially as "surro-moms" or even "surros." Still, readers should know that this terminology is contested in some quarters. As I will unpack further in chapter 2, some radical feminists criticize it for obfuscating exactly who is doing the substituting: they contend that a woman who gestates and births a child for someone else has done everything thus far a mother at that stage in the child's life could have done, which is why she should be regarded as the *real* (not substitute) mother while the person who intends to raise the child thereafter should be viewed as the (true) surrogate. Without malice, persons in the medical community sometimes restrict "surrogate mother" to refer only to a "traditional surrogate"—a woman who is the gestational and genetic mother of a child intended for others. They thus use "gestational carrier" to describe a woman like me who has borne or will bear a genetically unrelated child for someone else. Others in the medical community might also call a woman or trans man in a queer couple who undergoes "reciprocal IVF"[9] and gestates the resultant embryo formed by their partner's oocytes and sperm (from a third party) a "gestational carrier" since, from a medical point of view, they must undergo the same IVF and heterologous embryo transfer process as gestational surrogates must to become pregnant.

For the purposes of this book, however, I will *not* be considering them "surrogate mothers" because they would not be gestating a baby for someone else—they would be carrying and delivering a child for themselves (they and their spouse or partner) to raise in their newly expanded family.

Fifth and finally, my personal experience as a surrogate is inextricably connected to my friends' (Katie and Steven's) struggle to become first-time parents and my family of four's ongoing relationships with their happy family of three. There are portions of our shared story, however, that I am not at liberty to tell. In the pages that follow, I narrate key moments of our journey *as I have lived and reflected upon them* without speaking for my friends. I also omit some details about our collaborative reproduction to preserve their and their child's privacy as befitting a book entitled *My Body, Their Baby*.

1   A PRIMER ON SURROGACY: LOGISTICS, LAWS, AND TRENDS

THERE WAS ONLY ONE BRIGHT pink line—one short vertical line, instead of the two I had been counting on seeing. I had been taking home pregnancy tests every morning for the past several days, and the results were the same—I was still not pregnant. *But how could that be?* In the days following my embryo transfer (ET), hadn't I experienced nearly identical symptoms as I had years ago when expecting my own boys: dizziness when rising too quickly, tenderness in my breasts, and even an altered, metallic taste in my mouth (dysgeusia)? Weren't the two embryos we had transferred rated "high quality"? Hadn't my reproductive endocrinologist complimented me on my "beautiful uterus" at every check-up and told us my uterine lining had expanded to the optimal thickness for the transfer?

I was astounded that neither of the two embryos had "stuck" after all the work we had done over the past several weeks in preparation. On my end I had taken three different pills three times a day. Timed my meals with the somewhat nasty tasting progesterone lozenges I had to place underneath my tongue three times a day on an empty stomach. Conscripted my husband to administer all of my estrogen injections every third day so I could avoid having to see, much less handle, those large-gauge needles. Even taken artificial hormones vaginally three times a day with a tampon-like applicator. Like many others undergoing in vitro fertilization (IVF), I had also felt bloated and more tired than usual. I had even gained some weight—something that caught me by surprise until my hematologist-oncologist friend scanned the ingredients in one of my IVF meds one day and told me he prescribes something similar for patients who need to pack on the pounds after experiencing sudden, cancer-induced weight loss.

After several mornings of peeing on a stick and seeing only one bright pink line, I faced a dilemma: should I tell Katie and Steven about my "big fat negative" since I had previously shared with them my excitement about really feeling pregnant? Or would alerting them only increase their anxiety, since home pregnancy tests are prone to give false negatives if taken too early and are otherwise less reliable than blood tests? In concluding I had an obligation to tell since I had earlier raised their hopes of implantation success, I decided to let them know.

By the time the lab confirmed what I had already known, I had already begun feeling simultaneously betrayed by my own body for having given me such a powerful experience of a faux pregnancy and awed by the powers of modern science for having enabled such mimicry. My friends who did not have this experience of bodily duplicity, but were nonetheless counting on reproductive technology to bring them good news, were understandably devastated. To their credit, they never once made me feel badly about implantation failure, and I never blamed myself either since I had followed all instructions to a T.

Months later, I experienced the same strong pregnancy-like symptoms after our second transfer. This time, however, I had learned not to get my—or their—hopes up prematurely, so I didn't tell Katie and Steven about them. I'll never forget how elated I felt upon finally seeing two bright pink lines on my test early one Saturday morning before leaving to spend the day on the slopes as a parent chaperone for my kids' youth snowboarding program. Three days later, the lab confirmed I was indeed pregnant. I felt utterly confident my friends' ten-year saga with infertility would soon be over, though it was still mind-boggling to me that it would be my then-forty-year-old body that would help give them renewed hope.

———

When my husband (Nathaniel) and I formally entered into a surrogacy agreement with Katie and Steven in the summer of 2015, none of us had realized we had become part of a fast-growing trend: surrogacy in the U.S. had more than doubled in the last decade and increased by nearly 1,000% worldwide in a shorter time frame.[1] Our arrangement was what is conventionally called altruistic (versus commercial), meaning they did not pay me to carry their child beyond reimbursements for pregnancy-related expenses. My friends who had been yearning for a child would be described by industry insiders as the commissioning, contracting, intended, or social parents depending on where they were in the process: commissioning, contracting, or intended prior to childbirth and social thereafter. Because we knew one another beforehand, we did what is called an independent (versus agency) arrangement and found the professionals we needed to complete all steps instead of using a broker to coordinate them.

What we went through—and what the vast majority of surrogates and intended parents (IPs) go through today—differs markedly from surrogacy practices of yore. Because the baby was not genetically related to me, my surrogacy was gestational (versus traditional, genetic, or partial), which meant I had to get pregnant through science. However, when infertile couples in antiquity turned to surrogacy as a last-ditch attempt to bear progeny as per the tragic story of Abram-Sarai-Hagar-Ishmael in Genesis 16 and 21, those were traditional (versus gestational or full) arrangements. The surrogate was thus also the biogenetic mother and could only become pregnant through intercourse—however consensual—with the intended father (IF) until artificial insemination for humans was popularized in the mid-twentieth century. After the advent of IVF allowed for conception to take place outside of a woman's body and resulted in a live birth for the first time in 1978, gestational surrogacy became a technical possibility. In the years after Shannon Boff, the "world's first fetal baby-sitter," bore a genetically unrelated child in Michigan on April 13, 1986, gestational surrogacy eclipsed traditional surrogacy in usage.[2]

These and other advances have allowed countless persons who cannot bear a child without medical assistance to become first-time parents. While accurate numbers are impossible to obtain given imprecise tracking, a lack of mandated reporting in many jurisdictions apart from other assisted reproductive technology (ART) procedures,[3] and nondisclosure due to fear of social criticism or of punishment due to illegality in some contexts, an estimated several thousand children worldwide are born annually through surrogacy. These persons include HIV-positive gay male couples through the Special Program on Assisted Reproduction (SPAR) who, since 1998, have been able to bear genetically related children without transmitting the virus. Though rarer still, they also include postmenopausal grandmothers who have birthed their own biological grandchildren. The world's oldest surro-mom at the time of this writing is a sixty-seven-year-old woman from Greece named Anastassia Ontou who delivered her own granddaughter via C-section after her daughter, the baby's genetic and intended mother (IM), had endured seven failed pregnancy attempts.[4] In a different part of the world where surrogacy is "de facto banned," the one known doctor in Japan who performs surrogate births, Dr. Yahiro Netsu, has helped at least five grandmothers bear their own biological grandchildren since his first announced surrogate birth in 2001, with his oldest being a sixty-one-year-old grandmother who successfully bore her own daughter's child.[5] When commenting in an interview on the social stigma and medical establishment's disapproval of surrogacy in Japan, Dr. Netsu once said, "All I ask for is a society in which people can live complementing each other's weaknesses and consoling each other."[6]

In the rest of this chapter, I offer an overview of surrogacy for readers unfamiliar with the practice or industry: I describe what it involves medically and logistically, provide a snapshot of diverse laws and customs in the U.S. and across the world, and attempt to explain surrogacy's surging popularity. To transcend purely clinical explanations, I also draw throughout upon my journey of bearing a child for my friends in the State of California—the jurisdiction widely characterized as the surrogacy capital of the world.

What Happens Medically

The process of surrogacy today involves a series of coordinated steps, with details varying depending on the type of arrangement, fertility clinic protocol, policies of the surrogacy agency or charity (if used), and the jurisdiction(s) involved.

TRADITIONAL SURROGACY

Traditional surrogates require relatively few steps to get pregnant. While sexual intercourse was the only way possible for millennia, today most patients undergo artificial insemination wherein a doctor inserts sperm directly into their cervix, uterus, or fallopian tube following ovulation. To be sure, some traditional surrogates elect to inseminate themselves outside of a clinical setting such as their home or have one of the intended parents or another party do it.

GESTATIONAL SURROGACY

Getting Pregnant

Gestational surrogates like me must become pregnant through a more time-intensive, invasive, and costly series of steps involving IVF and heterologous embryo transfer (HET). Whether the intended parents are creating new embryos or using cryopreserved ones from previous cycles, the IVF process of embryo creation involves the same basic steps. First, eggs must be retrieved from either an intended mother or someone else (a donor) and then fertilized in a test tube or culture dish in a laboratory with sperm from an intended father or donor. After any resultant embryos have incubated for three or five days,[7] one or more (determined by prior agreement) are transferred into the surrogate's uterus using a syringe with a flexible catheter at the end and usually also an abdominal ultrasound to guide the reproductive endocrinologist's placement. As I was instructed to do so, the surrogate will also normally have followed a detailed regimen of hormones and other fertility drugs for approximately one month prior to the transfer to suppress ovulation and to prepare their uterus for implantation.

Surrogates and intended parents often experience a bundle of emotions on the day of the transfer, and the former may be advised to take antianxiety medication or undergo relaxation therapy beforehand (e.g., breathing exercises, guided meditation). The surrogate's ability to be as calm and relaxed as possible is believed to be of medical, not just psychological, benefit because hormones released under stress such as adrenaline can cause their uterus to contract, thus potentially impairing their reproductive endocrinologist's precision. My IPs had asked if I wanted to get acupuncture on the day of the procedure—a popular complementary therapy among IVF patients. But I declined because I did not anticipate feeling nervous but could foresee becoming so if I had to add one more unfamiliar (and in my mind, not scientifically proven) treatment to my list of things to do.[8]

Most surrogates experience the embryo transfer as a relatively quick and only mildly uncomfortable procedure—one resembling a pap smear. The worst part for me was our fertility clinic's requirement that I begin with a full bladder to enhance the doctor's visualization of my uterus for better alignment of the catheter, with the pressure on my bladder compounding as he moved the abdominal ultrasound probe around. In each of my two transfer attempts, only one other guest was permitted to be with me. We arranged it so one IP drove me to and from my appointment, watched the procedure on the ultrasound video screen in the room with me, and kept me company during the agonizing thirty minutes wait following the transfer when I was still not permitted to void but had to hold it while laying still on the exam table.

The IVF with HET is complete once the lab confirms all embryos meant for transfer have been deposited (i.e., a technician examines the catheter under a microscope). Depending again on protocol, we surrogates might be released with specific instructions of modified bed rest (i.e., to limit or re-strict physical activity without needing to be confined in bed) for some time thereafter: forty-eight hours per my doctor's orders, but other doctors may prescribe longer or shorter periods.[9] Likely the next time a surrogate will see their reproductive endocrinologist again will be to test for pregnancy.

In between the ET and the scheduled pregnancy test, the surrogate and IPs must undergo what is known colloquially as the "two week wait." Many IVF patients and IPs find this period to be excruciating—perhaps the most difficult part of any IVF cycle—as they remain cautiously hopeful for implan-tation success given all they have invested into achieving a pregnancy while also preparing themselves for reproductive failure, given a likely history of disappointment on this score if the IPs have long suffered from infertility. In contrast, most surrogates have been conditioned by their more positive repro-ductive history to expect success instead, just as I did in our first attempt. If one or more embryos implant, the surrogate will attend frequent check-ups with their reproductive endocrinologist involving physical exams, blood and urine tests, and ultrasounds while maintaining her IVF meds regimen before being discharged around the second trimester mark to regular ob/gyn care. Because IVF pregnancies are considered higher-risk for preterm birth, low birth rate, multiple gestation, and assorted pregnancy-induced complications due to advanced maternal age (AMA) of the genetic mother, gestational sur-rogates often see perinatologists or maternal-fetal medicine specialists as well, as I was directed to do so. If there is no confirmation of pregnancy, the IPs and surrogate must decide whether and when to begin another attempt, as the entire process of IVF medications for the surrogate (and perhaps embryo creation for the IPs if none remain) would have to be repeated if so. Though my contract with Katie and Steven only specified one embryo transfer attempt and we agreed we would determine later what next steps, if any, to take, if I didn't get pregnant after our first attempt, it was a "no-brainer" for me that we should try again: Katie and Steven still had embryos left and I didn't want all the work we had already done to be for naught if they were to end up childless.

Making Other IVF Decisions

The above is what gestational surrogacy involves on the medical front. Embedded within those steps are at least five other major medical decisions the IPs, as all IVF patients, must make. First, they must decide *genetic parentage*. For example, a gay couple must determine which of them will contribute the sperm and whether they will obtain the eggs from a known or non-identified donor and then from whom or where (i.e., which person or egg bank?). Second, they must resolve questions about *embryo creation and storage*, such as whether they will attempt to fertilize all their eggs and store any frozen embryos left for potential future use or only create the number of embryos they wish to transfer immediately and freeze any remaining eggs. Third and fourth, they must decide *how many embryos they will transfer at one time* and *which ones*, with this latter question requiring them first to either pursue or decline preimplantation diagnostic testing (PDT) to help them decide. Finally, they must resolve *what they will do with any excess embryos* once they have completed IVF, with common options being to destroy or allow them to die, donate them to research, donate them to another couple for another chance to be born, or to continue to keep them in cryopreserved storage due to indecision. All told, how IVF patients will determine these five matters will normally be influenced by nonmedical considerations as well: the degree of importance either of the IPs attach to being genetically related to their child, their willingness or ability to undergo another IVF cycle if they are not successful with this one, their openness to bringing a child into the world with fetal anomalies given statistical risks and probabilities, and their beliefs about the moral status of embryos—or at least how those the IPs have created or otherwise have custody over ought to be treated.

What collaborative reproduction does is add complexity to the IVF decision-making process. If the intended parents opt to use fresh (versus frozen) eggs for fertilization upon retrieval, the surrogate must synchronize her cycle with the genetic mother's (usually by birth control pills or other hormones), so as to prepare her uterine lining to receive the embryo(s) at the proper stage of embryonic development. If the parties collectively decide to transfer more than one embryo at a time in the hopes of increasing their chances at implantation success while reducing the time and money needed for another IVF cycle should this attempt fail, they would simultaneously be increasing the risks of multiple gestation (i.e., the presence of two or more embryos in the uterus) which holds dangers for both the surrogate and the

IPs' future child(ren).[10] Even the IPs' decision about *how* they will determine which embryo(s) to transfer may have implications for the outcome of the pregnancy and, thus, the surrogate's experience. Since the presence of chromosomal abnormalities is a leading cause of implantation failure and miscarriage, most fertility clinics conduct embryo grading as a routine part of IVF. At additional cost, the IPs could elect to discover even more information about their embryos through preimplantation genetic testing (PGT) to screen for extra or missing copies of chromosomes (e.g., Down syndrome) or to detect the presence of single-gene disorders (e.g., cystic fibrosis).

Making embryo transfer decisions based on predicted embryonic traits raises questions about the moral status of embryos, the parental good or right of preventing the birth of children projected to have certain congenital impairments, the quality of life of persons living with particular disabilities, and whether some uses of PGT—designed for prospective parents to reduce the probability of having an affected child—are beyond the moral pale. In a collaborative reproduction scenario, a surrogate would arguably be implicated in (for moral praise or blame) whatever decisions the prospective parents were to make on this score, since the surrogate would be an agent carrying out their wishes. She might accordingly think twice if the intended parents wanted her to help them have a *particular* kind of child, not just a (or another) child, such as a one born male, or one born with the same recessive congenital condition one or both of the intended parents have (e.g., deafness, blindness, dwarfism), or one born as a "match" to the parents' extant sick child for future donation purposes (of bone marrow or other tissue).[11] Or, consider a different scenario where the intended parents know or strongly suspect they would want their surrogate to abort in the case of a prenatal diagnosis of a particular fetal anomaly. Should they spare themselves and their surrogate from subsequently getting an abortion weeks after the pregnancy has already gotten underway by undergoing preimplantation genetic testing, not selecting any affected embryos for transfer, and thus dramatically reducing the likelihood of that hypothetical coming to pass? Or might they instead prioritize whatever concerns they have about the increased costs or risks of PGT and just take their chances?

Katie and Steven had to work through these five IVF decisions and questions in consultation with me about several of them. Because they had elected to use frozen, not fresh, eggs, I did not have to manage an additional layer of coordination with another person. We also collectively decided to transfer two embryos at one time—we all understood the risks of multiple gestation and were willing to take them, though it turns out only one embryo "stuck" after our second transfer attempt, who eventually became their baby girl. Because my IPs had no embryos they had created remaining when we were finished with our two rounds of IVF, they did not have to make any agonizing final disposition decisions about remaining embryos. But one of the most painful parts of the process for me was my experience of the scenario discussed above where we collectively entertained whether to undergo PGT and they did not respond in the ways I had hoped they would have responded. I explain what we ultimately decided to do in chapter 5 under the principle of medical self-determination.

Other Nuts and Bolts of Surrogacy

Surrogacy is obviously not for everyone. Most respectable fertility clinics and surrogacy agencies or charities will weed out whom they deem to be unacceptable candidates. Most will also not allow prospective parents and surrogates to formally begin the long and uncertain process until all parties have passed basic medical eligibility, cleared their psychological evaluation, and formalized their pre-conception contracts or agreements.

MEDICAL ELIGIBILITY AND SCREENING

Well before a surrogate either begins her fertility medications in a gestational surrogacy or is artificially inseminated in a traditional one, she will have been medically cleared to proceed. Specific eligibility criteria will vary, but most reputable doctors would rule out the following as acceptable candidates:

- women who have had difficulty getting or staying pregnant, have had complicated deliveries, or who have exceeded their maximum recommended number of previous C-sections
- women who have never given birth before, since it is unknown whether someone with no prior experience can even become pregnant and safely carry to term
- women who have pelvic or uterine abnormalities or obstructions (e.g., uterine fibroids)
- women who test positive for infectious diseases

- women who have a body mass index (BMI) below or beyond what is considered a healthy range

- women who abuse alcohol or drugs, do not live in a smoke-free household, or who have other lifestyle factors correlated with poor pregnancy outcomes

- women who have a medical history, including an underlying condition, where another pregnancy or the use of IVF medications is contraindicated

- women who are below or above a certain age

Prospective surrogates must undergo several tests and also have their medical history reviewed. Even though I was forty years old at the time, it turns out I was a good candidate: I had had two previous vaginal births at full term without incident, no (known) history of miscarriage, a healthy BMI and lifestyle, and that apparently "beautiful" uterus. Prospective IPs who hope to create embryos from their own genetic material must also have their medical and family history examined to ascertain genetic factors as well as the feasibility of using their own gametes.

Most reputable fertility clinics in the U.S. follow a protocol exceeding Food and Drug Administration (FDA) requirements when transferring an embryo into a third party. This protocol includes the surrogate and their partner, if any, needing to clear infectious disease screening and testing, screening and testing all gamete donors, and even screening and testing IPs whether or not they are also the genetic parents.[12] Still, as my spouse and I had to acknowledge on our fertility clinic's consent form, IPs and genetic parents who test negative for the human immunodeficiency virus (HIV) at the time of the embryo transfer could still transmit HIV to the embryo and thus to the surrogate (and then the surrogate to any partner), since there is a three-month window where an HIV-infected person does *not* register as positive.

PSYCHOLOGICAL EVALUATION

All reputable fertility clinics and surrogacy agencies also require their clients to clear psychological screening. A licensed psychologist might evaluate prospective IPs and surrogates for any history of mental illness, depression, addiction, or trauma; relationship instability or other life stressors; feelings about pregnancy and parenthood; adequacy of support system; fitness to pursue surrogacy and with the persons with whom they have been or may be matched; problems they anticipate occurring; expectations concerning the quality and frequency of contact during the arrangement and plans for future contact post-childbirth; and their position on privacy and disclosure. The surrogate's partner (if any) must also usually be screened to assess their understanding there would be no child at the end for them to parent and their willingness to support the surrogate throughout the process, including by complying with mandated periods of sexual abstinence from the start of injectables to a confirmation of pregnancy.

Increasingly, fertility clinics are requiring group evaluations in addition to individual psychological screenings, as what was required in our case. Though my husband and I found some of our psychologist's comments problematic, such as her insisting that Katie have a baby shower even though it is not uncommon for intended mothers to feel ambivalent about the presence of their visibly pregnant surrogate at the party (i.e., we felt our psychologist overstepped in speaking so imperatively to us), the group conversation was productive overall. My friends (the IPs) were able to articulate some outstanding concerns they had about their unconventional way of becoming parents. I, in turn, had an opportunity to distinguish between what I as their *surrogate* would minimally require from them and what my husband and I as their *friends* would advise them to do when deciding whether and when to reveal the irregular circumstances surrounding their child's conception and birth to others.

OTHER FERTILITY CLINIC OR SURROGACY AGENCY REQUIREMENTS

Other procedural requirements for surrogacy vary according to the jurisdiction, fertility clinic, and agency or charity involved (if any). Many reputable agencies in the U.S. conduct criminal background checks on prospective surrogates and their partners (if any), and these results might be given to a court system involved in approving or enforcing contracts. Others might also seek to confirm their clients' financial solvency, including by running credit checks to ascertain the IPs' ability to pay all fees. Most will exclude surrogacy candidates on governmental assistance (such as welfare, public housing, or section 8) to provide IPs some assurances their surrogates would neither be rendering their services only to escape a dire economic situation, nor compromising the public assistance they already receive since welfare recipients must report all sources of income. Some U.S.-based surrogacy agencies only accept surrogate candidates with their own medical insurance. Still, some health insurance companies exclude surrogate-pregnancies from coverage (fortunately, ours did not), thus requiring the IPs either to wait for their surrogate to switch insurance providers, purchase supplemental coverage, or cover all pregnancy costs out-of-pocket. Finally, to avoid criminal prosecution or other legal complications, some U.S.-based agencies will only work with clients who are U.S. citizens or permanent residents who reside within the same state. Others market themselves as a surrogacy destination for prospective clients who might be facing legal restrictions, limited markets, or inferior reproductive health care in their home contexts.

CONTRACTS OR FORMAL PRE-CONCEPTION AGREEMENTS

The final step in formalizing a surrogacy arrangement is to draw up a written agreement or memorandum of understanding (MOU) detailing each person's rights and responsibilities. Since contracts are designed to clarify mutual expectations and obligations to protect all parties and ward off potential areas of dispute, the persons involved commonly enter "voluntarily, transparently, and in good faith" into a "signed, written preconception agreement"—as per the American College of Obstetrics and Gynecologists' (ACOG's) recommendation. Even where surrogacy contracts are void and unenforceable such as in the U.K. or in particular U.S. states, the persons in the collaborative reproduction often still take their agreements seriously.[13] For liability purposes as it was explained in our case, many reputable fertility clinics in the U.S. will not allow the surrogate to begin taking injectable medications until all parties have signed their contracts or formal pre-conception agreements.

The contract stage in U.S. states where surrogacy is legally permitted typically proceeds as follows. The IPs work with their attorney to draft an initial document, which they then present to the surrogate and to their partner (if any and if required) through legal counsel for review. Common contract provisions include the parties' consent to various medical tests or procedures and acknowledgment of risks, the maximum number of embryos to be transferred and for how many possible total ET procedures over what specified period of time, the behavioral modifications and travel restrictions the surrogate will undergo while pregnant, matters pertaining to abortion and selective reduction, what the parties would do in specified worst-case scenarios, the compensation the surrogate will receive and payment schedule (if any), where (in which hospital) the birth will take place, and a specification of custody and parental rights. The surrogate and partner will then request changes as needed through legal counsel. Revised drafts are sent back and forth until the parties are satisfied with the terms. The contract is then signed, usually notarized, and perhaps also sent as part of the paperwork to be filed for the IPs to be eventually declared the legal parents.

MATCHING INTENDED PARENTS WITH SURROGATES

Surrogacy as a practice requires an individual willing to carry a child for someone else to be matched with parent hopefuls who will commission them to that end. How the two parties will come together will vary.

In most altruistic arrangements, prospective IPs and surrogates typically have preexisting bonds of love and care. My four women friends or acquaintances I had referenced in the previous chapter who had once entertained, but ultimately decided against, becoming a surro-mom had wanted to help a close friend or relative have their first child. Of the twenty-one surrogacy cases Japan's Dr. Yahiro Netsu oversaw in the first decade since he began in 2001, 100% were for relatives: five between mother and daughter (i.e., the grandmothers were the surrogates who bore their own grandchildren), and ten between either sisters or sisters-in-law.[14] Still, not all parties in altruistic arrangements start out as longtime intimates, which is why some nonprofit organizations in areas prohibiting commercial contracts have emerged to facilitate matches. To illustrate, the charity Surrogacy UK was founded in 2002 by former surrogates with an ethos of "surrogacy through friendship."[15] In addition to arranging for meet-ups among prospective surrogates and prospective IPs, they encourage everyone to develop relationships with one another for a minimum of three months before entering into a collaborative reproduction agreement. They also advise potential matches not to proceed further if they discover major areas of incompatibility on their responses to a questionnaire designed to assist them in their discernment.

For commercial arrangements, surrogacy agencies exist to recruit parent hopefuls and potential surrogates, provide a clearinghouse of information, and coordinate other logistics. If prospective IPs or surrogates pass the agency's screening for acceptable clients, the agency will eventually suggest a match or series of matches the individuals in question could either accept or decline. Almost all surrogacy professionals emphasize the importance of partnering with someone with whom one feels a sense of comfort, ease, and trust. Other important considerations include an alignment in values about any acceptable scenarios for pregnancy termination or selective reduction, the maximum number of embryos to be transferred in one procedure, prenatal care and nutrition, and the kind of relationship and frequency of contact desired during and after journey's end.

For parties pursuing an independent (not agency-facilitated) arrangement, the match can come about through an already existing relationship like my spouse and I had with Katie and Steven, by word of mouth, or through social media or message boards or ads in print or online. Through cutting out the middleman, IPs can save thousands of dollars by "going indy." Still, in the various online discussion forums I have read about or participated in, discussants consistently advise IPs to pursue an independent arrangement only if they have confidence in their own vetting abilities and for surrogates to do the same only if they are comfortable advocating for themselves, including on the sensitive matters of selective reduction/pregnancy termination and compensation. A common practice for surrogates is to work first with an agency and then—and only then—"go indy" for any subsequent journeys, such as to birth a sibling for a child they previously bore for their IPs.

Surrogacy Laws and Practices

In the Code of Hammurabi, an ancient set of laws ostensibly enacted by the Babylonian King Hammurabi (reign 1792–1750 BCE), surrogacy is prescribed for childless women to prevent their husbands from divorcing them or wedding another wife. Wives unable to bear children were permitted to "give" their husbands a maidservant for this purpose. If children were born as a result, the husband could not wed another wife and the surrogate could not be sold for money though could still be treated as a slave.[16] Though scholars debate the degree to which the Code actually functioned as part of ancient Babylonian law, Hammurabi's Code nonetheless reveals telling social attitudes about gender, class, marriage, consent, fertility, and progeny. Tales of handmaids or slaves being forced into surrogacy by their "barren" mistresses can also be found in the Genesis narratives about the first patriarch Abraham (Gen 16, 21) and the third in line in God's covenant with Israel—Jacob (Gen 30:1–24).[17]

Surrogacy practices and legal protections for all parties have since come a long way. When Michigan attorney Noel Keane drafted the first formal surrogacy contract between a woman and a married couple in the U.S. in 1976 and subsequently became known as the godfather of modern surrogate motherhood, the surrogate participated voluntarily and did not request payment.[18] In 1980, the pseudonymous Elizabeth Kane became America's first legally paid (traditional) surrogate after responding to a newspaper story about an involuntarily childless couple in Kentucky.

In the mid-to-late 1980s, the American public came to debate the meaning of parenthood and the wisdom of entering into pregnancy-for-hire contracts when the first U.S. court ruling on the practice received widespread domestic and international attention. In the media-sensationalized landmark case known as "Baby M," Mary Beth Whitehead had contractually agreed to be inseminated with William Stern's sperm and then to relinquish all paternal rights to William and his wife Elizabeth for $10,000.[19] Whitehead had a change of heart soon after childbirth, fled the state with the baby, and sought to return the money while suing for custody. The Supreme Court of New Jersey and a family court ultimately ruled commercial surrogacy contracts null and void, clarified that Mrs. Whitehead was and remained the legal mother (and William Stern the legal father), and awarded custody to William Stern using a "best interests of the child" analysis while granting Mary Beth Whitehead visitation rights.[20]

The legal fallout from and impact of this groundbreaking case reached far beyond New Jersey. Many jurisdictions instituted formal bans on traditional surrogacy out of concern for the welfare of women and children. Most IPs today the world over opt for gestational over traditional arrangements even when both types are legally permitted, as we did in our case. Several states in the U.S. and many nations across the world also prohibit commercial surrogacy contracts (whether traditional or gestational) out of a conviction that recruiting and then paying women for their reproductive labor is degrading, exploitative of their oft inferior economic status, and akin to baby-selling.

To date, there is no federal legislation governing surrogacy, leaving each state in the U.S. to regulate what they will prohibit or permit within their own borders. There are also no international laws concerning surrogacy, thus requiring each sovereign body to set its own standards. When my friends and I were trying to figure out the how-to of surrogacy while discerning its appropriateness for us, we thus needed context-specific information.

SURROGACY IN THE U.S.

Because each state handles surrogacy idiosyncratically, remarkable variation exists on the types permitted, what other fertility services can be sold (e.g., some states permit the sale of gametes for procreative but not research purposes), and what civil or criminal penalties might attach to violators. States also differ on whose name(s) can or must be included on the baby's birth certificate, IP eligibility requirements, and what parents must do to secure their parental rights.

On the most restrictive end of the spectrum, states have published statutes or case law prohibiting commercial surrogacy. In response to the neighboring Baby M saga in New Jersey, New York Governor Mario Cuomo introduced a bill in 1989 that took effect in 1992 rendering all surrogacy contracts "contrary to the public policy of this state and . . . void and unenforceable." During New York's nearly two decades of prohibition, an IP caught supplying, a surrogate caught receiving, or a surrogacy broker caught facilitating payment beyond "reasonable and actual medical fees and hospital expenses for artificial insemination or in vitro fertilization services incurred by the mother in connection with the birth of the child" faced the prospect of civil penalties and a felony conviction for any second offense. Though the New York law was repealed in April 2020, and came into effect in February 2021, prohibitive statutes at the time of this writing can still be found in Michigan, Louisiana, Nebraska, Arizona, and Indiana.[21]

On the other end of the spectrum lie the most surrogacy-friendly jurisdictions: states where there are no eligibility restrictions based on the IPs' marital status, sexual orientation, or genetic relation to the embryo(s); where the IPs can be officially recognized as the legal parents on the same day as the child's birth if a pre-birth order is filed correctly, and where both IPs can be named on the baby's birth certificate. California, the state in which my IPs and I are residents, falls in this category. Not only are there no prohibitions on advertising, soliciting, or receiving payment in connection to gestational surrogacy, but the state will not hold a surrogate legally responsible for raising the child if the IPs were, for whatever reason, to refuse to assume parentage post-childbirth. Traditional surrogacy is also permitted to the extent it is not expressly prohibited.[22] Given the state's ample surrogacy agencies, minimal legal restrictions, long-standing case law recognizing IPs' rights, and numerous Hollywood celebrities opting for surrogacy, California remains a trend-setting, top destination for persons seeking cross-border reproductive care.

In between the most prohibitive jurisdictions and the most permissive ones lie the vast majority of states with varying regulations. For instance, in Virginia where I moved after completing my doctorate to start my first full-time faculty position at Virginia Tech, surrogates can only receive payment for "reasonable medical and ancillary costs," and no third party can be paid to recruit or facilitate surrogacy matches or contracts. The IP(s) must be an unmarried individual or a married couple, they must provide "medical evidence" of their need for surrogacy, and at least one parent must be genetically related to the embryo(s) (or have "the legal or contractual custody of the embryo at issue"). The legal parents in Virginia are the woman who gives birth (the surrogate) *and her spouse,* if any, and a surro-mom can only relinquish her parental rights three days after childbirth by signing a "surrogate consent and report form naming the intended parent as the parent of the child."[23] While my arrangement with Katie and Steven would have met all qualifications under Virginia law, none of us would have been happy about my husband and me needing to be the legal parents of their child for any length of time if we had been Virginian, not Californian, residents.

While hovering between total prohibition on the one hand and maximal leniency on the other hand, the State of Tennessee, where some of our relatives live, has taken a different approach. Gestational surrogacy contracts are neither expressly permitted nor forbidden: surrogacy is simply defined in the section of the statute covering adoption. A "surrogate birth" has taken place when a woman either has contractually given birth to a child for a married couple who are both the child's genetic and intended parents or has been inseminated by the intended father's sperm out of a contractual understanding that she will relinquish the child once born to him "and the biological father's *wife* to parent" (emphasis added). In the absence of statutes expressly regulating surrogacy, Tennessee case law has covered whose names can or must appear on the birth certificate: the gestational surrogate must be named if a heterosexual or same-sex couple uses an egg donor until the second parent (intended father or mother) completes an adoption proceeding, and then that second parent will replace the surrogate's name; moreover, only the intended parent who is also the biological father can obtain a pre-birth order.[24] While Tennessee at least de facto permits surrogacy, the state's treatment of any nongenetic, intended parent as the "secondary" or adoptive one, view of the genetic parent as the original one, and mandatory listing of the gestational surrogate as the child's original, legal mother leaves much to be desired from the perspective of my surrogacy for my friends in California. This is because Katie and Steven and many other IPs documented in the literature understand themselves to be *equal* partners in their turn to surrogacy whether or not their child has both sets of their genes (not with one parent being primary and the other, secondary), and thus would take issue with any legal processes suggesting otherwise.

SURROGACY GLOBALLY

The lack of standardized surrogacy laws internationally mirrors the nonuniformity of state laws in the U.S. According to the Sexuality and Gender Law Clinic of Columbia Law School, nations have typically adopted one of four approaches: (1) prohibit surrogacy of any kind; (2) provide no protections or prohibitions on surrogacy and therein leave the practice in a legal vacuum; (3) explicitly permit and regulate only non-commercial surrogacies; (4) allow all types of surrogacy, including paid arrangements.[25]

Many Western European countries, including France, Germany, Italy, and Switzerland, fall into the first category. Common reasons for their total prohibition include the desire to protect children and to avoid exploiting, objectifying, and/or commodifying women and their reproductive capacities. For example, surrogacy has been condemned in France by the Court of Cassation since 1991 on the grounds that "only those things in commerce can be the object of contracts." France subsequently made their prohibition explicit in 1994 when specifying "any contract concerning procreation or surrogacy for others is void."[26]

The U.K., Australia, and Canada fall into the third category of countries permitting and thus regulating only non-commercial arrangements. In the U.K., surrogates can only receive funds for "reasonable expenses" without anyone profiting from recruiting or advertising for clients.[27] All U.K. surrogacy contracts also remain legally unenforceable under the Surrogacy Arrangements Act of 1985 and the Human Fertilisation and Embryology Act of 2008. Key provisions include the woman who gives birth being the legal mother regardless of genetics or any agreements they may have made with others and her husband, if any, being the legal father until she consents to relinquish post-childbirth and the courts determine it is in the child's best interests for legal parentage to be transferred accordingly.[28] Similarly in Australia, surrogacy laws and regulations vary at the state and territory level, with all only allowing for reimbursements of the surrogate's reasonable pregnancy-related expenses and preserving the surrogate's legal right not to hand over the child following childbirth.[29]

The final category allows for all types of surrogacy arrangements, subject to regulation, and thus can be regarded as a foil to the first, entirely prohibitive type. Russia and Ukraine had become popular destinations for reproductive travelers because of their lower expenses—in one estimate, one-third of what it might cost in the U.S.—and because their statutes expressly permit commercial surrogacy.[30] However, since the severe disruption to their markets following Russia's invasion of Ukraine on February 24, 2022, Ukrainian surrogates have been evacuating to neighboring countries, and Russian lawmakers took a step toward banning foreigners from accessing surrogacy in Russia altogether on May 24, 2022, in the wake of deteriorating relations with Western countries.[31] The long-term effects of the war remain unknown at the time of this writing.

Indeed, global surrogacy hot spots can suddenly change in response to world events, as even the story of how Russia and the Ukraine emerged for a time as leading surrogacy destinations cannot be understood in a vacuum. India was once touted as the world's top "baby factory" in the first decade of this millennium primarily for reasons of its reduced costs and formerly unregulated, multibillion-dollar industry. But India began barring foreign gay couples and singles from hiring surrogates in 2012 given an Indian sociopolitical climate of privileging heterosexual family units over other family composition types, then prohibited all internationals in 2015 following several scandals involving foreigners "abandoning" their surrogate-born children when they were legally prevented from bringing them back to their (more restrictive) home countries, and most recently banned commercial surrogacy altogether (even for Indian nationals) in December 2021 given ongoing concerns about the exploitation of poor Indian women.[32] In Nepal, the world was shocked by a different scandal following the Israeli government's airlifting of twenty-six surrogate-born babies to safety to their mostly gay Israeli parents (who, until January 2022, were legally prohibited from accessing surrogacy services at home) after a devastating 7.8-magnitude earthquake in April 2015 while leaving their mostly Indian surrogate mothers behind. Essentially, neighboring Nepal had emerged as an offshore hub for Indian clinics after India's first wave of restrictions in 2012. But the Supreme Court of Nepal halted surrogacy in the aftermath of that scandal and later announced a Cabinet decision to restrict surrogacy for only infertile (i.e., heterosexual) Nepali married couples.[33] To provide one last example, Thailand—a nation long known for its medical tourism, was also once a top destination for surrogacy but similarly blocked all commercial surrogacies in 2015 in the wake of global media firestorm following a Thai surrogate's birth of a set of twins in 2013 for a set of Australian intended parents. It was widely reported (though later determined erroneously) that the parents had "abandoned" the twin boy with Down syndrome to the care of the Thai surrogate who then crowdfunded money to support him; the media also later (correctly) discovered that the intended father was a convicted child sex offender now parenting their surrogate-born (twin) baby girl.[34]

LEGAL TRENDS AND DIVERSE EXPERIENCES

While the global trend in surrogacy is toward increased restrictions or even total prohibition, several U.S. states have swapped their decades-long ban on commercial arrangements for regulation: the District of Columbia, the State of Washington, New Jersey, and New York all between 2017 and 2021. This movement toward greater toleration of surrogacy across the U.S and lack of federal policies—and thus federal oversight—on the industry has led the U.S. to be dubbed the Wild West of third-party reproduction.[35]

To be clear, global variation in surrogates' lived experiences is due not only to heterogeneity in the law, but also to diverse local customs. In the heyday of India's international surrogacy trade, many clinics provided dorm-style lodging for their surrogates either upon confirmation of a pregnancy or in the final months of pregnancy: surrogates would often live with other surrogates apart from their own families and children, receive daily meals, be supervised by health-care providers until they gave birth, and did not have much direct contact with their IPs since the clinics encouraged communication through intermediaries.[36] In contrast, in the U.K., the U.S., Canada, and Australia, surro-moms normally live in their own homes and are in frequent, direct contact with those they are assisting. Even so, intended parents in those contexts where the birth mother is the legal one and where their legal parentage can only be secured later (after weeks post-birth in the U.K. or Australia or after several days in Virginia) obviously do not enjoy comparable rights as their counterparts do in California and elsewhere, and thus might understandably be more anxious throughout the process.

The variability of laws and customs has contributed to the rise of a multibillion-dollar global infertility industry wherein the policies of one place can reverberate beyond its borders. As alluded to earlier, when India blocked gay parent hopefuls from accessing their surrogacy services in 2012, several Indian agencies responded quickly by moving their operations to Nepal, Thailand, and Cambodia—literally flying out "frozen embryos that were awaiting wombs, and women who were already pregnant to give birth."[37] The prospect of saving money undoubtedly continues to motivate one demographic of prospective parents to engage in what some have dubbed "reproductive tourism." Still, others, like those gay Israelis contracting with Indian women in Nepal who were blocked from accessing surrogacy at home until 2022 or world-famous soccer player Cristiano Ronaldo who fathered his first three kids through California-based surrogates before his home nation, Portugal, lifted prohibitions on the practice in 2017, had been hoping to avoid the restrictive laws, eligibility requirements, or long waiting lists on ART they faced at home and thus might be more properly viewed as "reproductive exiles" even with their class privilege.[38] There is clearly a relationship between discriminatory adoption laws, ART policies, or otherwise difficult-to-access fertility services in one jurisdiction and reproductive travelers seeking cross-border reproductive care in another—the social justice implications I will explore later in chapters 5 and 6.

Accounting for Surrogacy's Popularity

The Centers for Disease Control and Prevention (CDC), the American Society for Reproductive Medicine (ASRM), and the Society for Assisted Reproductive Technology (SART) have reported exponential growth in surrogacy in the years before and after I became pregnant for my friends: usage has more than tripled from 2010 to 2019.[39] The UK in a comparable time frame (2011–2020) has experienced a fourfold increase in the number of parental orders filed for legal parentage to be transferred from the surro-mom to the IPs, with parental orders being a common way UK researchers track the number of surrogacy cases.[40] After launching the Parentage / Surrogacy Project in 2011 and providing a preliminary report in 2012, the Permanent Bureau of the Hague produced a lengthier study on surrogacy in 2014 that noted that several states (including Israel, New Zealand, Switzerland, Canada, Ireland, Norway, and Spain) had reported increased prevalence in international surrogacy contracts "over the past five years, in some cases significantly." The U.S. and India were also mentioned most frequently as the then most popular states of birth for cross-border surrogacy, followed by "Thailand, Ukraine and Russia, with Georgia and Canada also being mentioned frequently in responses" and a longer list of less frequently mentioned states of birth including "Armenia, Australia, Belgium, Brazil, Cambodia, China, Cyprus, Czech Republic, Greece, Israel, Italy, Indonesia, Kazakhstan, Kenya, Philippines, Poland, South Africa, Malaysia and Mexico."[41]

How might we understand surrogacy's soaring popularity beyond the cross-cultural preference for many couples to be biologically related to their child(ren) when possible, even if only through one parent? There is, of course, an increase in "delayed childbearing" among women in several contexts across the world, which is itself a multifaceted phenomenon, and the adverse effects older age has on their fertility.[42] In addition, as many patients undergoing infertility treatments come to learn, IVF success rates increase when IVF is paired with gestational surrogacy: by 8%–13% in one reporting period in the U.S. among intended mothers aged forty-two or younger and by 20%–32% for those older than age forty-two.[43] As the interaction of these three factors suggests, many infertile couples come to view surrogacy as their last chance for bearing progeny: they have likely already tried other ART and either have embryos remaining from previous IVF cycles or are willing to create new embryos (potentially by using donor eggs), which they would then hope to transfer into a younger and healthier surrogate.

A fourth consideration accounting for surrogacy's boom involves evolving societal norms about marriage and parenting, including a growing acceptance of diverse family types in some contexts. Beyond the nuclear model of one man and one woman bearing children together in matrimony, families today are increasingly blended, adoptive, or intergenerational as well as potentially headed by singles, unmarried cohabiting partners, or same-sex couples. Not surprisingly, same-sex (mostly gay male) couples are represented among IPs globally, just as single men in smaller numbers are also becoming fathers through this reproductive technique.[44]

Finally, another contributing factor to surrogacy's growing popularity is some couples' preference to become parents through this method over adoption when they cannot bear any or more children themselves. Beyond the common desire to maintain biological relatedness where possible, many prospective IPs also value the ability to be involved in their future child's life from conception to birth and therein monitor their prenatal care and development—prospects not ordinarily possible in adoption. Other IPs wish to avoid what they believe to be adoption's tragic dimensions, since relinquishment often comes as a result of an unwanted or crisis pregnancy. Still others cannot stomach putting themselves in a vulnerable position where the birth mother in an adoption scenario could legally refuse to hand over the baby post-childbirth should she experience a change of heart and thus opt for surrogacy instead, particularly if they reside in jurisdictions where their rights as intended parents would be more secure than they would be if they were instead adoptive parents. Gay men with means in particular are increasingly turning to surrogacy over adoption in the hopes that the genetic relatedness made possible by surrogacy for at least one parent could provide a "bulwark against gender discrimination in adoption and custody in many legal systems."[45] That said, other IPs chose surrogacy over adoption out of *adaptive*, not original, preferences, particularly when adoption laws or adoption agencies screen them out from eligibility or being selected because they are single, too old, coupled but unmarried, or in a same-sex relationship.

All told, the rise in surrogacy can be explained by a host of push-pull factors. Since parent hopefuls cannot realize their dreams of having children through surrogacy without the existence of someone becoming pregnant for them, we must also investigate what explains surrogacy's rise from their perspectives. I cover the topic of surrogate motivations in later chapters, though it may be helpful to know now that surro-moms in contexts as diverse as the U.S., U.K., Israel, and Thailand commonly report having had enjoyable or at least not difficult pregnancy and childbirth experiences, feeling compassion and empathy for involuntarily childless couples, believing they might be well-suited to help (i.e., believing it takes a special person to become a surrogate and that they fit this bill), and—in the case of those receiving compensation for their services—reasoning they could put the money they would earn to good use.[46]

2 DOES SURROGACY CAUSE PSYCHOLOGICAL HARM?

NEARLY EVERYONE WHO HAS SPOKEN with me about my unconventional pregnancy has told me they have never previously met or known a surrogate before. Their comments and questions thus gave me a window into how ordinary people around me think about the practice. While most of my conversation partners expressed curiosity if not explicit support, quite a few still had reservations about what my friends and I were doing, which they did not hesitate to share.

"Wait—how old are you, Grace? Are you sure that's wise and safe at your age?" queried a male colleague in whom I had confided during the period when I was taking hormones prior to my first embryo transfer. Others may not have been so blunt, but I could that tell they, too, were worried about my and the future baby's health given my advanced maternal age (thirty-five and over) and the risks of IVF.

In addition to the many women who would put themselves in my shoes and contemplate whether they could hypothetically carry a child for someone else (with most concluding they could not), some would imaginatively place themselves in the role of my involuntarily childless friends instead. They would say something like this: "We would have been devastated if I couldn't bear our own kids. Your friends must be so excited, but anxious. How are they holding up?" Through further conversation, I could tell they thought my friends were fortunate to have someone like me, but they themselves would not have opted for surrogacy because it would have been far too expensive, or too cumbersome a process, or too emotionally difficult for them to let go and trust another person without incessantly worrying whether she were eating and resting adequately or taking all IVF meds on schedule and so forth.

My husband and children were the objects of concern for other friends and relatives. They would ask iterations of "What does your husband [Nathaniel] think about all of this? What about your kids?" as if they were expecting to hear tales of him coming around only after a period of initial resistance or of awkward conversations we had to have with our presumably perplexed boys about how I managed to get pregnant with a baby who would not be their sister. Questions about my sons (then ages six and eight) made sense to me, since I, too, initially wondered how they would react. But my feminist "Spidey sense" would tingle when I sensed folks were implying I would have needed to have gotten Nathaniel's permission first instead of us talking through all major decisions together or if they saw him as extraordinary for "allowing" me to help our friends in this way, as if my body were under his control.

"Grace, this is just not the way God wants people to have children. Why don't your friends just adopt?" said my mom repeatedly in Taiwanese when attempting to dissuade me from going through with our plans. Due to the strangeness of assisted reproductive technology (ART), the impact another pregnancy—and an IVF one—might have on my professional and familial responsibilities, and their opposition to anyone taking unnecessary medical risks (n.b., my father is a retired surgeon), my parents did not want me to put my body on the line. To be clear, they weren't the only ones who interpreted our use of ART as a rejection of adoption—I could tell others in my community believed the intended parents (IPs) and I had some explaining to do.

But the most common questions I received from friends, strangers, and colleagues alike were—and still are—variations of "Weren't you afraid you'd grow attached to the baby and not want to give it up?" and "Is it painful for you to continue to see the child you bore being raised by someone else?" Even the intended mother, Katie, gently asked me versions of them before, during, and in the weeks after our journey together, as she was understandably baffled by my—or any other woman in my place—*not* wanting to keep the baby in the end due to her own intense longing for a child. The frequency with which I was asked, and continue today to be asked, these questions has shown me how pervasive belief in the inevitability of maternal-fetal bonding is.

———

The reservations expressed by my friends and relatives with diverse political and faith commitments show us a great deal about the concerns a progressive Christian account of surrogacy must address. While more and more people have been turning to this reproductive method to expand their families, the public's reactivity to the practice remains. Opponents often scornfully describe commercial surrogacy as "reproductive prostitution," "womb-renting," or "baby-selling." The media also tends to sensationalize the rare but real-life disasters of women refusing to relinquish post-childbirth because they have bonded with the baby in the process, IPs failing to accept parentage because they have broken up in the interim or the baby has been born with congenital anomalies, surrogates fleeing to jurisdictions with greater protections for birth mothers because the IPs want them to abort or selectively reduce against their will, or the whole arrangement being a ruse to con unsuspecting clients out of their money.[1] With less than 1% of all births in the U.S. involving surrogacy, the disproportionate attention the media devotes to this route to parenthood should prompt us to probe why surrogacy has so captivated—and unsettled—the general public.

This is my task in the next two chapters. The lion's share of the controversy centers on charges that the surrogacy industry exploits women who are in need of money to incur the physical risks and sacrifices of pregnancy for someone else while commodifying their bodies, pregnancy, and children in the process. But even in altruistic arrangements where surrogates presumably bear children for others out of compassion, not desire for profit, the general public still sometimes fears harm might nonetheless befall the persons most involved or affected by such arrangements. Distinctive feminist misgivings include allegations that surrogacy unacceptably redefines and fragments what motherhood essentially is, undermines a pregnant person's bodily autonomy and rights, has undesirable implications for the abortion debate, and perpetuates harmful stereotypes about women. Though Christian critics share many of the general public's discomfort with surrogacy, they tend to be "pro-life" on the abortion front and not especially critical of pronatalism in contrast to their mainstream feminist counterparts. Their distinctive complaints include the unnaturalness of reproductive technology contravening their understanding of God's design for sex, reproduction, and the family; the use of a third party in assisted reproduction compromising a married couple's vows of exclusive fidelity to each another; the IVF process in gestational surrogacy mistreating and destroying embryos—a grave sin for those who hold that life begins at conception; and the prospect of assisted reproduction tempting persons to expend sizable resources to produce a biogenetically related child instead of pursuing the presumably morally superior alternative of adopting an extant child in need of a stable and loving home.

While bracketing the popular exploitation and commodification charges until chapter 6 when I examine the ethics of commercial arrangements, I spend this chapter unpacking and then responding to widespread concerns about the psychological health of the parties involved in or affected by all kinds of surrogacy arrangements. I then take up what specifically troubles feminist and Christian critics in the next chapter.

The Charge: Surrogacy Impairs Psychological Well-Being

As I experienced in my own surrogacy journey with my friends, some well-wishers are concerned about the emotional and psychological impact a collaborative reproduction arrangement may have on the members of any given surrogacy triad—that is, the persons like me who become pregnant for others, the intended parents like Katie and Steven who commission them to that end, and the child(ren) like their daughter born as a result of their agreements. They are also worried or at least curious about surrogacy's impact on the families of surro-moms and of the IPs.

CLAIM #1: SURROGATE MOTHERS WILL EXPERIENCE
EMOTIONAL PAIN AND GRIEF UPON RELINQUISHMENT

As I witnessed firsthand when pregnant with my friends' baby, the general public generally believes it must be emotionally torturous for a woman to bear a child for someone else—that her service cannot but come at a high psychological price. They assume the handover will either prove traumatizing because any "birth mom" would have grown attached to the baby she has nurtured in her womb over the course of nine months or that surro-moms would eventually come to feel tremendous loss about it in the long term, after the immediate feelings of joy and satisfaction at the completion of their service subside.

What accounts for the widespread belief in deep surrogate pain and remorse following relinquishment? One factor must be the pervasive belief in the maternal instinct purportedly present in all women or at least all expectant ones—the understanding that women naturally crave motherhood and bond with the life growing inside of them when pregnant. Just as popular culture commonly characterizes birth mothers in adoption as grieving mightily and for a prolonged time after being compelled by tragic circumstances to "give up" their child, so it is widely assumed surro-moms would analogously yearn for the baby they once nurtured in their wombs but had to give up because their contracts or prior agreements prevented them from being able to keep them. More controversially, I suspect that just as women who have had abortions are commonly depicted as having made an agonizing decision— even by those who wholeheartedly affirm their legal and moral right to have done so—so it is presumed that anyone who agrees to become pregnant for others could only sever their bond with the baby which began in utero with great hardship.

That the first well-publicized surrogacy cases in the U.S. and U.K. ended tragically at a time when the public was first becoming aware of this simultaneously age-old and newer way of bringing children into the world has furthered sealed in the public imaginary this belief of motherhood as the commonly desired goal of any pregnancy. The first paid traditional surrogate in the U.S., Elizabeth Kane, originally touted the joys of surrogacy for infertile couples on the talk show circuit but later came to regret having served as a "human incubator" and fell into a depression with suicidal ideation that lasted for several months.[2] As noted in the previous chapter, the world also witnessed traditional surrogate Mary Beth Whitehead's anguished inability to cope following the birth and handover of Baby M. Across the Atlantic, the first (traditional) surrogate in the U.K., Kim Cotton, was similarly devastated because she never got to meet the Swedish couple she was recruited to assist (her arrangement was brokered by a U.S. agency, and they remained anonymous to her) and because she had agreed never to contact baby Cotton postbirth. The media headlines about her suffering led to public outcry. It also quickly spurred the Surrogacy Arrangements Act (1985) and subsequent laws in the UK which, among other provisions, render contracts unenforceable and permit surrogates to change their mind insofar as every birth mother remains the legal one until and unless a court issues a post-birth parental order to someone else if they believe it to be in the child's best interests.[3]

Popular culture has also reinforced this trope of surrogate grief. To provide two examples, I remember watching a story arc in the hit NBC sitcom *Friends* (1994–2004), when one of the main characters, Phoebe (played by actress Lisa Kudrow), carries triplets for her brother and his wife. In the October 1998 episode where Phoebe gives birth, she asks her brother if she can keep one of them. After he declines, Phoebe shares a moment alone with the triplets and says the following: "Everyone said labor was the hardest thing I'd ever have to do, but they were wrong. This is."[4] More recently, a 2017 best-selling book, Celeste Ng's *Little Fires Everywhere* which was adapted for a television mini-series in 2020, contains a surrogacy-gone-wrong plot twist. It turns out one of the two protagonists (Mia Warren, played by actress Kerry Washington) was once a traditional surrogate who couldn't bear the thought of parting with the baby once born, so she lied to the couple that she had miscarried and has been raising her daughter, Pearl, on the lam ever since.

CLAIM #2: SURROGACY WILL PSYCHOLOGICALLY TAX THE PARENTS

While intended parents are not the primary subjects of the public's worries about surrogacy, some commentators worry the practice will come at high costs for them, too. Beyond needing to determine how they will afford treatment and find a trustworthy person to bear their child, infertile couples are projected to undergo a long and stressful process in these ways:

> [They] must live throughout the pregnancy [once one is finally achieved] with the uncertainty of whether the surrogate mother will relinquish the child. . . . [They] must establish a mutually acceptable relationship with [her] . . . and ensure that this relationship does not break down. Not only is this situation likely to produce anxiety . . . , but it may also result in marital strain, particularly for couples with one partner more in favor of the . . . arrangement than the other. . . . [T]he commissioning mother's . . . relationship with the fertile and often younger surrogate . . . may result in feelings of inadequacy, depression, and low self-esteem. In addition, there is a great deal of prejudice against . . . surrogacy, and commissioning couples are likely to experience disapproval from family, friends, and the wider social world. Unlike other forms of assisted reproduction in which the mother experiences a pregnancy . . . , couples who become parents through surrogacy must explain the arrival of their newborn children.[5]

Other anticipated anxiety-ridden moments include the uncertainty involved following medical procedures (e.g., Will our embryos survive the thaw? Will the embryo(s) we transferred implant?), the wait before they can finally be declared the legal parents, and their determining whether, when, and how to disclose to others—including the future child—their use of third-party reproduction. Given these stressors, some psychologists fear the entire ART process would ultimately have a "negative impact [on] not only their psychological well-being, but also on their quality of parenting."[6]

Like their heterosexual counterparts, gay male commissioning parents are also projected to experience stress in their path to parenthood, including social disapproval for their "selfish" turn to this controversial method of family expansion in lieu of the more socially acceptable option (in some communities) of adoption. Of course, however gay male couples become parents, they will likely have to face gendered assumptions about male inferiority as their children's primary caregivers, "legal barriers at state and federal levels" to parenthood, and possibly even "accusations of paedophilia."[7] Those who opt for surrogacy must usually also face complex decision-making about *which* of the two intended fathers (IFs) will also be the genetic one, followed by intrusive questions from family and strangers alike about which one of them is the bio-dad.[8]

CLAIM #3: SURROGATE-BORN CHILDREN WILL NOT
EMERGE UNSCATHED

What now of the welfare of arguably the most vulnerable member of any collaborative reproduction—the child brought to life by the hopes, dreams, and great efforts of the adults involved? Just as the general public once worried about IVF-conceived children feeling odd or being ostracized by others about having begun their lives as "test-tube babies," so some commentators worry today about surrogate-born children coming to fret about the irregular circumstances surrounding their birth. Others fear surrogate-born children might become confused about who their parents "really" are, particularly when three sets of parents could arguably make a claim on them: the gestational one (the surrogate), the genetic parents, and/or the social parents. Still others speculate that surrogate-born children might experience emotional distress if they were to discover they had been created for the express purpose of being given away by their "birth mother" for money in compensated arrangements.

CLAIM #4: OTHERS MIGHT SUFFER HARM, TOO

Finally, just as some people in my community asked about how my spouse and kids were handling my being a surrogate, commentators have raised questions about how persons beyond the surrogacy triad might fare. For instance, it seems obvious that the surrogate's spouse or partner would likely have to endure sacrifices of their own as they accommodate her time and energy being diverted to a pregnancy that would not directly benefit their family, save any financial compensation she might receive for her service. In addition, any man married to or partnered with a traditional surrogate who lives in a socially or religiously conservative environment would also have to manage the social fallout caused by her impregnation by another man.[9] The family members of a surrogate might also seek to shield themselves from social criticism by being very selective about disclosure. As Heather Jacobson's Texas- and California-based surrogates report, "they and their husbands were cautious about to whom they divulge[d] information about surrogacy" because they understood "the larger social context surrounding [it] . . . which includes stigma."[10]

Members of the general public have also worried about the surrogate's own children coming to experience collateral damage from their mother's choices. Might they develop a low view of her if they were to learn their mother intentionally became pregnant for financial gain with no intention of ever raising that child herself? Or might they become sad, confused, or even fearful when anticipatorily watching their mother's stomach expand throughout the pregnancy but without ever being able to welcome a new sibling into their home? As columnist Katha Pollitt rhetorically asked when commenting decades earlier on the Baby M saga: "How can it not damage a child to watch Mom cheerfully produce and sell its half-sibling while Dad stands idly by? I'd love to be a fly on the wall as a mother reassures her kids that of course she loves them no matter what they do; it's just their baby sister who had a price tag."[11] Still others are troubled at the prospect of the surrogate's own children sharing in the social stigma if the arrangement takes place in a context where the practice is neither well understood, nor well received. Ann Beltran, a mother of four and two-time gestational surrogate in her early thirties, recounts being devastated by the "negative reactions from people in her church and school-based social circles" as they began to ignore her and talk behind her back during her second surrogacy, "saying 'Oh it's terrible what she's doing to her children!'" She was "particularly upset" when people began shunning her kids and found it odd that while her children "could explain the whole IVF procedure," they still "had no clue" why people were acting differently around them because they did not understand the broader context of social disapproval of the practice.[12]

Finally, it is worth noting that a surro-mom's parents might also be adversely affected by their daughter's decision to offer her body in the service of others. Elizabeth Kane reports that her father was proud of her for helping an infertile couple, but her mother could neither approve, nor even comprehend why Elizabeth agreed to bear a child for an infertile couple. It grieved her mother deeply to know she would have a grandchild in the world whom she could never meet, much less be in relationship. Kane chronicles how they were alienated from each other for some time. While my parents never mourned the loss of a future grandchild since the baby I carried for Katie and Steven was not genetically mine, they were likewise troubled by my decision. Because of the importance of the virtue of filial piety in Confucian-Christian communities, I knew in advance that my helping Katie and Steven would create tension in my relationship with my parents with whom I am close and visit most weekends. When my mom finally realized on Mother's Day no less that I had gone through with the surrogacy after all (n.b., I was then nineteen weeks pregnant), she became so upset that she refused to go to church with us that morning as we all then typically did and to the Mother's Day brunch following service for which I had made reservations.[13] Throughout the remainder of the pregnancy, both of my parents genuinely worried that something would "go wrong." While I continued to bring my family to visit and stay with them on weekends, our relationship was strained until I gave birth—something I only told them about days later after I was discharged from the hospital to spare them from further worrying.[14]

ADDENDUM: A NOTE ABOUT CONTEXT

The social or psychological risks and costs of surrogacy for members of the surrogacy triad and others outside of them will obviously vary according to context. The ones I have highlighted emerge from social scientists' and other commentators' predictions about the psychosocial impact of surrogacy on persons in the U.S., U.K., Canada, and Australia, assuming no extenuating circumstances. As I will unpack further in chapter 6, persons engaged in cross-border surrogacy arrangements usually face an additional set of risks and stressors due to their need to negotiate two or more sets of laws or customs in different jurisdictions. In addition, in contexts where the mechanics of surrogacy are not well understood by the public, the psychosocial risks and costs for those who become pregnant for others and their loved ones would arguably heighten. For example, in parts of India during the heyday of its multibillion-dollar industry where there was extreme stigma against surrogacy given its association with the bodies of poor women and sex work due to the widespread misunderstanding that impregnation occurs through intercourse with the intended father, many surrogates did not even selectively disclose to others their pregnancy, but kept their "surrogacy a secret from their communities, villages, and very often, from their parents." They did so by either hiding in clinics or other temporary accommodations in the last months of their pregnancies or "decid[ing] to tell their neighbors that the babies were their own and later say[ing] that they had miscarried."[15] Their spouses and their children left behind when the women were apart from them and the emotional toll on the surrogates and their spouses to keep the secret at all costs by evasion or deception thus must be factored into the total costs of the pregnancies they undertook for others.

Responding to Fears about Psychological Harm

I respect persons and other commentators who operate in good faith when describing their fears about surrogacy's impact on the welfare of women, well-being of children, integrity of the family, and dignity of vulnerable populations. It is with this spirit I address their concerns and reservations as the argument of the book unfolds, beginning with my initial responses below to this first set of worries about surrogacy's effects on psychological well-being. While I believe my conversation partners were sincere when asking whether I was dreading having to give the baby back at the end of nine months or how my family members were handling my unconventional pregnancy, I have also come to see how their lines of inquiry were nonetheless influenced by widespread myths about surrogacy. Decades of research on families expanded by this ART technique should put several of these popular fears and concerns to rest, as they are not well substantiated by the data.

MOST SURROGATES RELINQUISH HAPPILY AND
BOND WITH THE PARENTS, NOT THE BABY

Does a typical surrogacy arrangement usually come at a high psychological price for the persons who agree to them? In contrast to those early tragic court cases and fictional storylines about traumatic or at least emotionally fraught relinquishment, the vast majority of persons who bear children for others hand the babies over without incident.[16] Medical anthropologist Elly Teman estimates over 99% of the 25,000 women and counting in the U.S. who have become surrogate mothers since the late 1970s have gladly and willingly handed over the child, with less than "one-tenth of 1%" of cases end[ing] up in court battles.[17] Childlessness Overcome through Surrogacy (COTS), the oldest U.K. surrogacy charity founded in 1988 by the aforementioned Kim Cotton, estimates approximately 99% of the arrangements they have facilitated have "reached successful conclusions," with COTS being directly involved in 1,099 surrogate births as of November 2022 that have brought "unbounded joy" to IPs and "a great deal of satisfaction" to the women who carried their babies.[18] As of the time of this writing, there has never been a gestational arrangement contested in court by a surro-mom in Canada since the nation began regulating surrogacy in 2004. There have, however, been six cases where the *intended parents* abandoned the surrogate during her pregnancy mostly because they had divorced in the interim, with the child eventually being adopted by someone other than her.[19]

It is not simply that most surrogates follow through with their contractual obligations or pre-conception agreements, it is that the overwhelming majority give the baby back at journey's end with delight. A 2021 review essay published in the *American Journal of Obstetrics and Gynecology* found "the majority of research aimed at exploring surrogates' coping mechanisms during the relinquishment period unequivocally show feelings of joy, accomplishment, pride, and satisfaction."[20] Most of the surrogates in Heather Jacobson's U.S. study even identified the specific moment of transfer as a highlight and the very "reason they engage in surrogacy," since they finally got to "witness the making of parents and . . . [be recognized for] their important role in that process."[21] A Japan-based researcher who has conducted fieldwork in Thailand between 2010 and 2018 and in Cambodia in 2015 has concluded similarly: "When surrogacy takes place on good terms, an intimate relationship is engendered between the client and surrogate mother, and the altruistic aspirations of the surrogate mother are realized."[22] A testimonial from one of her subjects underscores this point: "During the delivery, my client stood beside my bed and we both cried when the baby was born. It was very emotional. When I got pregnant, I was very happy and I felt even happier when I handed the baby to the client. . . . I think I will be a surrogate mother once more for the same client."[23] That surrogates typically part with the baby with gladness as I did—not torment—not only comes as a surprise to the people with whom I have shared my post-childbirth feelings, but to some surrogacy researchers themselves. For instance, it was an "unexpected finding" for sociologist Hazel Baslington that the majority surrogates in her study had "coped very well," with half mentioning "the look on the faces of the couple as the baby is handed over to them as being 'the best' part."[24]

Though opponents and others ambivalent about the practice worry that surrogacy may be asking too much of a woman—to alienate herself from what she would "naturally" feel toward any child carried in her womb or to "promis[e] something it is not in anyone's power to promise: not to fall in love with her baby"[25]—countless surrogate mothers report never bonding with the child to begin with, so never needing to protect themselves from becoming attached. As five different surro-moms from four different studies conducted in Israel, the U.S., and Thailand explain:

> It's not mine and that is why I didn't have the kinds of feelings you'd expect.

> I have NO feelings of "mother" towards her . . . I do not in any way feel like I am giving up a child. I am giving a child to her parents after nine months of helping her grow.

> I nurtured, loved and would have died for my surro baby. . . . It was one of the best experiences of my life. I did however have to remind tons of people that I simply gave the baby BACK TO ITS PARENTS—NOT AWAY!! . . . I cried tears of JOY because sacrificing, giving life . . . was more rewarding than I ever thought it would be. BUT I STILL FELT NOTHING MATERNAL WHAT SO EVER TO THE BABY I BROUGHT INTO THE WORLD!!! [emphasis in original]

> I knew carrying babies that were not genetically related to me, I would not have a hard time separating. . . . I never felt like I was giving up babies. I was giving them back. If it were genetically mine, I think I might feel like I was giving it up.

It is no problem for me because that's what I intended to do from the beginning.[26]

The researchers who conducted a qualitative study of Indian surrogates in three sites (Mumbai, Chennai, and New Delhi) before India prohibited commercial arrangements had similar findings. They, too "observed no kind of maternal bond, which is consistent with other findings in India and observations in other countries such as Canada, the US and the United Kingdom." Their surrogates nevertheless described an "affective bond" or something like a "nanny bond" with the child they were carrying and noted they were "taking special care for this pregnancy . . . because the future baby represented an important investment for the intended parents and a large sum of money for them."[27] As I later explain in chapters 3 and 6, I too never bonded with Katie and Steven's baby: I never once felt she was ever mine to begin with or that I had wanted her to be at any point throughout my pregnancy or in the years after.

In contrast to this pervasive myth that pregnant women will become attached to the life growing inside of them, the literature shows instead that surro-moms are more likely to bond with the intended parents instead. As Olga B. A. van den Akker, British psychologist and author of *Surrogate Motherhood Families,* has seen from her clinical studies on families expanded by surrogacy:

> Many surrogates and commissioning couples develop a strong bond or friendship during the arrangements because both physical and emotional changes are relevant to both parties. Many . . . experience strong emotions when the result of a pregnancy test is positive and the experience of birth is shared. . . . These emotions are shared by both parties together under these intimate conditions. They therefore get to know each other well and most keep in contact well after the arrangement has terminated.[28]

Several other researchers have found that a surro-mom's most important relationship is with the IPs. In Yuri Hibino and Yosuke Shimazono's study of Thai surrogates, their subjects "expected that their compassion in helping an infertile couple would be reciprocated not only by monetary payment but by special treatment during pregnancy and after the delivery"—the surrogates understood themselves to be "forg[ing] a lasting personal relationship" with their couple.[29]

Thus, when "things go wrong" from the surrogate's perspective, it is usually due to tension or strain in their relationship with the IPs for a variety of possible reasons. For example, while surrogates are usually sympathetic to their IPs' desire to exert some control in a long process with no guarantees, some also resent being grilled about their diet, weight gain, work, or other activities. As one five-time mom and two-time surrogate annoyed at her intended mothers' "presumed expertise" exclaimed: "I don't need somebody to tell me how to be pregnant! This isn't my first rodeo! It sounds kind of harsh to say, but you see these IPs who are micromanaging [us] . . . and they've never had any [kids]."[30] Another possible negative outcome is hurt when the feelings of intimacy and closeness with their IPs abate at journey's end. While many parents send regular updates about their new lives with their baby and many other IP-surrogate pairs maintain lasting friendships particularly in contexts where ongoing friendship is expected,[31] there are also sporadic "anguish stories" of parents who abruptly wean themselves off from their previously chummy relationship, leaving the women who bore their child(ren) heartbroken.[32] The danger in insisting upon this trope of surrogate pain post-relinquishment after numerous studies have found it to be the rare exception, not the norm, is that we risk "eclipsing the meaning of the process for surrogates themselves"—we risk substituting our preconceived notions of what surrogacy is like for surrogates' firsthand accounts of their own feelings and experiences.[33]

MOST INTENDED PARENTS EXPERIENCE STRESS *AND* POSITIVE PARENTING OUTCOMES

Turning now to intended parents, psychologists are not wrong to have identified that long list of possible stressors for couples given the expenses and medical and other logistical uncertainties involved, the delicate relationships that must be negotiated with one or more third parties, and the social stigma infertile couples might already be facing for their childlessness, which might be compounded by their resort to the most controversial method of assisted reproduction. As I saw myself with my friends, Katie and Steven, and have come to learn through other intended parents I have since befriended, nearly every step of the journey can be nerve-wracking. Victories, large and small, are commonly celebrated: the successful creation of a good number of healthy embryos, the first time they all hear the fetal heartbeat via ultrasound, and so forth. Conversely, large and small setbacks can occasion fresh waves of anxiety, grief, or even despair, such as when only a small number of blastocysts survive the "thaw," when they receive bad news of implantation failure, or other crushing events.

Straight Couples

Despite some researchers' hypothesis that these stressors would accordingly have a "detrimental effect" on their psychological state and subsequent "quality of parenting," their own findings and the studies of others on surrogacy-created families suggest otherwise. One study involving forty-two British surrogacy families and a comparison group of fifty-one egg-donation families and eighty natural-conception families found that parents of surrogate-born children scored even higher on tests on psychological well-being and adaption to parenthood in the child's first year of life than the parents of naturally conceived children did, with the exception of their "emotional overinvolvement" or overprotectiveness. Those who became parents through surrogacy displayed lower levels of parenthood-related stress, "greater warmth and attachment-related behavior," and "greater enjoyment of parenthood," and these results also held steady when these same parents were assessed again two and three years later.[34] The researchers explained their unexpected finding thusly: the surrogate-born children (like their donor-conceived counterparts) were "extremely wanted" by those who had been trying for years to become parents, and the long and laborious process of assisted reproduction likely strengthened the IPs' desire and determination to succeed, which then translated into happier parenting.[35]

Gay Male Couples

Gay male IPs are comparable to their heterosexual counterparts in experiencing some anxiety and stress during the ART process, but similarly have positive parenting outcomes upon completion of a successful journey.[36] A study of forty gay men in committed relationships who had become fathers through a California-based agency specializing in gay clientele found that most experienced an enhanced sense of self-esteem and pride in finally being able to fulfill their dream of having both a loving partner *and* a child (or children) with him. Most also responded favorably to the "increased recognition of their family unit after having children" from their work colleagues or other acquaintances, friends, and families of origin. As one new father noted: "My family is more interested in what we're doing. It's just such a pleasure to watch my family react to the baby."[37] Others were moved by the support they received even from people to whom they did not feel especially close. As new father Randall recounted:

> I work in a medium-sized company, and as our due date approached, one of our secretaries . . . organized a baby shower for us. *The whole company gathered the next week at lunch hour.* . . . There was special food, gifts, and party games, and when they opened the presents they took each ribbon from the gift and put it through a paper plate to make two decorated hats. We have the photograph of Nathan and me in our hats on the mantel, right next to Audrey's baby pictures.
>
> It was a fabulous experience for us. While I work with these people, they aren't really our close friends. And who knows, maybe some people stayed away on purpose. *But it was like the world was welcoming Nathan and me and our baby. It really meant a lot to us.* (emphasis added)[38]

One key difference between infertile straight couples and gay male couples is that donor-assisted reproduction of some kind is "universally necessary for gay and lesbian couples" if they would like to have biogenetically related children, so their use of ART generally carries "none of the . . . sense of failure within the GLBT communities that many heterosexual couples must lay to rest."[39] Heterosexual couples who must typically mourn the "death" of a conventional parenthood story before turning either to adoption or collaborative reproduction to become parents may have something to learn from queer families who have been managing the presence of third parties since the beginning of queer families—a point to which I will return in subsequent chapters.

A second key difference is that while heterosexual IPs might also be biogenetically asymmetrical in relation to their child if only one but not both of them would also be the genetic parents, gay male IPs face a distinctive, potentially competitive situation where only one of them could be the biological father. Same-sex couples have nonetheless found ways of handling this oft-sensitive issue to preserve a sense of fairness, equality, and joint participation. Some attempt to work out which one of them cares more about biogenetic relatedness and then have that person become the genetic parent.[40] Others use a similar method and encourage the nongenetic father to play a more dominant role in *other* decisions as a way of bringing more parity into the situation. As one gay dad from Australia recounts:

I ended up taking the lead in screening and narrowing down the choice of egg donors from agency websites . . . , while my partner Ricardo (who ended up being the sperm donor) selected among the egg donors I presented to him. In that sense, I felt that I, too, had played a major role in genetically creating our baby from the start even though I wasn't the sperm donor. Sally [our upstairs neighbor] joked that not only had I selected the egg donor, but . . . the sperm donor too. The baby was entirely my genetic creation! We all laughed.[41]

Still others attempt to introduce as much symmetry as possible in each step of the ART process. One couple in a traditional surrogacy took turns providing sperm when their friend (their surrogate) was ovulating and then registered the nongenetic parent on the baby's birth certificate to "express their social equivalence as parents."[42] An interracial couple from Australia took a different route by arranging not only for both to have an equal chance of being the bio-dad, but also for the resultant child to physically resemble them both:

Sami: We decided we wanted to have mix [*sic*] race children because I'm Asian and Ian's Caucasian. So my sperm was mixed with a Western girl and Ian's with [an] Asian girl and then we selected one [embryo] of each and [went] from there.

Ian: We . . . wanted our children to reflect our backgrounds . . . . We wanted them to have not only exposure to and experience with each of our cultures, but we also wanted them to physically reflect them as well so when they look to us they'll see part of themselves in each of us.[43]

Other couples believe any approach where both contribute genetic material to see whose sperm or whose embryo would prevail could "detract from a sense of equity or partnership" by introducing "an unfavorable competitive element into the attempts to conceive." Rather than risk a situation where the man without the "'virile' sperm" could end up feeling a "potential loss of masculine dignity," some couples make a purely medical decision based on their doctors' assessment of which of them has the material more likely to "surviv[e] the sperm quarantine and freezing process and produc[e] healthy embryos."[44] However gay male couples resolve the question of genetic fatherhood,[45] studies show they tend not to disclose the identity of the bio-dad to outsiders. This choice is not typically due to shame or unresolved feelings about their use of third-party reproduction (as it is for many heterosexual couples) but to preserve their privacy, avoid perpetuating the idea that it is biological connection that makes a family, and allow them to reveal the truth to their children on their own terms someday without fear of accidental disclosure from others.[46]

FOUR KEY FINDINGS ABOUT SURROGATE-BORN CHILDREN

While the research amassed on surrogate-born children is not as extensive as that on adoptees or IVF-conceived children, peer-reviewed longitudinal studies have been conducted on their psychological health and well-being from ages one to fourteen. As I will unpack below under four key findings, the "kids are all right."[47]

First, mirroring the normalcy of the women who gave birth to them, studies of U.K. surrogate-born children of heterosexual couples done at ages one, two, three, seven, ten, and fourteen reveal the normal range of their psychological health in the preschool and early adolescent years. Contrary to assumptions that surrogacy would carry the greatest psychological risks for the persons involved given its status as the most controversial method of family expansion, the children did not differ in infant temperament in their first year of life from their donor-conceived or naturally conceived counterparts or in cognitive development and psychological adjustment at age two. They also did not differ on other psychological measures at age three, though did have more positive parent-child relationships than their naturally conceived counterparts.[48] By ages three, seven, ten, and fourteen, their scores on the Strengths and Difficulties Questionnaire (SDQ) also remained within the normal range, with one notable difference between them and their other family-type counterparts to be discussed below.[49] In a separate study, British children ages three to nine of gay male couples also showed "high levels of adjustment" with low levels of "behavioral and emotional problems" (below the cutoff for clinical problems) as reported by parents and teachers alike and even lower levels of "internalizing problems" than lesbian-headed households.[50]

Second, surrogate-born children are often told at a very young age that someone other than their parents bore them, and this early disclosure has been shown to be of psychological benefit to all persons involved. In one British study of forty-two families created by surrogacy, 91% had disclosed to their child by the age of ten how they came into the world, with approximately half disclosing before three and the other half disclosing between three and seven.[51] A British professor of health psychology has concluded from her own clinical studies and literature review that most surrogate-born children in the U.K. "fare well and are well cared for with a full understanding of their conception, their other 'mother,' and why they were conceived in this way."[52] These empirical findings should go some way in assuaging the fears identified above that children born of surrogacy arrangements would inevitably be "distressed by the knowledge that they had been created for the sole purpose of being given away to other parents."[53]

Third, to expand now on a point alluded to earlier, surrogate-born children showed higher levels of emotional and behavioral adjustment problems at the age of seven while still functioning within the normal range and below the cutoff for clinical problems than both their naturally conceived and donor-conceived peers.[54] According to several studies, seven is the age when most children can understand the concept of biological inheritance and the rudiments of surrogacy. As one child has articulated the matter: "Well my Mum's womb, I think . . . it was a bit broken, so . . . [my surro-mom] carried me instead of my Mum."[55] Interestingly, children adopted internationally as infants have also shown a "similar increase in behavioral problems" at age seven, though both groups eventually showed a reduction of problems: by age ten for surrogate-born children and early adolescence for international adoptees. The researchers explain this temporary uptick in difficulties thusly: both transnational adoptees (many who are trans-racial) and surrogate-born children struggle with identity-related issues at an earlier age than their peers given knowledge of their "difference." By age fourteen, surrogate-born children did not differ in self-esteem or psychological well-being from their counterparts in the other reproductive-donation family types.[56]

A fourth and final key finding is the *positive* correlation between the child's well-being and continuity in relationship with their surrogate mother.[57] Ten years following the formal conclusion of the surrogate-pregnancy, the majority of surrogate-born children in a U.K. longitudinal study had remained in close, regular contact with their surro-moms to the satisfaction of all parties whether or not they were previously acquainted with one another, thus allaying some researchers' concerns that her continued presence in the child's life might pose problems for the family over time. Most children at age ten either felt "positive" (24%) or "neutral/indifferent" (67%) about their surrogate birth,[58] with the majority "liking" their surrogate mother (93%), describing her with adjectives like "kind," "lovely," and "nice," and also addressing her with honorific, kin-like titles such as "auntie," "special auntie," "tummy mummy," or " 'other mum."[59] Regular contact between surro-mom and surrogate-born child thus seems to facilitate a number of goods, including normalizing the child's unconventional conception and birth.

At the time of this writing, there are no known peer-reviewed studies of surrogate-born children as adults, so what is known about such children pales in comparison to what we know about the other members of the surrogacy triad. My constructive framework of ethical principles for surrogacy nonetheless incorporates these findings, including by recommending early disclosure to the children the truth about their birth circumstances and encouraging the maintenance of relationships between and among the surrogate, IPs, and child(ren) following the formal conclusion of the arrangement.

OTHERS BEYOND THE SURROGACY TRIAD

As I witnessed myself when my well-wishers would ask about how my husband and children were handling my unusual pregnancy, commentators tend to suspect that surrogacy arrangements would come at notable costs to the surrogate's own family as well. The research shows a surrogate's own family members and others in the surrounding community typically respond in varied ways, with empirical studies providing evidence of being supportive on the one hand and disapproving and even resentful on the other depending on a host of contextual considerations.

The Surrogate's Spouse or Partner

Arguably the person most affected by a surrogate's involvement in the collaborative reproduction apart from all members of the surrogacy triad is their spouse or partner, if any. The issue is not simply most surrogates' need for emotional support. As discussed in my primer, this partner or spouse usually must also take part in the medical and psychological screening processes, perhaps also sign the contract or pre-conception agreement or even be listed as one of the child's parents on the birth certificate depending upon jurisdiction, and abide by the surrogate's mandated periods of sexual abstinence or "pelvic rest"—in my case, an approximately six-week period from the start of injectable medications to a positive confirmation of pregnancy in the first (failed) ET and again for another six weeks in our second (successful) attempt. They might also have to do more than their normal share of childcare or household chores during the times in their partner's pregnancy when she cannot resume her regular activities due to doctor's orders, must travel for medical appointments, or undergo other pregnancy-related best practices. Surrogates themselves generally acknowledge the additional work, inconveniences, and sacrifices their spouses or partners must undergo: one of the reasons why four-time surrogate Deana Meer in one study finally "retired" from bearing children for others after helping three different families was her husband's desire to "have [his] wife back."[60]

Indeed, the majority of surrogates in one Texas- and California-based study concluded that their surrogacy would have been impossible without the support of at least one close ally, who was usually their spouse or partner. Most of these subjects sought out and received their husband's support, with some only coming around after considerable resistance to the idea. As a different researcher who analyzed surrogacy message boards and online forums in the U.S. reports, a consensus has emerged that the partner's or spouse's support is essential, which is why veterans commonly advise newbies *not* to embark upon a journey unless the surro-mom's partner or spouse is firmly on board, as some know from their own experience the tensions and difficulties it can cause if they are not.[61]

My husband's response was very different from some of these surrogates' reports about having had an initially resistant partner. I never had to convince Nathaniel that I should help Katie and Steven in this way, as he knew pregnancy was relatively easy for me and that there was no danger of my bonding with my friends' child in utero (I explain why in chapter 6). Nathaniel not only did the requisite things noted above, but he also faithfully administered all of my IVF hormone shots every third day over what ultimately amounted to a five-month period. Unlike my parents, he did not worry about my health throughout my higher-risk IVF pregnancy, though he did find difficult—as we all did—the circumstances surrounding my need to have an emergency C-section and the operation itself. Finally, unlike Elizabeth Kane's husband, he did not feel stigmatized by his co-workers or others about my being pregnant with another man's (and another woman's) child. Sometimes he would even have some fun by telling people "Grace is pregnant, but here's the thing—I'm not the father" as he watched their eyes widen with alarm before assuring them that this wasn't a shocking case of infidelity but a happy one of my helping out our friends who would finally become parents after ten long years of waiting.

The Surrogate's Own Children

A U.K. study on the psychological health and experiences of the surrogate's own children has concluded they "overall . . . do not experience negative psychological health or family functioning."[62] These findings, corroborated by other research in the surrogacy literature, show that the children are able to understand and support their mother's decision to bear a child for someone else who could not on their own. Despite some critics' fears to the contrary, the surrogate's own child(ren) also tend to regard their mother as "special" rather than either develop a low view of her for "giving away" a baby or become fearful of being abandoned themselves.[63] The following is an example of one child's attitude among the 81% of them in one study who were coded as having "positive views" of their mother's surrogacy: "I think it's a really like nice thing to do for someone, obviously if they can't have children and they really want a child that's a bad thing, so if someone else is able to do that for you and help you through it then it's something that's compassionate really."[64]

At the start of my surrogacy journey, one of my two major unknowns was how my boys (then ages six and eight) would respond to what was about to unfold. It turns out that they were delighted to learn I would be helping Katie and Steven (whom they affectionately called "auntie" and "uncle") to have their first child, as they had independently observed they were the only married friends with whom we regularly socialized who didn't have kids. Like other surrogates' children, my boys proudly "shared the fact that their mother was a surrogate with other people in their lives: their friends, teachers, and class-mates; and people at church and camp."[65] They enjoyed watching my belly expand over the course of nine months and feeling the baby move around in my second and third trimesters. They even asked me a few times to recount if they had similarly once kicked and fluttered about when they were growing inside of me—questions they had never previously asked. My surrogacy had not only deepened their understanding of pregnancy, but also how they them-selves once came into the world.

Still, the research shows the surrogate's own children do have to contend with their share of inconveniences and sacrifices. Since what a surro-mom does is "woven into the fabric of the day-to-day lived experience" of familial life, all members participate either directly or indirectly in her arrangement "but not without tension."[66] Family members have sometimes reported being unhappy with their mother's mood swings from pregnancy hormones, her time spent away due to frequent medical appointments or other pregnancy-related behavioral restrictions, and the extra work they may have had to do in light of it, such as an older sibling being called upon more frequently to watch younger siblings. Indeed, many infertility clinics (including the one we used) do not permit surrogates to bring their own children with them to their appointments out of sensitivity to other patients struggling to bear any children at all, thus obliging surro-moms to arrange for childcare. In my own case, my kids missed me when my first embryo transfer attempt prevented me from going on a Cub Scout camping trip with them, when I could not snowboard with them on the weekends out of an abundance of caution when pregnant, and when I was apart from them for what amounted to a five-and-a-half-day hospital stay for childbirth and recovery. While this was not my experience, some surro-mothers report having felt guilty about the times when they "had to put their own children's needs to the side" either for the sake of the surrogate-pregnancy or because they felt unwell during portions of it.[67]

What I find both remarkable and true in our case is that the surrogate's own children can sometimes even "maintain contact and develop positive relationships with the intended parents and the surrogacy child" once born. In one of the previously mentioned U.K. studies, the surrogate's children would refer to the surrogate-born child using a range of siblings terms ("sister/brother," "half-sister/half-brother," "tummy sister") or as someone who was "like a cousin or a sister," a "family friend," or by name—with none of these terms being associated more with traditional or gestational arrangements. The researchers speculated it was possible that the terms "reflected the closeness of the relationships between the surrogate's family and the intended family which were not dependent on whether or not the surrogate used her egg for the surrogacy."[68] In my collaborative reproduction with my friends, my sons donned a somewhat protective role over Katie and Steven's unborn child once they learned I was carrying her and then took on an older cousin–like role after she was born. Once when we were thinking about watching a particular movie for Halloween and my then six-year-old worried that if the movie was scary, it might also scare the baby inside of me and so maybe we better not? My boys have continued to see and play with her on a semiregular basis, though the frequency of our meet-ups diminished during the Covid-19 pandemic in the interests of public health.

One question common among first-time surrogates is how to tell their own children what they are doing. Many surrogates, particularly if they are on repeat journeys, try to normalize surrogacy by explaining the mechanics to them, which in some cases requires them to accelerate the timing of their talking about sex and reproduction. My husband and I decided to wait to tell our kids (then ages six and eight) anything about our plans with our friends until I had crossed the twelve-week mark—past the first trimester when miscarriages are more common. To my relief, our kids were able to understand the basics of what we told them through a book we used called *The Kangaroo Pouch: A Story about Surrogacy for Young Children* (2006) which plays out a version of the popular "broken tummy" explanation in the context of friendly marsupials.[69] Perhaps because they had not known for long how babies are made naturally, they were not confused by our explaining to them how others like Katie and Steven would come to have a child through a different route.[70] As Linda Kirkman, the first gestational surrogate in Australia who carried her sister's child, explains: "People underestimate children's ability to understand a clear explanation. Children can be confused and unhappy if they are aware something is happening and secrets are being kept from them." She reports how her own kids (Heather and Will) handled the news of carrying her niece (Alice) for her sister (Maggie): "Heather and Will have always known what is going on and why . . . They have always accepted without question that [Alice] is their cousin, not their sister, and are slightly disdainful of others who cannot understand what to them is perfectly clear. She is Maggie's baby who grew from Maggie's egg and was always intended to grow up as Maggie's daughter."[71]

Conclusion

I have come to see that many in society do not only presume it must be psychologically torturous for a woman to hand over the child she has carried in her womb to others to raise, but they actively *want* that to be the case, lest their belief in the solidity of maternal love be shaken. As Australia's first intended mother and second known intended mother in the world wisely observed, "part of the horror inspired by surrogacy is fear of a world in which the mother-child bond is fragile and transient—a world in which a mother can give away her baby."[72] Surrogacy as a practice threatens public confidence in the naturalness of motherhood and the universality of the maternal instinct. But just as the myth of abortion regret persists even though numerous studies have found that the majority of persons who terminate their pregnancies feel relief after the fact and affirm even years later that it was the right decision for them to have made, so I and other surrogates must gently correct people's assumptions about our painful "loss" over the child we once carried and gave back at journey's end.[73]

Something similar can be said about popular fears about the well-being of the children born of or affected by surrogacy. Of course, segments of the general public have been raising concerns for decades about families that deviate from the nuclear model of a married mother and father raising their biological (and naturally conceived) children together, whether those families are headed by single parents or queer couples or have donor-conceived children or are blended and so forth. But the research on families expanded by surrogacy should pacify some folks' worries about psychological risks, as studies have shown both surrogate-born children and the surrogate's own children are generally able to cope well when told the truth about these irregular pregnancies, with their greatest risks stemming from social disapproval or misunderstanding about what their families have done.

3   DOES SURROGACY VIOLATE DISTINCTIVE FEMINIST OR CHRISTIAN COMMITMENTS?

IT WAS VERY LATE ONE fall evening. I had already been in the hospital for thirty-six hours and counting after having been admitted for a medically indicated induction. My husband had stationed himself behind my head, gently whispering words of reassurance. He could sense my alarm at how much my body was involuntarily shivering and shaking from the epidural, IV fluids, and labor hormones. Katie, the intended mother of the baby I had been carrying for thirty-eight and a half weeks, was standing to my left, nervously awaiting what was to unfold. Her husband, Steven, had not been permitted in the operating room given the two-guest limit. I could see in front of me a large curtain and several doctors and nurses scurrying about in surgical scrubs and masks. While months before, I had nearly spit out my drink during office hours when a graduate student recited John 15:13 upon learning of my surrogacy and thus compared me to Jesus ("No one has greater love than this, to lay down one's life for one's friends"), it wasn't lost on me that I was now lying down on a T-shaped operating table with my arms outstretched and strapped down in what some nurses have called the "crucifix position."

Of the many memories I have of the events surrounding my emergency C-section, one stands out above the rest: the moment when my ob/gyn pulled the baby out and we all heard her cry. I remember closing my eyes, releasing

59

a fresh surge of tears from relief, joy, and exhaustion, and thinking silently to myself, "Hot damn, we did this." I also remember sensing my doctor's hesitation as he held the baby girl and slowly moved toward me. He seemed uncertain—or perhaps he had simply forgotten—to whom he should give her: my friend (Katie) or me (her surrogate). So I quickly exclaimed "Katie! Give the baby to Katie!" and then uncharacteristically stuttered "K-K-Katie, hold your baby!" to end the confusion by barking out orders of what was to be done. As my unconventional pregnancy came to an end, so did Katie and Steven's ten-year saga of involuntary childlessness.

———

I turn in this chapter to discussing common fears and objections to surrogacy among feminists who are largely but not exclusively operating out of a secular framework and among Christians who are not necessarily committed to feminism. Feminists who oppose surrogacy have long criticized both the industry and practice for redefining and fragmenting motherhood, impeding the autonomy and rights of persons who contractually bear children for others, undermining the case for abortion rights, and advancing harmful gender stereotypes. In turn, Christian opponents of surrogacy fault the practice for its alleged incompatibility with God's vision for sex, marriage, reproduction, and the family; routine mistreatment of embryos in the IVF process required in gestational arrangements; and purported inferiority to adoption.

Feminist Concerns about Surrogacy

Feminists as a diverse group do not hold one unified position on surrogacy. Some welcome reproductive technologies for augmenting people's choices and self-determination in reproductive matters while others, including friends and colleagues, cite a litany of reservations.

THE CHARGE: SURROGACY REDEFINES AND FRAGMENTS MOTHERHOOD

Some feminist critics fault surrogacy for disrupting the unity of maternity in ways they do not believe serves women's best interests. Among others, sociologist Barbara Katz Rothman finds the practice "horrific" for "reinvent[ing] motherhood, mak[ing] it imaginable or understandable that a woman is not necessarily the mother of the baby with whom she is pregnant." Surrogacy in her view puts all women in harm's way, for "if any pregnant woman is not necessarily, inherently, legally, morally, and obviously the mother of the baby in her belly, then no woman can stand firm before law and the state in her motherhood."[1] *The Nation* columnist Katha Pollit expressed similar discomfort in the late 1980s about even calling persons who bear children for others "surrogate mothers":

> "Mother" describes the relationship of a woman to a child, not to the father of that child and his wife. Everything a woman does to produce her own child Mary Beth Whitehead did, including giving it half the genetic inheritance regarded by the judge as so decisive an argument on behalf of William Stern [the intended father]. *If anyone was a surrogate mother, it was Elizabeth Stern*, for she was the one who substituted, or wished to substitute, for the child's actual mother. (emphasis added)[2]

This view led her to prefer the term "contract maternity" instead, just as it led philosopher Rosemary Tong to call surrogates "contracted mothers" instead, since a woman who gestates a child in her judgment "*is* the mother of that child."[3] Decades later, fifteen self-identified "feminist academics and advocates" who submitted an *amici curiae* (friends of the court) brief in support of the pregnant woman in a tragic 2017 California custody dispute argued similarly: "A pregnant woman is not a 'surrogate' for someone else. She is a pregnant woman whose body causes a child to exist; being forced to deny this biological reality constitutes grievous harm."[4] These critics find it atrocious for the institution of surrogacy to be privileging the projected relationship between a couple and their hoped-for child over the pregnant woman's real, embodied relationship to this same child developing inside of her, particularly since patriarchal thinking has long prioritized spirit over flesh and mind over body.

To be sure, this prioritization of the mental over the physical is arguably what happened when California made surrogacy headlines as the first U.S. state to declare gestational surrogacy contracts compatible with existing federal and state laws. *Johnson v. Calvert*, 851 P.2d 776 (1993) was a precedence-setting case involving a contractual surrogacy arrangement that had soured. In dispute was legal motherhood and custody: should the gestational surrogate (Anna Johnson) be recognized as the child's legal mother, or should the contracting mother (Crispina Calvert), since Ms. Calvert and her husband (Mark) had originally deputized Ms. Johnson to gestate the embryo created from their own (the Calverts') gametes? The California Supreme Court found both "genetic consanguinity" and "giving birth" were sufficient to establish motherhood under the Uniform Parentage Act, though there could only be one "natural mother" under California law. Since the court viewed both Ms. Calvert and Ms. Johnson as having an equal claim, they turned to the "intention" of all parties to settle the matter. They found in disputed cases where the genetic mother is not the same as the gestational one, "she who intended to procreate the child—that is, she who intended to bring about the birth of a child that she intended to raise as her own—is the natural mother."

THE CHARGE: SURROGACY DIMINISHES WOMEN'S AUTONOMY AND RIGHTS

A second fear among feminist critics is that surrogacy would leave women worse off than they were before—that any woman who would contractually agree in advance to forsake her maternal claims following childbirth would be signing away the power she would otherwise have had if she had signed nothing at all. When reflecting on Baby M, Katha Pollitt noted the ways surrogacy erodes women's power and autonomy:

> Right now a man cannot legally control the conduct of a woman pregnant by him. He cannot force her to have an abortion or not have one, to manage her pregnancy and delivery as he thinks best, or to submit to fetal surgery or a Caesarean. Nor can he sue her if, through what he considers to be negligence, she miscarries or produces a defective baby. A maternity contract could give a man all those powers, except, possibly, the power to compel abortion.[5]

Decades later, Gloria Steinem articulated similar concerns in her Open Letter in June 2019 calling upon the Governor of New York not to legalize commercial surrogacy since it "undermines women's control over their bodies" when the "rights over the fetus [women are] carrying are greatly curtailed" and they "lose all rights to the baby."[6]

This fear that surrogacy curtails, not augments, women's rights to bodily autonomy and integrity taps into the radical feminist critique that the rise of reproductive science has eroded the maternal power of childbearing which was previously the exclusive purview of women. Poet Adrienne Rich, among others, has criticized the medicalization of pregnancy and childbirth in her *Of Woman Born: Motherhood as Experience and Institution* (1985). In contrast, in the purported superior method of "natural" childbirth, pregnant and laboring women would resist medical or technical interventions to preserve women-centered knowledge (i.e., midwifery) and a sense of their own control. Gena Corea, a journalist and founding member of the Feminist International Network of Resistance to Reproductive and Genetic Engineering (FINRRAGE) similarly argued in *The Mother Machine* (1985) that "reproductive technologies from artificial insemination to artificial wombs" (her book's subtitle) do not serve women well. For under the guidance of a historically and still largely male-dominated scientific and medical community, poor women are being coerced not to reproduce through either sterilization and other campaigns shaming them for childbearing while wealthier women are being encouraged to address fertility issues through the use of harmful drugs, invasive procedures, and prenatal tests which alienate them from their own bodily experiences.

THE CHARGE: SURROGACY UNDERMINES ABORTION RIGHTS

A third fear for some feminists is surrogacy's unwanted implications for the abortion debate. In discussions about what has been called the "metaphysics of pregnancy," philosophers have been discussing how to characterize the relationship between the maternal organism (in this case, a pregnant person) and the embryo or fetus growing inside of them as well as how the relationship changes over time. On the *parthood* model, the developing life is *part* of a pregnant person like your hand is part of you or a tail is part of a dog or cat: colloquially, the developing life is a pregnant person's "bump." On the *container* model, a pregnant person is hosting a separate entity in their uterus: colloquially, the entity is their "bun in the oven."[7]

Whether to valorize or to condemn, commentators often use *container* imagery when describing surrogacy as a practice where a pregnant person provides nurturance to a life distinct from them. Surrogacy professionals in India often explain to prospective surrogates that their wombs would be temporarily housing a "separate entity"—a baby who would not otherwise have a place to live and grow.[8] The Israeli surrogates Elly Teman interviewed thought of themselves as an "'oven baking a cake' and a 'kiln baking a sculpture.'"[9] I have observed how U.S.-based surrogates who take part in maternity photo shoots often appear with the two intended parents (IPs) (or with sometimes just the intended mother of a heterosexual couple)—with signs saying variations of "their pea, my pod" or "their bun, my oven." Some feminists fear the *container* imagery pervasive in surrogacy not boding well for abortion rights advocacy, particularly if the embryo or fetus is regarded as being under the control or possession of someone other than the expectant person. Put simply, activists fear they would have a more difficult time defending a pregnant woman's "right to choose how her body is used" if her decision were widely regarded as resulting "in the termination of a separate organism" as per the *container* model.[10] As feminist movement leader Phyllis Chesler explains:

> Viewing a woman as merely a *vessel* for property that contractually belongs to "intentional parents" [sic] erodes and is in direct conflict with the grounds for a woman's right to an abortion. The *embryo/fetus/developing child is part of the woman*, it *belongs to her* because it is in her body. This fact gives her the right to terminate a pregnancy. If others—the surrogacy profiteer, the sperm or egg donor—claim this right, then what is to stop the state or the church from making this same claim? (emphasis added)[11]

It may be no coincidence that reproductive health, rights, and justice activists often campaign for maintaining access to safe and legal abortion by implicitly drawing upon a *parthood* model of pregnancy instead—"my body, my choice" or "our bodies, ourselves."

THE CHARGE: SURROGACY PERPETUATES NEGATIVE
GENDER STEREOTYPES

Finally, some feminists fault surrogacy as an institution for perpetuating pernicious ideas about women and men. They allege the great effort IPs undergo to have a biogenetically related child, which is matched by the extraordinary measures surrogates undertake to become pregnant for them, reinforces patriarchal beliefs about women's worth being tied to reproductive functioning and therein bolsters the compulsory motherhood ideal the feminist movement has been keen to interrogate instead of promote. Thus, for all of the talk about the newness of reproductive technologies, some feminists view ART as ultimately advancing traditionalist ends and thus being more conservative than truly progressive.

A variant of this concern about surrogacy perpetuating negative gender stereotypes is that the institution reinforces social expectations for women to serve others sacrificially, especially through pregnancy and childbirth. According to radical feminist Gena Corea, because women in patriarchal societies have been conditioned to place the needs of others before their own and because society values women's childbearing more than their career trajectories, it is "not surprising that some women only feel special when they are pregnant and assert that they love reproducing."[12] Similarly, some aspects of altruistic surrogacy might be commendable according to radical feminist Janice G. Raymond, but the social practice still leaves intact "the image and reality of a woman as a *reproductive conduit,* someone through whom someone passes" and thus fails to unmoor the "social definition of women as breeders."[13] Finally, while Catholic feminist Lisa Sowle Cahill's goal is neither to "judge [or] condemn . . . couples . . . [who] find the new birth technologies virtually irresistible" in their yearning for a child, she finds the radical feminist critique of ART instructive for directing us to "look below the surface of free and informed consent" to recognize that "powerful social forces always shape choice and define the options that we are able to discern as available to us." She would thus similarly draw our attention to the "collusion of gender stereotypes and market forces" that has produced a clientele for infertility services, particularly when women have been socialized since birth "with images of mothering as crucial to their identity," men have been "taught to see virility and sexual potency as confirmed in the ability to 'father' a child," and both men and women have been "led to see the sexual and reproductive services of women as men's natural right and due."[14]

Christian Concerns about Surrogacy

The Ethics and Religious Liberty Commission of the Southern Baptist Convention (SBC) confidently proclaims "almost all Christian bioethicists agree that most forms of surrogacy are theologically and morally problematic."[15] Although the SBC as an organization does not speak for all Christians, their statement may well be correct as an empirical matter since Christian leaders and bioethicists across the ecumenical spectrum tend to express more condemnation than commendation for this unconventional way of bringing a child into the world.

THE CHARGE: SURROGACY VIOLATES GOD'S WILL FOR MARRIAGE, SEX, AND THE FAMILY

First, Christians who denounce surrogacy normally take issue with other nontraditional sexual and reproductive practices as well while often showing compassion for—and providing guidance to—married infertile couples despondent over their involuntary childlessness. The Congregation for the Doctrine of the Faith (CDF), the body responsible for defending and promulgating Catholic doctrine, has addressed the morality of reproductive technologies in a 1987 document called *Donum Vitae* ("Instruction on Respect for Human Life in Its Origin and on the Dignity of Procreation"). The CDF instructs that medical technologies assisting the conjugal act toward pregnancy (e.g., fertility drugs, surgery to overcome tubal blockages) may be morally licit, though any medical technique or practice replacing sexual intercourse even between husband and wife to beget a child remains prohibited (e.g., artificial conception including artificial insemination by husband, IVF, the use of donor gametes). While *Donum Vitae* also insists everyone deserves to be treated with dignity and respect as a blessing from God no matter how they came into the world, "truly responsible procreation" would entail each "unborn child" being conceived naturally in marriage as "the fruit and the sign of the mutual self-giving of the spouses, of their love and of their fidelity."[16]

Importantly for our purposes, *Donum Vitae* judges the practice of surrogacy to be "contrary to the unity of marriage and to the dignity of the procreation of the human person." Surrogate motherhood "represents an objective failure to meet the obligations of maternal love, of conjugal fidelity and of responsible motherhood; it offends the dignity and the right of the child to be conceived, carried in the womb, brought into the world and brought up by his own parents; it sets up, to the detriment of families, a division between the physical, psychological and moral elements which constitute those families."[17] As Catholic moral theologian John Berkman explains in his concurrence, the Church objects to the practice's "multiplication of 'parents'" for the ways it corrodes familial cohesion, "instrumentalization of women's bodies for the benefit of others" whether or not the surrogate is paid for her labor, and trivialization of the "moral significance of the biological and emotional bond that typically forms in gestation"—a bond both he and the *Magisterium* believe to be natural.[18]

We can detect two notable differences when shifting from Catholic to other Christian moral reasoning about these matters. First, many Protestant and Orthodox thinkers, like their dissenting Catholic counterparts, reject the Vatican's insistence for each and every act of marital intercourse to remain open to procreation: they usually permit the use of artificial contraception so long as the general connection between marriage and childbearing is maintained and, for some "pro-life" Protestants and Orthodox, so long as the contraceptive method used does not cause harm to any new life a couple may have already procreated.[19] Second, most Protestants and the Orthodox ground their positions on marriage, sex, and the family more explicitly in reference to biblical teaching and on centuries of theological commentary about it than on what "reason" or "nature" may reveal as per the natural law. Despite these differences, we can detect practical convergence on their opposition to surrogacy.

Consider the following sample of views. While acknowledging no explicit biblical condemnation of the practice can be found, Russell Moore, a former president of the Ethics and Religious Liberty Commission of the Southern Baptist Convention, still urges evangelicals to avoid resorting to surrogacy because it "severs the one-flesh union God has designed as being the place where children are born" and commodifies children rather than treating them as God-given gifts.[20] Bioethicist Scott B. Rae similarly seeks to hold up the "Genesis ideal" of God's original design, which is for sex and procreation to take place within "permanent, monogamous, heterosexual marriage"—and without any third-party involvement.[21] According to bioethicist and former Society of Christian Ethics president Allen Verhey, the infertility industry threatens the "integrity of medicine" and distorts a proper view of ourselves as "embodied and communal creatures" by permitting persons to treat "pro-creative behaviors . . . as if these could be regarded merely as matters of physiology and . . . contract."[22] More specifically, because providers of sperm, ova, and wombs "engage in acts of begetting without an intention to care for the children who might result" and because society ordinarily insists "biological parents have a responsibility to care for their children" even as we permit and even encourage adoption in some cases, Verhey faults these ART techniques for "demean[ing] the 'good' exchanged . . . corrupt[ing] the community of parent and child . . . and . . . distort[ing] the way we think and talk about children and about ourselves."[23]

THE CHARGE: SURROGACY INVOLVES INFIDELITY

Second, one way of articulating the argument that surrogacy contravenes God's plans for marriage goes beyond the popular belief discussed in the previous chapter that third-party reproduction would be difficult for any couple to navigate interpersonally. According to a subset of Christian critics, any outsider's presence in a couple's act of procreation, even if no intercourse or intimate physical contact with that third party were involved, would necessarily constitute an abuse of the marital vow of exclusive fidelity. The Russian Orthodox Church understands third-party reproduction to be a violation of "the unique nature of marital relations."[24] As paragraph 2376 of the Catechism of the Catholic Church also instructs, it would be "gravely immoral" for a couple to use a "donation of sperm or ovum, [or] surrogate uterus" in childbearing, for doing so would "betray the spouses' 'right to become a father and a mother only through each other.'" According to the Southern Baptist Convention, the use of a third party in surrogacy or donor conception would be a "violation of the marital covenant" due to the couple's refusal to "share the burden" of infertility as God intended, since "if God has chosen to withhold that blessing [of children] from one spouse, He necessarily chose to withhold it from the other."[25]

This line of argumentation would obviously render any married surrogate, not just any married couple she were helping, guilty of spousal betrayal as well. Several Catholic thinkers judge both traditional surrogacy and heterologous embryo transfer (HET) into a married woman, even if the latter is for the well-intentioned practice of "prenatal adoption" (to be discussed further below), to be tantamount to adultery because "it involves [her] seeking pregnancy apart from marital intercourse."[26] In addition, the (non-Catholic) Rev. Mark Lones draws upon thirteenth-century medieval Jewish scholar Nachmanides's novel interpretation of Leviticus 18:20 to likewise proscribe surrogacy for married women. Following the Hebrew language and Nachmanides's commentary, Lones translates Leviticus 18:20 not in the more usual manner: "You shall *not have sexual relations* with your kinsman's wife and defile yourself with her" (NRSV), but much more literally: "And you shall *not give your semen* to your neighbor's wife for seed for defilement in her" (emphasis added). Both adultery and surrogacy accordingly run counter to God's will: "God, in His infinite wisdom, prohibits surrogacy as evidenced by the author use of specific words shifting emphasis from the sexual act, defined as penetration, to deposit of semen. Surrogacy provides for procreation outside the context of the marital union of a husband and his wife, by the insertion of another person's 'seed' into another woman's uterus, and thus would be forbidden in this text."[27]

THE CHARGE: THE IVF PROCESS MISTREATS EMBRYOS

A third central area of concern for Christian opponents of surrogacy is the way embryos are routinely treated during the IVF process required in gestational arrangements. As noted in my chapter 1 primer, embryos are usually graded for their quality and sometimes even biopsied as part of preimplantation genetic testing (PGT), potentially subjected to multifetal pregnancy

reduction (MFPR) in the event of multiples, and also perhaps not even transferred into a womb for a chance to be born but stored indefinitely in a tank
of liquid nitrogen in the event of a "surplus" until those who created or have
custody over them make a "final disposition" decision about their fate.

These standard practices horrify the segment of Christians invested in
protecting the dignity of embryonic human life. The Catholic Church holds
that each human being is to be "respected and treated as a person from the
moment of conception,"[28] just as the Russian Orthodox Church condemns
the "purposeful destruction of 'spare embryos'" in light of the Church's
"biblical and patristic teaching" of the sacrality and preciousness of "human
life . . . from its origin."[29] Former Southern Baptist leader Russell Moore urges
fellow evangelicals to remember an "'embryo' isn't a thing; he or she is a
'who'"—embryos are fellow "brothers and sisters of the Lord Jesus" who are
"persons" created in the image of God whether they remain cryopreserved or
are given an opportunity to be born.[30]

While the Vatican remains staunchly against IVF, it is worth noting that
some "pro-life" Protestant thinkers have cautiously permitted IVF for married
heterosexual infertile couples who follow certain constraints. For instance,
for the sake of "safeguard[ing] the dignity of unborn human persons," Scott B.
Rae and Joy Riley have counseled Christian married couples to eschew the use
of donor gametes, create only as many embryos as they are willing to give an
"opportunity for implantation and development" into a (born) child without
cryopreservation, and transfer only the number the wife can safely carry to
term for the couple to rear if all implant.[31]

Finally, it is worth acknowledging how some Christians are so committed
to protecting embryonic life that they encourage a practice they call *embryo*
or *prenatal adoption*.[32] The movement to save embryos began when a clause
in a 1990 British statute mandating the destruction of cryopreserved embryos
left unclaimed after five years led to widespread media coverage about the
endangerment of approximately 3,300 embryos in fertility clinics across Britain.[33] Catholic moralists spearheaded a vigorous debate about the propriety of
women gestating cryopreserved embryos as a form of "adoption" or "rescue,"
particularly due to a gray area in *Donum Vitae* (1987) about the permissibility of HET and after more than two hundred women from a small Italian
village unsuccessfully petitioned the British government to stop "what they
saw as mass infanticide" by attempting to adopt them.[34] In turn, evangelicals
started "embryo adoption" programs. The evangelical-based Nightlife Chris-

tian Adoptions agency pioneered a "Snowflakes embryo adoption" program in 1997 with this rationale: "Just as each snowflake is frozen, unique and a gift from heaven, so are each of our embryo adopted Snowflake Babies. We hope to help each donated embryo grow, develop and live a full life."[35] Some Christians have been so keen to save cryopreserved embryos that they have even permitted "rescue" surrogacies as an exception to their general prohibition of the practice.[36]

As should be clear, even if some Christian critics can countenance surrogacy in "rescue" operations or permit heterologous embryo transfer to save unwanted embryos from destruction, their harsh judgment against IVF remains. Since IVF is required in the vast majority of surrogacies today (by some estimates more than 90%), they urge conscientious Christians to pursue alternative ways of fulfilling their yearning to become parents.

THE CHARGE: ADOPTION IS PREFERABLE TO ASSISTED REPRODUCTION

The final objection to surrogacy widely held among Christians, which is also common to feminists and members of the general public, is the conviction that adoption would be the better path for couples to take when they long for a child but natural conception is not (or is no longer) possible for them. While adoption when legal and ethical is a child-centered practice, feminist attorney Susan L. Bender and feminist psychologist Phyllis Chesler condemn surrogacy for being an institution where children "are being conceived in order to be adopted."[37] Even as adoption is widely understood as involving grief and loss (not just joy) and even as almost all infant adoptions today in the U.S. are either open or mediated (versus closed) to allow adoptees to stay in some contact with their first families to mitigate some of that loss,[38] a key difference between adoption and surrogacy is that birth mothers in adoption have not intentionally become pregnant with the goal of surrendering the baby once born to others to raise like surro-moms have. As in the report commissioned by the Conservative British Government in 1982 whose conclusions led to the banning of commercial surrogacy in the U.K. and the clarification that any woman who gives birth to a child is the child's legal mother, the mother-child relationship is distorted when women intentionally become pregnant for the purpose of handing over the child once born to someone else to raise.[39]

What is distinctive about the Christian encouragement of adoption over assisted reproduction is its grounding in the broader Christian mandate to help relieve the suffering of the most marginalized and vulnerable, the afore-mentioned criticisms of both IVF and third-party reproduction, and the long-standing valorization of adoption as a theological motif and actual practice. To unpack this last point, New Testament texts frequently explain the Gospel or God's plan for salvation using adoption language (*huiothesia*) (Rom 9:4, Gal 4: 4–6; cf. Rom 8: 14–17). Gentiles, or those who do not share blood con-sanguinity with the predominantly ethnically constituted Jewish people, are nonetheless depicted as having been incorporated into God's eternal covenant with Israel through the metaphors of adoption and of grafting two plants into one (Eph 3:5–6, Rom 11: 11–31). Other scriptural passages seemingly prioritize spiritual over biogenetic kinship: Jesus's teaching disrupts ordinary family re-lations (Matt 10: 34–36), Jesus's true kin are those who do God's will, not nec-essarily his biological relatives (Mark 3: 31–35), and Jesus's references to God as Father (Matt 12:46–50, Luke 2: 41–51) establishes his personal relationship with God and shows God—not one's kin—as the One who should command a person's highest loyalty. The long-standing ecclesial practice of baptism even ritualizes each baptizand's new identity in Christ and new place of ultimate belonging in the body of Christ—their spiritual family (1 Cor 12:12–13).

The Christian tradition has not surprisingly a long, albeit imperfect, prac-tice of bearing witness to the beauty of adoption in their earthly families alongside of caring more generally for children. Christians have established schools and orphanages, created "foundling wheels"—often in convents—where persons in crisis pregnancies could anonymously place their newborn infants in the care of others, established other child welfare and adoption agencies, and issued exhortations from the pulpit for congregants to adopt.[40] Lisa Sowle Cahill, herself a mother of two biological children and three ad-opted ones from Thailand, joins other Christian leaders in commending adoption for Christian married couples as a form of hospitality to strangers. While soberly acknowledging that children might only become available for adoption from past or ongoing social injustices as well as the need for all par-ties to "come to terms with their 'loss' of a unified bio-social child-parent relation," she holds out for the possibility of "transform[ing] a reproductive 'failure' on the one side, and a disrupted birthing situation on the other" into a "constructive reconformation of family relationships" through adoption.[41]

All told, these Christian pro-adoption advocates tend to view surrogacy as fulfilling only the private interests of the privileged because only a tiny fraction of involuntarily childless couples the world over could ever afford or otherwise have access to fertility treatments. In contrast, they see adoption as ideally serving the common good if arranged in such a way where the "needs of the child, the needs of birth parents, and the needs of potential adoptive parents meet and are mutually served" in the words of Gilbert Meilander, a respected Christian ethicist and member of the President's Council on Bioethics (2002–2009) under the George W. Bush administration who has likewise encouraged Christians to avoid thinking of adoption and ART as being "two ways of doing essentially the same thing—acquiring a child to rear."[42] When the goods of adoption are calculated together with the problems or at least moral complexities of both third-party reproduction and IVF, these Christian opponents essentially reach the same concluding question as my mother did: "Why don't couples who want kids but can't have them naturally just adopt?"

Responding to Feminist and Christian Concerns about Surrogacy

The constructive part of this book begins in the next two chapters when I present my progressive Christian vision and framework of guiding principles for surrogacy. To clear the conceptual underbrush and pave the way for it, I address below the aforementioned concerns and objections.

RESPONDING TO FEMINIST MISGIVINGS ABOUT SURROGACY

Turning first to distinctive feminist concerns, my overall approach is to affirm areas of common ground while noting what some of their objections overlook or unacceptably imply.

Radical Feminists' Objections Are Not Progressive

As I previously noted in one of my Introduction's disclaimers, I insist upon calling persons who bear children for others "surrogate mothers" even though some radical feminists believe them to be the *real* mothers and any person who plans on parenting the child thereafter the true *substitute* or surrogate. Not only is my terminology consistent with social convention, but persons like me who become pregnant for others frequently call ourselves surrogates (or surro-moms or surros) with the full expectation that the intended parent(s), not us, will raise the child thereafter. This phenomenon also holds true for persons who bear children for others in contexts where they must be registered on the birth certificate as the mother and thus regarded as the legal mother at the time of birth such as in the U.K. and Australia—they still identify themselves as the "surrogates."[43] I thus understand this first, radical feminist way of reversing our ordinary way of talking about surrogacy as disrespectful to these persons' self-understanding of themselves and dismissive of their interpersonal agreements with others. In short, the surro-moms I have come to know informally through discussion boards and I do not wish to be viewed as the "true" or "real" mother of the child we have born for others, since we are already the true or real mothers of our own children.

What about the feminist concern that surrogacy distorts the idealized unity of maternal work? Since this part of their accusations gets to the heart of what surrogacy as a social practice facilitates—the uncoupling of gestating a child from rearing them thereafter—I address more fully the ethics of disaggregating parenting roles in the next chapter when I present my overall vision for surrogacy. But to preview my argument: the logic behind this objection is ill-suited for a progressive Christian account of the family because it is heterosexist to lament the separation of carrying and delivering a child by one parent from raising them thereafter by another: lament necessarily betrays one's disbelief that gay male couples could ever be good or even sufficient parents without the child's birth mother (whether through surrogacy, adoption, or still other paths to parenthood they might pursue) as a co-parent. In addition, while it might be disorienting for members of the general public to distinguish between genetic, gestational, and social mothers in this rapidly changing world of reproductive medicine, it is shortsighted for anyone to refuse to embrace, much less acknowledge, how maternal work is already commonly shared—and thus divided—in non-surrogacy contexts, such as between mothers, stepmothers, and mothers-in-law. As I explain more fully in the next chapter, these ways of dividing and sharing maternal work need not threaten family cohesion so long as everyone knows and respects their place.

Surrogacy Can Be an Expression of Women's Bodily Autonomy and Rights
Second, critics who condemn surrogacy for neither being good for the surrogates themselves nor for women overall because the practice allegedly diminishes women's rights are discounting each person's agency to decide for themselves, in conscientious discernment with trusted others, the potential risks and rewards of engaging in collaborative reproduction. To illustrate, my rights were better protected—not weakened—when I signed a surrogacy

contract with my friends. Among other provisions, our contract shielded me from having to assume legal parental responsibilities for a child post-birth I had never planned on raising as my own just as it provided greater safeguards to their unborn child and my friends when we identified specific persons who would assume legal guardianship in the unlikely event both Katie and Steven were to become incapacitated or die in the process.

Though there can be more than one acceptable way for legal regimes to specify the parameters of our human rights to bodily integrity, to found a family, and to make reproductive decisions, a guiding principle in my progressive Christian framework for surrogacy to be unpacked later in chapters 5 and 6 is for all societies to "trust women" to determine what is in their best interests to do in matters pertaining to pregnancy, including any pregnancies they might undertake for others. Thus when feminist critics including Gloria Steinem decry commercial surrogacy for "put[ting] disenfranchised women at the financial and emotional mercy of wealthier and more privileged individuals,"[44] they are offering a one-sided portrayal of surro-moms as naïfs or victims of tragic circumstances—not as persons who, even assuming for the sake of argument are less well-off than their intended parents, might still be able to assess their life circumstances and the potential risks and rewards of surrogacy to make a conscientious decision to undergo a pregnancy for someone else.[45]

What may be driving these concerns that surrogate mothers would be putting themselves in a more, not less, precarious position when they enter into surrogacy contracts with others is their fear that they would therein have to undergo whatever medical procedures or behavioral restrictions the intended parents would request of them. To assuage such concerns, everyone, including health providers, just needs to remember who the true patient is in any pregnancy—the pregnant person—and therein recognize the surrogate's final decision-making power regarding prenatal care. Another possible driver behind this fear is the widespread assumption that any pregnant person would naturally bond with the life growing inside of them and thus would ultimately want to renege on their prior agreement to relinquish the baby post-birth. But to draw again upon material presented in the previous chapter, the four decades and counting of research on surrogate mothers does not substantiate this widespread myth of surrogate duress or regret: most surro-moms happily hand over the child at journey's end and do not become attached to the baby they knew from the start was never theirs. Frankly, it is odd for me to understand how any pro-choice or pro-reproductive justice feminist would object to surrogacy on the grounds that pregnant person would naturally be anguished at the prospect of not being able to continue to parent them post-childbirth when the mainstream feminist movement has historically defended the right of each pregnant person to severe their relationship with the embryo or fetus developing inside of them if they came to conclude either pregnancy termination or adoption after carrying the fetus to term would be in their or their fetus's best interests.

Surrogacy Need Not Undermine Support for Abortion Rights

Third, how might we respond to feminist concerns that the institution of surrogacy undermines the philosophical basis for abortion rights, insofar as the embryo or fetus growing inside of a surro-mom is widely understood to be a separate from her and "belonging" to others? In an era where there is neither the full realization of reproductive justice nor the security of an individual's rights to pregnancy termination, we should first acknowledge that these fears are not unwarranted. Of course, a feminist could support both abortion rights and surrogacy by emphasizing different metaphysics contextually: *parthood* in the abortion debate, therein affirming each person's human rights to their own bodily integrity and autonomy, and *container* for surrogacy, so as to allow each person the right to offer (or decline) their reproductive services to others. But doing so would not be philosophically tenable once these underlying assumptions were made explicit, since embryos or fetuses cannot be *parts* of the pregnant persons only when the latter want the option to terminate pregnancy and *separate* from them when they want to be permitted to accept or decline requests to bear a child for someone else.

Fortunately, as I will explain in greater detail in the next chapter, we need not resolve the metaphysics of pregnancy to dig ourselves out of this quandary. We need only insist upon certain safeguards, particularly the legal right for all pregnant persons to retain medical decision-making in all aspects of their prenatal care (including about termination or selective reduction), even with pregnancies undertaken for others.[46] Just as a person cannot and should not be legally compelled to donate an organ, blood, or any other part of their body upon their death to save another person's life even in a hypothetical scenario where no one else could be a match, so a pregnant person cannot and should not be legally coerced to carry out a pregnancy even if we assume the "bun" versus "bump" model of pregnancy—that a separate living being inside of them would die as a result.[47]

The Case That Surrogacy Perpetuates Stereotypes about Women Is Overblown

Finally, we should also acknowledge that there is truth to the radical feminist observation that surrogate motherhood as a practice does nothing to thwart—but itself arguably perpetuates—stereotypes about women as breeders or as self-sacrificial persons risking their own well-being in service of others' wants and needs. We should quickly see, however, that any call to denounce surrogacy for these reasons would logically have to denounce a wider range of practices many more women engage in as well. This latter list includes women bearing children they intend to raise themselves, volunteering their time for worthy causes without receiving financial remuneration, and prioritizing the needs of others above their own in either professional or interpersonal matters. Surrogacy, in short, is hardly the activity which only or most perpetuates a view of women as altruistic breeders or as self-sacrificial do-gooders. It should thus not be singled out as if it were. Nonetheless, as Cahill suggests, all persons should nonetheless be aware of the way culturally transmitted gender scripts can exert extraordinary pressures on persons to become mothers and fathers, including in ways which may be incompatible with their own good and the common good.

RESPONDING TO CHRISTIAN MISGIVINGS ABOUT SURROGACY

Turning now to distinctive Christian concerns about ART, it is worth pausing to acknowledge how traces of the Catholic "natural law" and Protestant and Orthodox "Genesis creational norm" objections can be found in the broader society in diluted form. A *New York Times* reporter, Alex Kuczynski, who was raised in a liberal Catholic tradition had to wrestle with the "philosophical weirdness of it all" when watching her and her husband's baby emerge from another woman's body—the gestational surrogate they had hired after a decade of reproductive losses including eleven failed IVF cycles. Though she firmly believed both "nature and science derive from the divine," she confessed to experiencing her "chest seize" and "electric impulses" prick at her skin one night following her son's birth as she thought to herself: "What had we done? Was it right to have circumvented the natural order of things? Why had I been chosen to miss out on the act of giving birth, to be left out of the circle of life?"[48] Even Italian fashion designers Domenico Dolce and Stephano Gabbana of Dolce & Gabbana in a 2015 interview denounced adoption by gay couples, called both IVF- or surrogate-born children "synthetic" ("no chemical offsprings and rented uterus: life has a natural flow, there are things that should not be changed"), and reaffirmed their belief that children should be procreated in an "act of love" between mother and father.[49] Though their defense of the traditional family and of traditional childbearing shocked people like me who assumed gay men as such would have celebrated the queering of sexual and reproductive norms instead, we need only recall that radical feminists—several of whom are lesbian—are ardently opposed to reproductive technology.

I myself went through a range of feelings and experiences in my surrogacy journey with my friends—many beautiful and some difficult—but neither existential panic nor guilt about having violated some sort of divinely mandated cosmic ideal. I certainly did not worry about whether my welcoming of a heterologous embryo in my womb meant *I* had committed adultery or otherwise had broken my wedding vows, as I found that line of reasoning absurd. In having Katie and Steven's embryos transferred into my womb with my husband fully onboard with our plan, I was neither "choosing to give [myself] in an act of genital union to someone other than [my] spouse, nor [was I] choosing to engage in the conjugal act or in any sexual act."[50] Nor did I believe the intended father, Steven, had been unfaithful to his wife, Katie, when combining his genetic material with that of another woman's ex vivo to produce several embryos. Katie had wholeheartedly endorsed every step of their collaborative reproduction, and no intimate contact between Steven and these third parties was required. Rather than viewing us third-party donors as impairing the IPs' marriage, an argument could be made that we helped them realize an aspect they could not realize on their own—extend their love for one another outwardly to produce a child and therein fulfill one of the traditional goods of marriage for those who have discerned a vocation to parenthood.

Moving Beyond the Inseparability Thesis

Because the argument of *My Body, Their Baby* is grounded in feminist and progressive Christian commitments, my starting point differs markedly from those of many of the surrogacy opponents detailed above. This is to say my responses are neither likely to be persuasive to those critics, nor even direct rebuttals to their objections because of our different baseline assumptions. For one, my account does not subscribe to the "inseparability thesis" between union and procreation which holds that "each and every marital act" must be open to the procreation of human life and conversely, that the begetting of offspring must stem from "sexual activity, in which husband and wife are intimately and chastely united with one another".[51] My rejection of this cornerstone of Catholic sexual ethics is based upon several reasons, one being that its underlying logic equally condemns other practices such as the use of artificial contraception (which my husband and I practiced for years) and any same-sex activity even among married couples (which I say as an ally to the LGBTQIA+ community support). As with the twenty theologians who authored "The Religious Declaration on Sexual Morality, Justice, and Healing" in January 2000 which became the founding document of the Religious Institute, my account is founded upon a Christian sexual ethics more focused on "personal relationships and social justice rather than particular sexual acts."[52]

In the next chapter, I provide a fuller explanation for why I support several mainline Protestant denominations in their endorsement of the conscientious use of IVF. With feminist Catholic Margaret Farley, I, too find it to be a "failure of imagination" for Christian critics to hold that the only way to maintain the integrity of marriage or sex is to prohibit assisted reproduction, since IVF could still accord with "feminist understandings of embodiment, norms of relationships, and concerns for the common good" if its purpose were to enable "women who would otherwise be infertile to conceive a child" and the relevant parties observed appropriate "limits to its ethical development and use."[53] In addition, many mainline denominations' affirmation of the equal and nondiscriminatory participation of queer persons in all aspects of the church and broader society, including in marriage, leads me to acknowledge the significance of a third party of some sort necessarily being involved in any same-sex couple's path to parenthood, given the facts of reproductive biology. I then combine this progressive Christian affirmation of marriage equality with existing mainline Protestant support for IVF to argue for gay male couples' use of third parties in reproduction, including in surrogacy.

Addressing the "Just Adopt" Objection
Of all the Christian objections to surrogacy discussed above, the one exerting the greatest pull for me personally has been the argument that adoption is the better path for conscientious Christians to take when they yearn to become parents but "natural" childbearing is not (or is no longer) possible for them. I do not wish to reverse this valuation by now advancing surrogacy over adop-

tion, but to show how opposition to the former premised upon the purported superiority of the latter leaves something to be desired. Namely, some critics overplay the real or perceived benefits of adoption, assume facts about both practices that are only contingent, and unfairly even if unwittingly place the responsibility of adopting "needy" children on the socially or medically infertile.

Overplaying the Perceived Benefits of Adoption over Use of ART

First, some opponents of ART who attempt to steer prospective parents toward adoption instead tend to exaggerate what the latter can yield in comparison to what assisted reproduction purportedly cannot. Recall the idea behind the "surrogacy involves marital infidelity" charge is that it would be objectively unjust and unfair to the spouse whose reproductive role would be substituted by an outsider's genetic or gestational contribution which is why they extol adoption for, among other goods, allowing both parents to stand in symmetrical non-biogenetic relation to their child. No doubt some couples pursue adoption for this reason in concert with others, as there are goods to be had in biological symmetry (whether of joint relatedness or joint unrelatedness) between the two prospective parents and their child. However, the perceived benefit of foregoing ART to maintain reproductive symmetry is not only heteronormative, but it also comes with its own relational costs. As some adoption social workers have observed, the "fertile" one must normally work through grief about losing out on their ability to be genetically related to their child, the "infertile" one (or nongenetic parent) might "particularly in times of stress, feel guilty about this," and the "fertile" one when sensing their partner's guilt may have difficulty acknowledging their feelings of sadness or loss about genetic unrelatedness for fear that it "may be hurtful to their mate."[54]

Critics of third-party reproduction who stress the importance of infertile couples sharing in the otherness of the child through adoption may also be unwittingly assuming equal biogenetic relatedness (or lack thereof) is or will be the most significant factor in a family's sense of belonging when parents biogenetically symmetrical to their child may be asymmetrical to them in other important ways. To name some possibilities, only one of the two in an interracial couple may physically resemble their biogenetic child while the other (genetic) parent gets frequently mistaken by outsiders as an adoptive parent or the child's nanny. Or only one of them in a multicultural coupling may be fully comfortable speaking the language or living in the community in which they are raising their child. In short, biogenetic symmetry or asymmetry is only one part of what any given family must manage in their shared life together. In our family's case, while my husband and my children are both of our biological offspring, only three out of four of us are Taiwanese and Asian while my husband is not (he is white), and only three out of four of us are male and identify as men while I do not. This is to say that all families, whether or not the parents are biologically symmetrical to all of their children, must negotiate commonalities and differences between and among their individual members.

Assuming the Truth of Contingent Matters

Secondly, critics of ART who seek to steer folks instead toward adoption also tend to assume adoption would represent greater stewardship of the couples' time and resources. While an assumed cost differential may be warranted as a general assumption, whether adoption would actually prove less cumbersome or costly in any given case will depend on contextual considerations. Since there are an increasing number of U.S. states with mandates for insurance coverage for infertility treatments and some employers are either covering or offering coverage for the same, the IVF portion of a gestational surrogacy arrangement might be paid for in full or in part by one's public or private healthcare plan. Under those scenarios, the commissioning parents would only have to pay for any remaining IVF expenses, any legal fees, and any other out-of-pocket expenses associated with their surrogate's pregnancy including her compensation if relevant. In comparison, adoption from foster care in the U.S. might cost little to nothing, while an independent adoption by some estimates could range from $15,000 to $40,000 and from $20,000 to $50,000 or more according to some estimates in the case of an intercountry adoption depending on the country, service provider, and the needs of the children available for adoption.[55] Of course the same public or private plans offering coverage for IVF might also be offering tax incentives, subsidies, or other reimbursements for adoption as well.

Placing the Responsibility of Adopting "Needy" Children on the Socially or Medically Infertile

To be sure, the "better stewardship" argument against ART in favor of adoption is not necessarily tied to speculation about how much either course of action would cost or how long the entire process would take for any given couple, but to a broader calculation about more good resulting overall when prospective parents satisfy their longing for a child by adopting one or more children whose birth parents are for whatever reason unable, unwilling, or otherwise prevented from serving as the primary parents themselves. When reframed in this way, critics often accuse couples intent on pursuing ART of being selfish for expending so much time, energy, and resources to have a biological connection to their child when they could pursue adoption instead. But beyond the practical barrier of adoption not being accessible to all prospective parents in all contexts given variables of age, sexual orientation, marital status, and the pool of available children, what is missing in this anti-ART/pro-adoption position is an explanation for *why* the criticism of narcissism or selfishness is directed primarily at couples who use ART, not also at those intent on bearing children the old-fashioned way through intercourse. Why must those who cannot reproduce "naturally" be put in the position of having to justify their desire to have "their own" child—why isn't every prospective parent pressed to give an account?

Indeed, not all couples who are ultimately able to beget children without assisted reproduction have done so effortlessly, as natural conception can be extremely hard work for some. As per the experiences of several of my women friends and colleagues who put off childbearing for years for a variety of reasons, some couples had to chart the woman's menstrual periods or take their basal body temperature to detect ovulation and therein time intercourse to occur at their most fertile window. Several had to undergo significant behavioral modifications or lifestyle changes, such as lose or gain a considerable amount of weight or quit smoking. Others had to subject themselves to invasive medical procedures to be able to get pregnant (e.g., a urological evaluation to rule out male-factor infertility, surgery to correct fallopian tube blockage or to repair uterine anomalies), or even be put on medical bed rest to safely bring their chil(dren) to term. This is all to say persons who ultimately turn to ART are not the only ones who have made significant investments to become the parents of their biogenetically related children.

A second, related question I have is why most opponents of surrogacy who argue "adoption is *better*" do not carry out their logic further to conclude "adoption is *best*" for anyone who has discerned a call to parenthood, particularly for those who live in contexts where there are extant children "available" for adoption. Given the aforementioned Christian responsibility to respond to the needs of the poor and vulnerable, the good of environmental stewardship, and reality of already born children whose first families for various reasons cannot adequately care for them, it is not clear why adoption is commonly or primarily raised as an alternative for the socially or medically infertile as opposed to being a serious consideration for *any* and all prospective parents. To play out this line of reasoning: surely heterosexual couples capable of natural conception could seek to prevent pregnancy to make room to adopt children. Recall, many Protestants and Orthodox do not believe themselves to be prohibited from using artificial contraception; persons who extol the virtues of adoption could accordingly model it in their own lives. To be sure, Catholics in conformity with the *Magisterium* on reproductive matters might bristle at the suggestion that they should seek to preempt pregnancy for the sake of adoption by arguing that procreation in the context of a heterosexual marriage is not a decision that ordinarily requires moral justification because children born from conjugal union are to be understood as the fruit of the spouses' mutual self-giving in love. Even so, Catholics themselves have ways of licitly engaging in natural family planning and might elect to do so to create more space and resources in their lives to adopt. Among others, feminist Catholic theologian Darlene Fozard Weaver has encouraged Catholics to consider adoption as a "salutary form of procreation in its own right" and an "option any lay Catholic" might consider—not just a second-best choice for only those struggling with infertility.[56] Even *Humanae Vitae* teaches that "responsible parenthood" requires couples to consider the "physical, economic, psychological and social conditions" in their discernment in family planning (§10).[57]

The thrust of my argument, to be clear, is not to mandate adoption as a requirement for faithful Christian discipleship even though ethical and legal adoption should continue to be lauded as an important, even necessary, social institution. My point is to draw attention to the undue responsibility of adoption placed upon socially or medically infertile couples, or in Catholic feminist Maura A. Ryan's words, to expose how the "call to adoption is almost always applied selectively" when a case could be made that "all Christian families have obligations to take the needs of abandoned, neglected, or endangered children into account in making procreative decisions."[58] While I lack the space the develop this additional point here, the reality is that adoption carries its own complexities and ethical issues particularly but not exclusively in transnational or transracial cases and should not be presented as a "morally unambiguous solution to infertility."[59] I take no position on the question which set of issues (adoption or surrogacy) will be more difficult for any given couple to navigate or society to regulate than the other, but I do seek to identify where anti-ART/pro-adoption critics have and have not successfully made their case.[60]

Conclusion

Surrogacy continues to be the most controversial way of bringing children into the world, with opposition creating strange bedfellows among opponents. The original outcry in the mid-1980s following the landmark Baby M case saw secular feminists supporting the anti-surrogacy side along with priests defending the sanctity of motherhood and adoption advocates concerned about abandoned babies in inner-city hospitals and other children forced into foster care due to the "crack epidemic."[61] More recently, the Stop Surrogacy Now campaign launched in May 2015 counts as initial signers more than sixteen organizations ranging from La Lune and L'Association Strasbourgeoise de Femmes Homosexuelles (France) to the Center for Bioethics and Culture (U.S.A.), which is headed by a Christian president "who cares about the embryo and the unborn," and more than one hundred individuals ranging from radical feminist Janice Raymond to pro-life Catholic theologian Charles C. Camosy.[62] Even the Catholic press in the run-up to the ultimately unsuccessful attempt to prevent the State of New York from legalizing commercial surrogacy in February 2021 was keen to call feminist icon Gloria Steinem an "unlikely ally" in their fight.[63] Persons and groups not commonly aligned on other issues have clearly found common cause in their opposition to this method of bringing children into the world.

4 A PROGRESSIVE CHRISTIAN VISION FOR SURROGACY: ADVANCING THE ARGUMENT

WHEN PEOPLE LEARN I WAS once a surrogate for a husband-wife pair of friends, they usually assume I must have been so close to them to have been willing to help in that way. The truth, however, is more complicated. The overwhelming love I felt was directed at my own children—not principally at them. During Barack Obama's term as president, I remember First Lady Michelle explaining in an interview how her daughters were the first people she would think of when waking every morning and the last on her mind when drifting off to sleep at night—and thinking I felt similarly about my boys, too. Over the years, I have come to empathize with people I knew who yearned for children but were grief-stricken by infertility, miscarriage, and other reproductive losses.

In late fall of 2014, I caught up with another friend, Melissa, who I had not seen in over a decade who was then a single woman in her early forties.[1] While she had been public about recently surviving breast cancer and a double mastectomy, she told me then privately that she had also frozen and banked some of her eggs prior to treatment in the hopes of having kids someday with a future partner and future surrogate. Still, Melissa lacked confidence those grand plans would ever come to pass because her country prohibits commercial surrogacy, and she was baffled by the prospect of anyone doing it "for free"—out of the goodness of their heart. To Melissa's surprise, I responded I didn't think the scenario strange at all. I explained the reasons why I could imagine serving in this capacity myself under the right conditions—and thus could picture other women like me adopting similar reasoning. My being reassuring about the matter seemed to give Melissa comfort, even though we both knew it would be nearly impossible for me for geographical reasons alone to stand in her place someday. This conversation nonetheless prompted me to talk with my husband afterward about surrogacy in the hypothetical, with him agreeing if the situation were different, he could see me carrying a baby for Melissa or for someone like her. In Nathaniel's words, "there are some things we should be willing to do for friends we love who have suffered so much."

Several months later, I was at a party with a cluster of good friends talking about our forays into parenting, specifically how we determined when we were ready for kids and what it actually took for us to have them. Since we were all professionals who had become parents later in life to pursue advanced degrees and launch our careers, there was no shortage of stories to tell. One couple shared how they had waited until they were at a certain point in their graduate school and ministry before the wife had to take fertility drugs to get pregnant which ultimately resulted in their having twins. Another couple regaled us with tales about needing to provide semen samples for various infertility treatments before deciding to adopt their child overseas. I first mentioned how Nathaniel and I fortunately hadn't encountered fertility problems when we wanted to become parents after spending three early years of our marriage in a dual-residence commuting situation. But to contribute to the fund of stories, I outlined my recent conversation with Melissa about surrogacy. Katie then turned to me and asked in front of the others in a tone suggestive of one part jest and one part boldness, "If you were hypothetically willing to do it for her, would you be willing to do it for us?"

Suffice it to say, the answer was yes. Over the next few months, she and I with our spouses discussed what collaborative reproduction might look like in our case. By summer's end, we had completed all steps required by the State of California, and I began my first course of IVF drugs in the fall. We four had concluded that surrogacy was not only something we wanted to do, but that the practice was also compatible with our identities and commitments as Christians. Were we right to have reasoned as such?

———

The constructive heart of *My Body, Their Baby* begins with this chapter. I advance a positive vision for surrogacy where the presence of a third party into a couple's childbearing plans is welcomed as a gift, not regarded as an intrusion.[2] As a work in Christian ethics, my account draws upon the four sources of moral wisdom to which Christians have historically turned for guidance—Scripture, tradition, reason or secular modes of inquiry, and experience. Before unpacking these sources and describing the goods a successful journey could bring about, I first explain the seven parameters surrounding the type of surrogacy initially under investigation. To repeat my rationale from the Introduction, there is wisdom in first considering the practice's sine qua non—a person intentionally becoming pregnant to deliver a child for someone else to raise—before assessing other important, but ultimately secondary, matters in subsequent chapters, such as when surro-moms are paid for their service.

Seven Assumptions about the Surrogacy Arrangements

Given variation in the types and contexts surrounding surrogacy, the positive vision and framework of seven ethical principles I offer in this chapter and the next are premised upon seven basic or simplifying parameters about the collaborative reproduction.

The first is that the surrogacy arrangement is gestational, not traditional: the surrogate is not biogenetically related to the child. This stipulation has the advantage of capturing the vast majority of surrogacies in the world today, by some estimates, well over 90%. It also allows us to avoid additional complexities that might arise when surrogates offer their IPs the use of their own eggs as well.

The second condition is that the arrangement is what the industry calls non-commercial or altruistic, meaning the surrogate is not being compensated beyond reimbursements for reasonable, pregnancy-related expenses. By removing the profit factor, this idealization allows us to bracket for the time being the exploitation, objectification, and commodification charges that tend to dominate—even overwhelm—discussions about surrogacy. While non-commercial, altruistic surrogacies are admittedly less common, they do occur even in contexts permitting payment above expenses (as per my agreement with Katie and Steven in California) and are the only types legally permitted in some states in the U.S. and some nations across the world, including the U.K., Canada, Australia, India, and Thailand.

The third requirement is that the arrangement takes place in the same jurisdiction where both the surrogate and the commissioning parents reside and where all parties involved agree to abide by all relevant laws and policies. This simplification allows us to bypass having to address the morality of either breaking the law or attempting to circumvent it. It also enables us to temporarily sidestep the difficulties that could otherwise emerge in interstate or intercountry cases where one or more of the jurisdictions have prohibitive policies, including the remote but catastrophic possibility of a surrogate-born child becoming legally stateless or even legally parentless in the process.

The fourth stipulation is that all parties will have access to the standard of care and the capacity to provide informed consent to all the medical procedures and other screenings they might undergo. These baseline conditions are of critical importance because every pregnancy and ART technique carry risks, and all IVF pregnancies are higher-risk.[3] Because no surrogacy could possibly be judged good or even acceptable if the persons involved in them were not fully appraised of these risks or if they could not have reasonably consented to them (e.g., if the contracts were written in a language or used terminology the surrogate or IPs could not understand), these stipulations must be maintained in the more complex arrangements I consider in chapter 6.

The fifth assumption concerns the status and quality of relationship among the intended parents: they are married or are involved in a marriage-like relationship such as a covenantal partnership guided by norms of consent, equal regard, and a shared commitment to the well-being of others.[4] The Christian tradition has long valorized marriage as the context best suited for childrearing: the couples' love extends fruitfully toward the child at the same time the child benefits from being raised by two parents who bear special responsibilities to one another and to them. That said, my progressive Christian framework does not insist upon marriage among the IPs since some couples reside in jurisdictions or are members of ecclesial traditions that do not recognize marriage equality, or there may be other valid or extenuating reasons for couples, whether same or opposite-sex, to be fully committed to each other without being wed. The question whether the Christian tradition should consider other arrangements beyond monogamous couples for childrearing (e.g., single parenting by choice, polyamorous relationships, or communes) as acceptable or even as good as marriage or covenantal partnership are important questions, though lie beyond what can be examined here.[5] That said, empirical studies and my own surrogacy journey reveal that the practice simultaneously *fortifies* traditional notions of the family—with married or otherwise partnered parents raising their biogenetically related children together—while *expanding* traditional notions of kinship—such as by the IPs and the child coming to regard their surrogate to whom they have become close(r) as the child's "auntie" or the surrogate's own children and the surrogate-born child(ren) treating one another like cousins, even though there may be no ties of blood or marriage formally binding them.

The sixth condition is that the prospective parents only pursue surrogacy after a period of serious discernment because they cannot feasibly gestate a child themselves—and the gestation cannot occur in any other way given the current state of ART. For this condition to apply, a pregnancy would either be contraindicated or physically impossible because the IPs lack a suitably functioning uterus between them perhaps due to biological maleness or the female(s) having undergone a hysterectomy or having been born without a uterus. The IPs would thus need someone else to gestate their child, since ectogenesis (gestation outside of a biological womb) is not currently possible for us humans and since uterine transplantation is only at an experimental stage of clinical trials at the time of this writing.[6] To be clear, my account takes no position for or against either uterine transplantation or ectogenesis—it simply situates its evaluation of surrogacy within the current state of reproductive technology.

The seventh and final assumption is that antinatalists have not persuasively made their case against anyone continuing to bring forth new human life at all, whether through ordinary or extraordinary means. Antinatalists are a small but growing movement of persons who have questioned the wisdom of continuing to birth children into an already overpopulated world because they judge the latter would inevitably encounter "more bad than good" while themselves contributing to—and experiencing the negative effects of—anthropogenic climate change.[7] My account of surrogacy assumes what antinatalists deny: the human right to have a child should be recognized and respected universally,[8] the parental care and nurturance of children remains a valid vocation for those called to it, and the tragic reality of sin and suffering in the world does not mean the created order holds more disvalue than value. To be clear, I affirm conscientious efforts both individuals and corporate bodies make to decrease adverse human impacts on the environment, including by reducing overconsumption and resource depletion, encouraging families to have fewer (versus zero) children, or personally electing to go child free. But one need neither prescribe a draconian zero-child public policy nor morally condemn procreation as such to advance such ends.

Sources of Moral Wisdom

When drawing upon the four traditional sources of normativity in my progressive Christian account of surrogacy, I seek to find points of contact among them where possible while leaning especially on feminist, Reformed, and other progressive traditions of biblical and theological reflection. My secular sources of wisdom include international human rights standards, professional medical ethics committee opinions, and the reproductive justice framework. When lifting up the moral salience of experience, I draw prescriptively from ethnographic and social scientific findings on surrogacy, on families expanded by other methods, and on my own collaborative reproduction with my friends while giving pride of place to those who have had the relevant transformative experiences.

SCRIPTURE

Though the Bible remains an authoritative source for Christians seeking moral wisdom, my approach is neither one of proof-texting, nor of relying primarily upon biblical tales of surrogacy for counsel. The former represents bad hermeneutics, the latter overlooks the fullness of what can be mined from Scripture. My reading of the Bible is feminist insofar as core feminist principles serve both as a "negative limit" and a "positive key" to the way the Bible can help "shed light on human experience."[9] It is simultaneously intersectional insofar as it draws upon scholarship of those who engage the Bible through the lenses of race/ethnicity, class, sex/gender/sexuality, colonialism, ableism, and other ways the texts have been used to empower and to marginalize. I accordingly "re-rea[d] for liberation" in the words of womanist Hebrew Bible scholar Renita J. Weems in my non-hesitation to "read against the grain of a text if needed, and . . . stand against those texts whose worldview runs counter to one's own vision of God's liberation activity in the world."[10]

When seeking to applying the Bible's wisdom to our topic at hand, we would first have to acknowledge the problematic stigmatization of infertility and obvious son bias in numerous biblical passages "mark[ed]—and mar[red]" by patriarchy.[11] The biblical mandate to "be fruitful and multiple" (Gen 1:28) has historically led several Jewish and Christian communities to regard procreation as such as a religious duty (*mitzvah*). Given the importance the ancient Israelites attached to offspring to continue the family lineage, provide labor, and enhance the power of the tribe, the Bible also describes several cases of forced surrogacy and mandates levirate marriage (Gen 16:1–4, 30:1–10, Deut 25: 5–10). Feminist and progressive Christians are right to interrogate these and other passages that link together fertility, male progeny, and divine blessing (Ps 127:3–5, 2 Kgs 4:8–17), in addition to those connecting infertility with sin or divine displeasure (e.g., 2 Sam 6:20–23, Hos 9:1–14, Gen 20:1–18, Num 5:11–31, Ex 23:26, Deut 7:14).

This is not to suggest the Bible has nothing of value to offer for our purposes. Feminist Catholic theologian Gina Messina has written poignantly about finding solace in tales of "biblical foremothers who shared [their] barren state," such as by identifying with Sarai's anguish and bitterness, Rachel's envy, and Hannah's hope in her years-long struggle with infertility (Gen 17:15–21, 21:1–7, 30:1, 1 Sam 1:1–20, 2:21).[12] Others similarly pained by childlessness can draw comfort from the book of Job's categorical refutation that suffering is necessarily a sign of divine punishment and in Jesus's disavowal that a person's congenital impairment invariably stems from their or their parents' sin (John 9: 2–3). In addition, Christians experiencing judgment from others due to an uncertainty about or disinterest in a future as parents should know that the Bible also reveres several figures for reasons disconnected to their parental status. Consider the following encounter: "While he [Jesus] was saying this, a woman in the crowd raised her voice and said to him, 'Blessed is the womb that bore you and the breasts that nursed you!' But Jesus said, 'Blessed rather are those who hear the word of God and obey it!' " (Luke 11:27–28). As Lisa Cahill observes, this Lukan passage "disassociates the honor of women from biological maternity" and "deflects praise of [Jesus's] own mother" from the role she played in birthing and nursing him.[13] Relatedly, the married couple Priscilla and Aquila are esteemed as house church leaders and the Apostle Paul's tent-making ministry partners without ever being described as parents (Acts 18: 2–3, Rom 16:3–4, 1 Cor 16:19).

These biblical notions about calling, the unsuitability of marriage or parenthood for some, and the importance of delinking suffering from punishment all inform my progressive Christian account of surrogacy. Other relevant biblical norms include the prophets' and Jesus's special concern for the most vulnerable, the vision of the church functioning as a community of moral discourse and deliberation, the conviction that every person bears the image of God, and a covenantal understanding of key relationships.

TRADITION

Tradition encompasses the wisdom and practices of the community of faith across time. It is simultaneously a second source of Christian theo-ethical reflection and what has shaped the first source (Scripture), given different ecclesial communities' decisions about what to include in the biblical canon. When Christians turn to the tradition's major and minor strands to assist our understanding of biblical texts for Christian discipleship, we are asking—as Catholic feminist ethicist Margaret Farley has aptly summarized—"how to excavate historical layers of meaning, find lost treasures, take account of historical and cultural contexts for church life, [and] hold on to gems of revelatory experience and shared faith."[14] The church's embrace of medicine as a continuation of Jesus's healing ministry and overall regard for science as a "discipline through which we explore God's creation" in a way different from "but not opposed to theology" are obviously relevant to our topic.[15] The tradition's cherishing of children and affirmation of ways of being apart from marriage and parenthood (i.e., singleness and celibacy), valorization of adoption as both an important theological motif and institution, and charge to be faithful stewards of creation and to work for justice and the common good are also important aspects we should retain.

Beyond this shared inheritance, my account takes its particular point of departure from progressive theological positions several mainline denominations and other theologians and ethicists across the ecumenical spectrum have taken on two matters: full inclusion for LGBTQIA+ persons in the life of the church and broader society and on equipping individuals and couples to make their own conscientious decisions about reproductive matters, including on IVF. My starting point accordingly differs from where many Christian critics canvassed in chapter 2 began with their heteronormativity, upholding of the inseparability thesis, and condemnation of IVF for its treatment of embryonic life.

Marriage Equality

My positive vision and framework for surrogacy is grounded in the progressive Christian convictions that the goods and ends of marriage or a covenantal partnership are realizable among couples who are either opposite- or same-sex and that heterosexism must be overcome in the church and broader society.[16] To provide a sampling of these views, my own denomination, the Presbyterian Church (U.S.A.), views marriage covenantally as a "gift God has given to all humankind for the wellbeing of the entire human family" and since 2015 has understood marriage as involving a "unique commitment *between two people*"—no longer necessarily one man and one woman.[17] Theologian Eugene F. Rogers has argued that marriage of either type can be regarded as an "aesthetic practice" where two persons practice the mutuality of love characterizing God's triune life and a "means of grace" modeled after the mysterious union between Christ and his Church.[18] The Rev. Dr. Patrick Cheng, an Episcopalian priest formerly ordained in the Metropolitan Community Church (MCC), has drawn upon the freedom professed from the law in Christ and the equality professed in baptismal unity to contend that those who discriminate against LGBTQIA+ Christians in marriage, ordination, or in full participation in the life of the church are acting contrary to the Gospel: they can be compared to the "false teachers" who once sought to require new male Gentile converts to be circumcised before full acceptance into the fold (Gal 1:6–10; 3:28).[19] Womanist theologians have built upon the legacy of poet Alice Walker who coined the term "womanist" to mean someone who not only is a "black feminist or feminist of color," but is also, among other characteristics, "a woman who loves other women, sexually and/or nonsexually."[20] That Christian feminism has long opposed heterosexism is further supported by the work of the scholar-activist widely hailed as the mother of feminist Christian ethics, Beverly Wildung Harrison, given her understanding that Christian defenders of "the institution of normative heterosexuality" are almost always also anti-feminist in their upholding of male superiority and valuing of women primarily as wives and as mothers.[21]

To be clear, my account of surrogacy is compatible with multiple theologies of marriage and progressive Christian accounts of sexual ethics but is not premised upon any one of them in particular.[22] Though there is not yet consensus on the good of same-sex relationships or marriage across the worldwide church, I treat its fidelity to authentic Christian discipleship as a settled matter in the vision of collaborative reproduction offered here.

Conscientious Decision-Making about Reproductive Matters, Including IVF
When evaluating the ethics of using ART to bear children, I draw particularly
from the Reformed tradition of theological reflection, particularly the lived
theology of the Taiwanese American church of my childhood church (Evangelical Formosan Church of Orange County), and my ecclesial home since my
late twenties: the PCUSA. I ground my overall approach to sexual and reproductive well-being on the Reformed tradition's understanding of a "God . . .
at work to alleviate human suffering and offer wholeness, often most miracu-
lously through the wonders of medical science."[23] Just as a Special Committee
on Human Sexuality of the Presbyterian Church (U.S.A.) has regarded the
use of medical technology when responsibly exercised as "instruments of a
gracious God for healing and the promotion of well-being,"[24] so I was formed
by an immigrant Taiwanese church community who has historically associated Christianity with the provision of healthcare and practice of "Western"
medicine.[25]

The PCUSA and my Taiwanese immigrant church traditions of theo-
ethical inquiry have encouraged the development of *each* person's (and each
couple's) moral agency to decide matters pertaining to marriage and family
planning after a period of discernment with trusted others. In the words of
the PCUSA, the use of contraception when pregnancy is not desired can be a
"responsible exercise of stewardship of life" because parenthood is a serious
undertaking involving "covenant initiation."[26] Since 1983, the PCUSA General
Assembly has also affirmed the plausibility of abortion as a "responsible moral
choice" in the event of an unintentional pregnancy, a "grave genetic disorder"
of the fetus, or when a particular "kind of problem . . . prompts its consideration" as a matter of stewardship.[27] These PCUSA statements make explicit
the norms of the Taiwanese church in which I was raised: not only did the
ob/gyns in my home congregation regularly prescribe birth control and perform abortions when requested by their patients, but our deacons, elders, and
other respected members assumed the good of contraceptives for the purpose
of family planning as well as the importance of abortion to allow couples to
space or limit children when their prophylactic measures have failed, prevent
the birth of infants who would otherwise suffer with severe congenital anomalies, or end the ordeal of a crisis pregnancy.[28]

The PCUSA along with several other mainline denominations have explicitly supported advancements in the "enhancement and control of fertility"
for creating "new options for families" while recognizing the vulnerability of

all human undertakings to mishandling as well as the implications for the "community, society, and even the species" in the decisions persons make. The PCUSA recognizes the potential for IVF to be a "responsible alternative for couples for whom there is no other way to bear children."[29] Similarly since 2004, the United Methodist Church (UMC)—the denomination in which my spouse was raised and with which my institution, Claremont School of Theology, is affiliated—has endorsed the conscientious use of IVF by calling for vigorous standards of informed consent for clinicians and couples considering it with respect to "the procedures, the physical and emotional risks, and the associated ethical issues" involved.[30] In contrast to the Christian opponents of IVF discussed in the previous chapter, the UMC, like the PCUSA, supports embryonic stem cell research under certain constraints and permits IVF patients to obtain and then fertilize multiple ova at a time to spare themselves from having to incur the medical risks of every successive egg retrieval attempt if their first IVF cycle(s) failed to eventuate in a live birth. Other mainline denominations with official statements or positions in support of IVF include the Episcopal Church (TEC), the Evangelical Lutheran Church in America (ELCA), and the United Church of Christ (UCC).[31]

Importantly, the PCUSA in 1983 did not oppose the use of third parties in reproduction, as say, the Episcopal Church did that same decade when they approved IVF "for the purpose of providing children in [an otherwise childless] marriage."[32] Instead, my denomination encouraged further study on the "psychological, ethical, and legal ramifications of *surrogate motherhood and artificial insemination donors* for all parties, including the child" (emphasis added).[33] Today, the PCUSA has proverbially "put their money where their mouth is" by offering employee benefits plan coverage for "advanced reproductive technology" such as IVF, ZIFT, GIFT, ICSI, cryopreserved embryo transfers, ovum microsurgery, and "the supplies and prescription drugs related to such therapies" for up to three procedures per member in their lifetime. Their maternity plan also does not exclude surrogate pregnancies, which is to say the PCUSA is prepared to pay for, or perhaps already has, prenatal care for surrogates.[34] My account of surrogacy builds upon these ecclesial communities' support for the conscientious use of IVF while aiming to contribute to their tentative and underdeveloped reflections on surrogacy.

REASON AND SECULAR MODES OF INQUIRY

We must obviously use reason when evaluating plausible sources of insight about a contested issue. When reason is named as a distinctive third source for Christian ethics, what is meant is what can be known by our own lights apart from special revelation or supernatural means. As Margaret Farley has astutely observed, there is wisdom in conceptualizing this third source in terms of both reason and every secular discipline "offer[ing] the possibility of insight into the aspects of creation we seek to understand."[35] The secular sources I draw upon include the social sciences for their studies of families expanded in multiple ways; philosophy, as Christian theologians and ethicists have long done; the medical sciences; and the discourse and legal apparatus of human rights.

To say more about these last two beginning with the medical sciences, professional medical societies' ethics committee opinions on reproductive technology are especially helpful, as they outline potential benefits and risks of particular treatments; describe their ethical, legal, medical, and psychosocial ramifications; and provide clinicians with recommendations for patient care. Some of the principles I offer in my constructive framework for surrogacy are thus guided by the standard of care in the subspecialty fields of reproductive endocrinology and maternal-fetal medicine as well as from organizations such as the American College of Obstetrics and Gynecologists (ACOG), the Society for Assisted Reproductive Technology (SART), American Society of Reproductive Medicine (ASRM), the Centers for Disease Control and Prevention (CDC), and their analogs in other countries. While these organizations remain vulnerable to political pressures and error like all institutions are, their guidance is importantly grounded in clinical experience—not simply abstract reasoning.

Another important source for our progressive Christian ethical assessment of surrogacy is the large body of law and scholarship on human rights. There is a long history of Christians manifesting concern for human dignity through the moral language and legal apparatus of human rights, including in the original articulation of the concept during the formation of the United Nations and in the catalog of provisions in the International Bill of Human Rights.[36] Human rights offers cross-cultural standards with gravitas which we can use to evaluate diverse surrogacy practices and laws across the globe. Particular human rights of relevance here include the right to marry and to found or establish a family. They also include every child's human right "as far as possible . . . to know and be cared for by his or her parents"—with UNICEF interpreting "parents" to include the child's genetic, birth, and social ones. [37] Because several states, nongovernmental organizations, and individual critics have condemned surrogacy for infringing upon the human rights of women and children, any positive account must establish the practice's compatibility with—and advancement of—the human rights provisions allegedly under assault.

EXPERIENCE

Like reason, we can understand experience as either simultaneously embedded in the three other sources of moral wisdom or as a distinctive fourth source. In the former, we would regard the Bible as a record of some people's experiences with and reflections on God, tradition as capturing the experiences of the community of faith across the centuries, and some secular fields of inquiry as offering analyses of the lived experiences of particular groups in accordance with disciplinary norms. In the latter, experience as a distinctive fourth source of normativity would entail, as again per Margaret Farley, the "contemporary actual living of events and relationships, along with the sensations, feelings, emotions, insights, and understandings that are part of this lived reality." Experience is thus something which provides us with "data to be interpreted," while itself being "already interpreted" or mediated by the conceptual lenses we bring to our analyses.[38]

In drawing upon experience in ways consistent with methodology in both Christian and feminist ethics, I will emphasize the lived experiences of women and other historically marginalized groups. Both intersectional feminism and the Christian "preferential option for the poor and vulnerable" direct us to pay special attention to the real or potential vulnerabilities of surrogate-born children and of the persons who endure a higher-risk pregnancy to bear them, particularly if there are reasons to believe they might opt for surrogacy out of pressure from others or from economic desperation. Others meriting special consideration include involuntarily childless couples who are priced out of ART but might otherwise have explored it as an option and same-sex couples who may be facing disproportionate—or entirely prohibitive—barriers to adoption and access to fertility treatments.

As important as it is to attend to this fourth source of normativity, experience as a distinctive font of wisdom remains contested in Christian ethics. Questions remain about what kind of information or evidence experience provides, how the deeply felt authority of firsthand experience relates to other sources of normativity, and what kind of comparisons can be made between and among different accounts of people's experiences. "Women's experience" likewise remains contested in feminist theology given the temptation for some scholars to focus on commonalities in ways essentializing all women or at least subsets of them ("Third World women") or to overgeneralize about "women's oppression" in ways insufficiently attentive to differences between and among them due to race, class, nationality, age, religion, marital status, sexual orientation, or still other factors.[39]

One way to minimize problems in drawing upon women's experience is to be cognizant of the particular context, and thus limitations, of each ethnographic study or personal account referenced. For instance, social scientific findings about the experiences of mostly white and largely Christian middle-class surrogates in Great Britain should not automatically be assumed to hold constant for working-class, mostly Buddhist surrogates in Thailand, just as we should acknowledge how surrogacy experiences among women in India during the heyday of their surrogacy tourism industry may vary markedly from those of surro-moms in Israel or still elsewhere.

Beyond the importance of attending to particulars, the argument and progressive Christian framework of guiding principles I construct for surrogacy draws upon two additional concepts or conceptual paradigms.

Transformative Experiences of Pregnancy

The first is Lauri Ann (L. A.) Paul's concept of "transformative experiences" and Fiona Woollard's extension of this concept in her work. An experience is "epistemically transformative" if the only way to know what an experience is like is to have it yourself. Paul's examples include seeing a color for the first time or trying a fruit like the foul-smelling durian for the first time. An experience is "personally transformative" for a person if it changes their point of view or core preferences—if they undergo a fundamental change of a type where there is a demonstrable "before" and "after." Transformative experiences are thus experiences which are both epistemically and personally transformative. Paul's own examples include fighting in a war, enduring the loss of a loved one, undergoing a religious conversion—and, importantly for our purposes, becoming a first-time parent.[40]

Fiona Woollard's adaption of Paul's concept of "epistemically transformative experiences" can be productively applied to various debates involving pregnancy, including abortion and surrogacy.[41] When conceptualizing pregnancy as a transformative experience, we acknowledge that those who have been pregnant before have a kind of knowledge about pregnancy that those who have not been pregnant do not and that this disparity in knowledge should matter when evaluating whose perspectives to privilege in discussions about pregnancy-related matters. I draw upon this concept of transformative experiences to advance my "trust women" principle in the progressive Christian framework for surrogacy I unpack in the next chapter.

The Reproductive Justice (RJ) Framework

The second paradigm important to my understanding of experience for surrogacy is the collective wisdom forged by those who originally crafted and are still advancing the "reproductive justice" framework. Twelve pioneering Black women in the U.S. first coined the term in 1994 at a conference in Chicago co-sponsored by the Illinois Pro-Choice Alliance and the Ms. Foundation. They hoped to respond to the Clinton administration's proposed plans for health-care reform and to center the needs of Black women in anticipation of the upcoming U.N. International Conference on Population and Development (ICPD) in Cairo. These women who would soon call themselves the Women of African Descent for Reproductive Justice (WADRJ) had judged the dominant "pro-choice" platform insufficiently attentive to the structural barriers in their daily lives, as they understood the central question for Black women was not whether reproductive choice was protected by law, but whether they as Black women in the U.S. could exercise such liberties if so. Sixteen organizations representing women of color from four communities—Native American, African American, Latina, and Asian American—further developed RJ when forming the SisterSong Women of Color Reproductive Justice Collective in 1997.[42] RJ from its inception has thus been both grassroots and one linked to the global women's health movement in its understanding of the interrelationships between and among "poverty, underdevelopment and women's reproduction."[43]

Asian Pacific Islanders for Reproductive Health (APIRH) was one of the founding organizations of SisterSong in 1997. When APIRH renamed itself as Asian Communities for Reproductive Justice (ACRJ) in 2004, it became the first original SisterSong member organization to "rebrand itself using the phrase 'reproductive justice.'"[44] ACRJ's groundbreaking paper, "A New Vision for Advancing Our Movement for Reproductive Health, Reproductive Rights and Reproductive Justice," outlines three main frameworks for addressing reproductive oppression: (1) Reproductive Health, focusing on the delivery of a full range of health services in culturally competent and accessible (low cost or no-cost) ways to all women, (2) Reproductive Rights, focusing on legal and public policy advocacy to protect women's legal right to reproductive health care services, and (3) Reproductive Justice, focusing on movement building by connecting the RJ principles to various communities' social justice struggles toward self-determination, the transformation of structural power inequities, and the realization of human rights.[45]

I was first introduced to RJ by one of the twelve founding foremothers of RJ and one of the movement's best known activists today, Dr. Toni Bond, when she was then a doctoral student writing a dissertation under my direction. I then went through RJ training led by another founding foremother, Loretta Ross, the co-founder and national coordinator of SisterSong (2005–2012), in a series of Religious Scholars Convening meetings sponsored by the Religious Coalition for Reproductive Choice (RCRC) beginning in 2016. Though the RJ movement as a whole has not yet reached a consensus on surrogacy, I see the collective wisdom of RJ scholar-activists as holding exciting possibilities for my progressive Christian vision for the practice. The framework's centering of women of color bridges womanist reflections on surrogacy in the Bible with contemporary fears about the well-being of surrogates of color today, particularly from the Global South. RJ's grounding in international human rights and four-pronged understanding of the rights everyone should be recognized as having might also provide room for individuals to decide for or against surrogacy (as either surrogates or intended parents) in their own case. That said, the framework's long-standing intersectional approach to social problems, warnings that the hazards of pregnancy and childbirth vary dramatically with respect to race, and community-centered ethos should push anyone promoting an RJ-sensitive account of reproductive matters to concern themselves with the good of entire communities, not just the choices available to individuals. Though RJ is largely conceptualized as secular, RJ's requirement to look beyond individual reproductive choices and decisions to the social contexts in which they occur are a fitting complement to the attention paid in Christian social ethics to structural issues when analyzing social problems.

Advancing a Progressive Christian Vision for Surrogacy

Having named the seven simplifying assumptions undergirding the type of surrogacy under initial consideration and described my four sources of normativity, I now advance a positive vision for the practice where third-party reproduction enhances, rather than impedes, flourishing and relationships and where the pain of involuntary childlessness is transformed into a celebratory though unconventional way of bringing a child into the world. In my own surrogacy journey, I have experienced the friendships between my IPs and my husband and me deepen to previously unreached levels of intimacy. I have seen their bubbly daughter bring healing and sheer delight to her parents who had been longing for a decade to have a child of their own as well as to her grandparents who had likewise been hoping and praying fervently for her arrival. I have also been party to many others outside of their kinship networks who have been awed by the wonders of modern science *and* the goodness of God when learning how my "advanced maternal age" body was able to nurture their child in my womb. When the collaborative reproduction goes well, surrogacy can serve as a metaphor for a deep truth of our Christian tradition—the caring and rearing of children was always intended to be a communal affair, not simply the task of the parents alone.

In a gift surrogacy arrangement, a surrogate shares in the hopes and dreams of a couple who cannot bear a child without medical assistance. Though the analogy is imperfect as all analogies are, we can compare altruistic surrogates to altruistic living organ or tissue donors, since both are responding compassionately to others' medical needs by undergoing inconveniences, physical risks, and bodily sacrifices for their sake.[46] If and when the adults are preexisting friends or relatives, a surro-mom undergoes these hazards and joys with the knowledge she would be helping someone she already cares about satisfy a deep and unmet yearning. If and when the IPs have previously struggled with infertility, a successful outcome can be a cause for celebration insofar as the IPs' medical problems have been overcome, even if not directly cured. If and when the IPs have had a tragic history of failed embryo transfer attempts or miscarriages and have embryos remaining from previous IVF cycles, some thinkers have suggested we could even view the surrogate as a good steward of God's creation for bringing to birth a baby the couple would statistically have been more likely to have lost on their own.[47] If and when the IPs are a same-sex couple, we can laud a successful surrogacy for helping them overcome the difficulties of social infertility while also allowing most couples to maintain one parent's genetic relatedness to their child—something both straight and queer couples tend to value.

All of the aforementioned cases of gift surrogacies can be contrasted with tales of surrogacy in the Hebrew Bible where surrogates did this work either out of coercion or poverty. In the first and most significant of these, Sarai directed her husband to "go into [her] slave-girl" to bear them a child out of her desperation (n.b., she is then sixty-five years of age or older) and to bring to fruition God's promise for Abram to father a great nation through his descendants (Gen 12:2, 4, 15:4, 16:2, 17:17). Not only did the intended parents force "Hagar the Egyptian" sexually and reproductively, but their relationships further deteriorated: Hagar looked upon the woman who arranged for her forced pregnancy with contempt, Sarai blamed Abram for the situation she herself orchestrated and called upon God to judge between them, Abram refused to take responsibility for the worsening situation between his two wives, and Sarai ultimately "dealt harshly" but more accurately "violently abused, *t'a'nneha*" Hagar according to womanist Hebrew Bible scholar Wilda Gafney—prompting Hagar to flee while still pregnant (Gen 16:3–6).[48] The surrogate ultimately returns, the intended mother rejects the child she originally directed a foreigner to bear for her, and the surrogate and child are cast out into the wilderness to an uncertain and precarious future (Gen 21:9–10, 14–16).[49]

This pattern of a more powerful woman exploiting a less powerful one under conditions of patriarchy repeats in other biblical texts. The sisters and co-wives of Jacob, Rachel and Leah, took turns "offering" their slaves to him either to produce children for the first time (Rachel, through Bilhah) or to bear more children after secondary infertility (Leah, through Zilpah) (Gen 30:1–24). Even Ruth the Moabite, the eventual great-grandmother of King David, could be viewed as a surrogate because (1) her mother-in-law, Naomi, is the one who orchestrated Ruth's birth of a son, (2) Naomi (the intended mother on this reading) is the one who nurses the resultant child (Obed), and (3) the townspeople recognize Obed as Naomi's—not Ruth's—son (Ruth 3:1–4, 4:16–17). Whether Ruth's surrogacy should be regarded as similarly coercive is less clear since Ruth herself stood to gain from the arrangement and since she is famously depicted as voluntarily binding herself to her mother-in-law's fate and thus following Naomi's directions willingly. However one resolves that question, the story's tragic dimensions remain insofar as these two childless women who have undergone widowhood, famine and displacement, and marginalization as foreigners could only secure their economic futures in the land of Judah by capitalizing on Ruth's sexual and reproductive abilities.[50]

In contrast to these cautionary biblical tales of surrogacy, the non-commercial surrogacies under consideration here are neither coercive nor exploitative. They are better understood as embodied expressions of love and of reproductive generosity as each surro-mom graciously welcomes an alien life in her womb out of her willingness to help the intended parents do something they cannot do on their own. As an act of solidarity, the surro-mom accompanies the intended parents in their struggle as she puts her body on the line when extending hospitality to them and their hoped-for child(ren). When the surrogacy goes well, the IPs care and support their surrogate throughout pregnancy's various stages, including during the important postpartum recovery period. In these ways, surrogacy as a gift provides a powerful testimony of reproductive solidarity and generosity in a world where reproductive frustration and oppression are unfortunately all the more common.

MAKING A PROGRESSIVE CHRISTIAN CASE FOR SURROGACY

The progressive Christian case for surrogacy as a legitimate path for couples to consider when they yearn for children but their sexual activities are not "naturally" procreative is especially strong for married couples, since the Christian tradition still largely regards children (*proles*) as one of matrimony's goods or ends.[51] The argument for the moral acceptability, even good, of surrogacy for heterosexual married couples thus brings together this (1) valuation of children for those who have discerned a call to parenthood, the (2) conscientious use of IVF when there is no other way for a married couple to bear a child, and the (3) reproductive generosity of a person (the surrogate) willing to help them.

My argument for surrogacy for same-sex married couples ends in a similar place of involving the radical hospitality of someone else who will assist them, but begins differently with the progressive Christian point of departure articulated above: belief in the equal goodness and sanctity of marriage among same-sex and opposite-sex couples alike. As I see it, any progressive Christian committed to marriage equality should likewise view the rearing of children, too, as a possible good or end of a same-sex couple's marriage. But because spousal relations among same-sex couples are not "naturally" procreative like they are not among infertile straight couples, both types of married couples would need to pursue a different route to parenthood if they have discerned that parenthood is an appropriate vocation for them. Since many mainline Protestant denominations already affirm adoption and the conscientious use of IVF when there is no other way a heterosexual married couple can bear a child, it stands to reason they should advocate for same-sex married couples to have equal access to both adoption and IVF as well.[52] If not, these same progressive Christian denominations would be guilty of holding an untenable position: one that professed marriage equality but did not actually advocate for equality of access to marriage's various goods, blessings, or opportunities beyond the de jure legal right or religious rite of marriage.

WELCOMING ANOTHER PERSON INTO A COUPLE'S CHILDBEARING PLANS

As we have discussed in earlier chapters and I have observed in my own case, the concept and practice of surrogacy is disconcerting for a segment of the public. But those who find only alarm or tragedy in the division of maternal work may be failing—or simply unwilling—to see the beauty of one party's inability to bear a child on their own being overcome by another's willingness to do so on their behalf. Research on women who are involuntarily childless has shown they have levels of anxiety, depression, and other psychological symptoms comparable to persons who have been diagnosed with cancer.[53] As detailed in chapter 2, women who become pregnant for others frequently report feeling deep sympathy for those who cannot have children without third-party assistance and thus wanting them to prevail against the anguish of involuntary childlessness. Rather than view surrogates as intrusive or disruptive to a couple's relational intimacy, we should come to view them as partaking in an act of embodied solidarity with them. Of course, couples who would find unpalatable the presence of an "outsider" in their family expansion plans need not avail themselves of a gamete donor or surrogate, but they need not deter others who have decided differently from doing so.

As alluded to previously, a third party must always be involved in any same-sex couple's path to parenthood, even if the third party in question is the birth mother in an adoption scenario. As many gay male IPs themselves report, the use of a third-party surrogate and egg donor is an especially attractive way for them to expand their families. While of course same-sex couples also pursue adoption in jurisdictions where they legally can, other couples are reluctant to do so because they hope to maintain a biological connection to

their child and fear either still being discriminated against in the legal processes or having their adopted child taken away if the birth mother were to
return and reassert her maternal rights. Other gay couples become parents by
"enter[ing] into a heterosexual relationship or a co-parenting arrangement"
with someone outside of their marriage or covenantal partnership. Those who
choose surrogacy over that alternative generally do so because of the potential
for the biological mother or female co-parent to legally restrict their access
to their child in the future should their arrangement or other circumstances
change or their relationships sour over time.[54] This is all to say that while surrogacy represents for many heterosexual couples the last resort, when there is
nowhere left on the "infertility treadmill" to turn, it is not uncommon for gay
male couples today who can afford to do so to turn to surrogacy as their *first*
choice after weighing all options.[55]

Straight couples with unresolved feelings about their use of ART and a
third party might thus be wise to learn from the experiences of queer families.
While infertile straight couples must move past the grief of infertility if they
are to pursue either adoption or ART, same-sex gay intended fathers typically do not bemoan their inability to have played a gestational role in their
child's birth, nor feel sad or threatened by other women (such as their surro-
moms) providing breastmilk to their child—something IPs sometimes ask
their surrogates to do. The research shows that IP-surrogate relationships involving gay male couples are not as emotionally fraught as some IP-surrogate
relationships involving an intended mother (and her male partner) can be
because there are not usually issues of unresolved sadness, jealousy, or even
"womb envy" among the intended mothers that the surrogates must gingerly
manage.[56]

My point, to be sure, is not to suggest third-party reproduction among
queer couples is or would always be seamless. As sociologist Maureen Sullivan has shown in her research on lesbian mothers, while some deliberately
choose to "expand the boundaries of their family to include donors, donors'
partners and spouses, and even donors' extended families," other same-sex
couples worry about third-party intrusion like some of their heterosexual
counterparts do, and thus do not seek open and known relationships with
gamete "donors."[57] Still, the division of maternal work between two or more
women need not be a sad or alienating affair, particularly when the literature shows that lesbians commonly conceptualize their mothering in terms
of *shared,* rather than *fragmented,* activities. When ART is involved, some-

times one woman will gestate their child created by intrauterine insemination (IUI) while the other will later induce lactation to provide their child with nourishment. Sometimes one will manually inseminate the other to be "both symbolically and literally part of the conception process."[58] Or sometimes the couple will undergo reciprocal IVF instead, where one will supply the eggs and the other will carry to term the embryo(s). While those examples do not exhaust all possibilities, the point is to acknowledge that families expanded by collaborative reproduction normally will have had to manage more steps to arrive at the live birth of their child than families expanded by natural conception, but they are not to be regarded as inferior. To think otherwise would be to judge families comprised of straight couples and their biogenetic children as necessarily superior to all adoptive families or families headed by same-sex couples—and this is not a judgment any progressive Christian should be prepared to make.

AFFIRMING THE SHARING OF TRADITIONALLY MATERNAL ROLES

A key component of what makes ART transgressive is its disruption of traditional notions of maternity: one woman could contribute the egg, another could gestate the resultant embryo(s) and then fetus(es), and a potentially a third woman could raise the child(ren) once born. In these scenarios, society is forced to determine for legal and other purposes who the mother is, since the long-standing adage, *mater est quam gestatio demonstrat* ("by gestation, the mother is demonstrated") and *mater semper certa est* ("motherhood is always certain") no longer holds. That is, while a child's paternity prior to the era of DNA testing required assumption and guesswork, motherhood was for centuries prior to the advent of ART a given during pregnancy and at childbirth. Social discomfort at "maternal multiplicity"[59] and the disaggregation of motherhood into its component parts through surrogacy and other ART remains strong today.

Recognizing and Upholding Plural Motherhood

One way of assuaging societal discomfort with maternal multiplicity is to recall the ways plural motherhood—a variety of women serving maternal functions in the life of a child—is nothing new. Some children are being mothered and also step-mothered in the case of a parent's remarriage or new partnership after a divorce or a break-up, and these relationships can be harmonious and serve the child's interests if the parties are mature and responsible enough to work toward those ends. Birth mothers and adoptive mothers have also long been negotiating the different roles they will play in a child's life and therein have been maintaining relationships with one another in open adoptions. Other children are being mothered while receiving other forms of maternal care ranging in frequency and intensity from their grandmothers, foster mothers, "bonus moms," and "othermothers."[60] Still other grown children are managing relationships with both their own mothers and their mothers-in-law and these relationships, too, can be sources of support and strength when they go well. What the social practice of surrogacy adds to these varieties of plural motherhood is "gestational" mothering, in addition to making explicit that another woman could be the "intended" mother of a child by committing to do the work of rearing without having played a gestational (or perhaps even a genetic) role. Indeed, feminist philosophical support for this idea of separating the work of "mothering," a set of practices involving the care of children that either men or women could do, from "birthwork" or biological maternity can be found in no less than Sara Ruddick's 1989 classic *Maternal Thinking.*[61]

As I have intimated previously, heterosexual couples may have something to learn from the queer community since their members have been managing the presence of third parties and thus the division of maternal work since the beginning of same-sex-headed families. There are, of course, examples of heterosexual parents who can accept—even welcome—the presence of other mothers who helped to make the life of their child possible. In her memoir on infertility, Canadian feminist Alexandra Kimball recounts a powerful moment following her surrogate's labor and delivery five weeks preterm, when her surrogate still had "slick skin and . . . tubes twisting off her like seaweed" and her newborn Charlie was asleep on her [Kimball's] chest. As Kimball caught her surrogate's eye, she thought to herself: "Oh. . . . [t]his is what she wanted me to have. This is what she was talking about. . . . [T]hat there was so great a feeling I had not known—and that another woman had been willing to give it to me—overwhelmed me as much as Charlie's existence."[62] Elsewhere Kimball writes of being forever conscious of "two stories" every time she would either see her baby or interact with her child's surro-mom or genetic mother with whom she has stayed in contact: in one story she "had to have other women help make my baby (how sad!)"; in the other, she "got to have a baby with other women (pretty cool!)." Kimball concludes these two other women ultimately did not diminish her motherhood but "added to it" by allowing her to have "another partner in the process" beyond her husband. Though she did not become a mother through the typical processes of genetics, gestation, and birth, she believes she nonetheless shared in the "bodily work of pregnancy and childbirth" through the "medical experience of [her] infertility—all the miscarriages, surgeries, tests, and IVF, as well as the physical burden of the attendant grief."[63] I think she is right.

Wet-Nursing and Milk-Sharing as Cross-Cultural Precedents

Wet-nursing as a practice provides us with cross-cultural precedence for intimate maternal work of a different kind being divided among two or more persons. In wet-nursing, one person breastfeeds the child of another because the latter has died, is unable to do so for other reasons, or has elected not to nurse herself and can pay—or perhaps can force (as in the antebellum South and elsewhere)—another person to do it for her.[64] Because my framework for surrogacy initially assumes unpaid arrangements, the more apt comparison here would be between altruistic gestation and altruistic wet nursing or milk-sharing—not cases involving coercion or the sale of breastmilk. Even after the advent of reliable and accessible dehydrated milk and infant formula in the nineteenth century, women have still been performing the bodily service of expressing their own breastmilk to nourish the children of others in times of need. For instance, the feminist sociologist author of a book on reproductive tourism understands wet-nursing as a "historical example of reproductive outsourcing" and recounts her own grandmother's stories of nursing both her father and another child during the time of the Nazi occupation of Hungary because the other mother "was so nutritionally deprived she had stopped lactating."[65] Today, organizations such as Le Leche League International provide guidance on both milk sharing (the sharing of one's expressed breastmilk to others) and wet- or cross-nursing (where someone directly breastfeeds others' children) for prospective donors and recipients alike, such as advising all parties to be informed of potential risks and rewards and for donors to make sure their maintenance of "an oversupply with the intent of donating" will not cause hardship for either themselves or their own children.[66]

In the informal local Human Milk 4 Human Babies (HM4HB) group with which I have been involved, I have witnessed real connection and community form as members post their breastmilk needs and others voluntarily give of their excess. Recipients of these gifts—including parents of preemies, gay male couples, adoptive parents, and others with low or no milk supply—have shown heartfelt gratitude and would often post pictures of their growing babies in appreciation. Those who have offered these nourishing gifts have spoken of their deep satisfaction in donating their "liquid gold" to babies in need, despite all the extra time and work required to do so: pumping, cleaning pump parts, storing.[67] No doubt milk-sharing and cross-nursing can be off-putting and controversial for some people outside these informal networks, and the American Academy of Pediatricians (AAP) does not recommend it from a risk management perspective.[68] Still, those who partake in these ex-changes typically know the risks involved (e.g., bacterial or viral contami-nation through handling, disease transmission, exposure to medication or drugs) and still share or receive breastmilk because they have judged the gains of doing so outweigh them.

Because the ethics of gift surrogacies are separate from the ethics of either altruistic milk-sharing or cross-nursing, care should be taken to remember that support for one practice does not logically entail an endorsement of the other. Still, I have considered these practices in tandem not only to draw attention to another way intimate, embodied "women's work" can and his-torically has been shared across two or more persons, but also to describe another aspect of my surrogacy journey with my friends, as I, too, expressed breastmilk for their daughter for several months post-childbirth.[69] Just as the difficulty of providing breastmilk if neither parent can lactate or produce a sufficient quantity can be overcome by milk donors who are willing to give freely of their body's production, so the problem of a couple who cannot ges-tate their own child can be overcome by a surrogate willing to help in this most embodied way.

Conclusion

A plural understanding of motherhood and recognition of possible divisions in maternal work could not only help make the case for surrogacy, but also clear up common misperceptions about other matters as well. Just as it is both wrong and hurtful to identify the birth mother in an adoption scenario as the "real" one as if the adoptive one were not, something similar can be said about collaborative reproduction. Persons like me who have carried and delivered a child for someone else have not only done so voluntarily, but also played maternal roles in the process. In contrast to the insistence of radical feminists, however, there is no need to identify us as the child's "real" mother as if there could only be one, particularly when the child once born will be raised by another set of parents—perhaps even another mother. Beyond many societies' recognition of plural motherhood in situations other than surrogacy, theologian Ted Peters has observed many also have ample experiences with "parenting and childrearing beyond immediate family members" through nannies, childcare workers, babysitters, and other non-relative elders in the community (affectionately called "aunties" or "uncles" in mine). In short, we need not fear this third party's presence in the child's life undermining parental authority or family cohesion unless the surrogate deliberately attempts to do so in ways exceeding their welcome.[70] Frankly within the Christian tradition, it should not be odd to envision a third party maintaining a role in the child's life indefinitely, given that selected biblical texts hold the entire community responsible for the nurturance of children (Exod 22:22–23, Jm 1:27), entire church congregations in many branches and denominations of Christianity vow to care for *all* infants at baptism or at child dedication services, and a tradition of naming godparents who sponsor the child's entrance into the church and take an active interest in the child's personal and spiritual development is alive and well in many ecclesial communities.

5   A PROGRESSIVE CHRISTIAN FRAMEWORK FOR SURROGACY: SEVEN PRINCIPLES

I REMEMBER FEELING ALARMED after receiving positive results from my first trimester screen, meaning the fetus I was carrying for my friends had a higher than normal risk of chromosomal abnormalities. I had walked a variant of this road before when I was pregnant for the first time at thirty-three. My husband and I had to wait several weeks after my screen before I could have an amniocentesis, as the procedure is normally done between pregnancy's fourteenth and twentieth weeks. We could then only exhale after receiving reassuring news from our preliminary F.I.S.H. (fluorescent in-situ hybridization) results several days later—a diagnostic test for a more limited set of chromosome conditions that can be performed at the same time as the amnio.

Despite my past experience, this scenario felt different because IVF pregnancies are already higher-risk, I was pregnant for Katie and Steven not for me, and we had transferred two embryos with different genetic parentage without knowing which one of them had implanted. *Were the results a clue I was carrying the "snowflake"?* After all, that donated embryo had been "on ice" for the past seventeen to nineteen years and we did not know how long cryopreserved embryos could still be viable once thawed.[1] *Or was I carrying the fetus my IPs had created from some of their own genetic material and there was something abnormal about it?* If so, I'm not sure what, if anything, we would have done. *Or maybe our positive results were simply due to the screen factoring in maternal age and the powers that be had inputted my "geriatric" forty years—not the ages of the two younger genetic mothers of the two embryos we had transferred?*

My speculation about the baby's health was compounded by dread I might be heading toward pregnancy termination. I only knew my intended parents (IPs) believed abortion to be a morally serious matter, would prioritize my life over their fetus's if it tragically came to it, and had not wanted me to carry multiples beyond twins. Despite my repeated, gentle questions to them both prior to and during my pregnancy about other abortion or selective reduction scenarios, these were issues left unresolved—or at least not something they ever told me they had resolved. So while they were coming to terms with the distressing news, I was living with low-grade worry I would end up having my first abortion. While I was not opposed to the procedure in principle and support abortion rights, surely none of us wanted our journey to end in such a way. I had even asked my IPs to undergo preimplantation genetic testing (PGT) prior to our second transfer not only to boost our chances for implantation success and reduce our risks for miscarriage,[2] but also to preempt the situation we were now in. They declined for reasons of their own. When our perinatologist could not suppress her disapproval of my IPs' foregoing of PGT and point blank asked them why, I remember feeling shocked by her bedside manner and strangely affirmed by her tacit censure.

We had to wait one week to meet with a genetic counselor and then one more to receive my cell-free DNA screening test (cfDNA) results. I occupied myself in the interim with an intellectual exercise of working through what additional moral disapprobation I might face from "pro-life" moral theologians were I to abort upon my friends' request. *Would they judge me as the one with primary moral culpability, since I would be the patient consenting to the procedure? Or would they identify my friends as the principal agents of wrongdoing and me as formally having "cooperated with evil," since any abortion I would undergo would be because they had asked?* This speculation led me to ponder in the abstract who should have the final say about abortion or selective reduction in collaborative reproduction: the surrogate, since any decision would affect her body and pregnancy, or the commissioning parents, since her pregnancy would have been undertaken for their sake and a selective reduction or pregnancy termination would affect how many children they would end up with—including none at all?

———

The above is just one cluster of urgent questions any surrogacy arrangement should ideally have settled from the start. My consternation about abortion while already several weeks pregnant as a surrogate made me realize how much my friends and I would have benefitted from having had a framework of ethical principles to guide us, which is what I now provide here. Having already unpacked my sources of normativity and advanced a positive vision of surrogacy in the previous chapter, I offer seven principles or norms to guide the formation of ethical surrogacy relationships: (1) discernment without haste, (2) covenant before contract, (3) empathy, care, and stewardship, (4) medical self-determination, and (5) disclosure, not secrecy, (6) "trust women," and (7) social justice.

Given variability in the types of surrogacy as well as in the material conditions under which any arrangement could take place, these principles assume the same seven simplifying parameters named in the previous chapter. That is, the surrogacy arrangement in question is (1) gestational, (2) financially unremunerated, (3) lawful and intrastate, (4) for IPs who are married or in a committed relationship, (5) taking place under conditions where all parties have access to high-quality healthcare and have provided informed consent, (6) the only safe or feasible way the IPs' child could be birthed given the current state of ART, and (7) enacted under extant, non-dystopian conditions where anti-natalism does not hold.

Principles to Consider Prior to Embarking upon Surrogacy

My framework's first two principles are designed to guide persons and couples contemplating the feasibility of surrogacy for themselves. "Discernment without haste" encourages prospective surrogates and prospective commissioning parents to conscientiously examine whether this method of ART is appropriate for them given the totality of who they are, their life circumstances, and their social context. "Covenant before contract" engages the moral, not just legal, dimensions of any collaborative reproduction and also includes the future child as a member of the covenant to whom the adults will bear special responsibilities.

PRINCIPLE 1: DISCERNMENT WITHOUT HASTE

Having previously established that medicine, including reproductive medicine, could be a channel for God to bring about health, well-being, and flourishing, we must now discern the boundaries of responsible conduct concerning sex, reproduction, and family formation. My framework stands with the Presbyterian Church (U.S.A.)'s call for persons to be guided by "individual conscience" and to consult their "families, pastors, health-care professionals, and scientifically accurate medical information" when attempting to make "good moral decisions . . . about infertility, parenthood, and responses to problem pregnancies.[3]

Prospective Intended Parents

Conscientious decision-making about surrogacy should begin with persons ascertaining whether they are even called to parenthood. While the Christian tradition has largely endorsed Augustine's three goods (*bona*) of marriage—offspring (*proles*), fidelity (*fides*), and unbreakable bond (*sacramenti*)—and interpreted the first to mean each heterosexual married couple should be open to children as the fruit of conjugal love, the Christian tradition has also counterculturally valorized singleness and celibacy for those persons called instead to live differently (1 Cor 7:7–8; Matt 19:11–12). In an era when progressives in every Christian branch or denomination view marriage among two persons of the same gender as equally blessed even if not naturally procreative, affirm the responsible use of contraception, and support other pathways for couples to show "fruitfulness" without themselves bearing progeny,[4] parenthood as such should *not* be regarded as a necessary component for a marriage to be regarded as mature, legitimate, or otherwise good, despite cultural pressures suggesting otherwise.[5]

While there is no simple answer to the question of how a person or couple discerns what they are properly called to be or to do, this much is true: the inability to conceive naturally or to sustain a pregnancy should not be taken as a definitive lack of a call to parenthood, just as intact fertility should not be taken as a sign persons ought to rear children. In ways analogous to how feminists affirm women being called to ordained ministry even in ecclesial traditions that do not recognize women clergy, parenting need not be limited to those who have the biological capacity to conceive and bear children: current constraints, whether institutional or biological, ought not stand in the way.[6]

Given other pathways to parenthood beyond natural conception, whether surrogacy would be appropriate for a couple who cannot bear children without medical assistance would require further discernment. Would paying for IVF and surrogacy's other associated expenses (even when the surrogate herself does not charge a fee) be a wise and proper use of their and others' resources, time, and energy? Could they manage the logistical complexities of a collaborative reproduction, uncertainties and physical risks of the IVF process, and introduction of one or more third parties to their intimate family life? Could they handle their extended families' or community's reactions to their contemplated path, including those of their hoped-for child should their long and uncertain journey eventuate in a live birth? Which alternative path to parenthood, adoption or surrogacy, would pose greater social or legal risks for them given the particularities of who they are or their social context? Is ART truly best for them, all things considered, or might they be unwisely succumbing to the lure of the "infertility treadmill" where they cannot remove themselves from seeking successively more infertility treatments "once the 'reproductive team' has been assembled and IPs have been given hope that a baby . . . awaits them at the end of the process?"[7] As feminist memoirist Alexandra Kimball who underwent several miscarriages, IVF cycles, and multiple surrogacy attempts explains:

> The next procedure might work, the fallopian tube could always clear, the next fetus might not miscarry. . . . It's not that motherhood is out of reach, it's that it's just out of reach. It's not that motherhood didn't happen, it's that it almost did and, in fact, still could. The difference between the grief of infertility and other reasons for mourning . . . is in that promise of "just," in "almost," in "still could." This . . . [is] why . . . a woman might put herself under the knife ten, twelve, twenty times to get pregnant, why she might spend hundreds of thousands of dollars in the effort. The end to her grief is just so near. The tragedy of infertility is one of proximity, and the thing about this proximity is that it is . . . potentially solved—by technology.[8]

All couples contemplating surrogacy should carefully weigh the projected risks and rewards of pursuing this reproductive technique given who they are, what they have already done in their quest to have children, and the extent of the resources and other support available to them. They should also consider the likelihood of initial disagreement among themselves, which they would have to reconcile before proceeding.[9]

Prospective Surrogates

A person contemplating carrying another's child would obviously need to undergo discernment of their own. As British psychologist Olga B. A. van den Akker helpfully acknowledges, they may be facing interpersonal pressures to help when solicited by friends or family or when they get to know the IPs in another way.[10] To be sure, the Ethics Committee of the American Society for Reproductive Medicine (ASRM) does not object to surrogate-IP partnerships among relatives, though emphasizes the need to protect the surrogate's autonomy at all times from potentially "manipulative or undue influences by family members who would benefit from their participation."[11] Of course, as the literature on live organ donation has shown, decisions to perform a bodily service for another family member (e.g., donate a kidney) are often determined by "relational concerns . . . not adequately captured in terms of individual autonomy and voluntariness," given the complexities of "intra-familial decision-making dynamics and their implications."[12]

Each prospective surrogate should conduct an honest self-assessment with input from trusted others and accurate medical information about what agreeing to undergo an IVF pregnancy might look like in their case; that is, what are the risks and costs of a surrogate pregnancy on their overall health and well-being given their age, physical condition, previous pregnancy and childbirth experiences, and other life circumstances? As the reproductive justice (RJ) movement has warned, they should consider whether their race would make an already higher-risk pregnancy even more potentially dangerous for them.[13] They should also assess whether they might face social ostracism by their community or instead commendation and support, as others' reactions to their unusual pregnancy would likely affect their own feelings about and experience of it. Prospective surrogates should also consider the impact an additional pregnancy—especially a logistically and medically complex one—might have on their loved ones' abilities to handle the various changes, inconveniences, and sacrifices their pregnancy might have on them. Red flags include if persons contemplating surrogate motherhood have not resolved whether their own family is complete since they could possibly damage their reproductive capacities in the process, if they ordinarily experience pregnancy as difficult or more bothersome than joyful, or if they already have relational difficulties with the IPs.

Collective and Mutual Discernment

Discernment is often not—and ideally should not be—an individualistic affair. As it was in our case, the parties might be immersed in a religio-cultural context which values communal and intergenerational decision-making and where persons ordinarily must navigate "social taboos and traditions . . . in making reproductive decisions."[14] Ideally all parties would welcome selected others into their discernment process because these others most likely already care about them, the safety and well-being of their prospective surrogate, and the welfare of any child who may be born as a result.

A final part of the discernment process would involve the parties deliberating about the suitability of any potential IP-surrogate match. The IPs would need to vet their prospective surrogate carefully, especially if they suspect her health were less than optimal, motivations were less then commendable or truthful, or personality or lifestyle might be difficult for them to deal with during the long journey ahead. Conversely, each surrogate should ascertain whether she could affirm her prospective IPs' reasons for electing surrogacy as good or as minimally acceptable as well as foresee partnering amicably with them. When the parties in a possible arrangement are relatives or close friends, they should soberly discern whether the collaborative reproduction would be more apt to deepen their relationships or unnecessarily complicate them, particularly if things were to go wrong. Red flags include a surrogate requesting either special recognition from the IPs or a special role in the future child's life in ways the IPs would be unwilling to grant, the IPs being likely to direct anger at the surrogate if she were physically unable to achieve or maintain a pregnancy, or the surrogate being likely to blame herself—or be blamed by family or close friends—for implantation failure or miscarriage or if the child were to be born prematurely or with anomalies. In such cases, the parties should seriously weigh whether surrogacy would be worth the risk of jeopardizing their relationships.[15]

It made a tremendous difference in my discernment that adoption, not surrogacy, had been the path Katie and Steven had first conscientiously pursued after dealing with infertility for years. Their original choice mattered not because I had judged adoption necessarily superior, but because my IPs' earnest attempts at open adoption showed me how they had already begun preparing themselves to raise a biologically unrelated child and, thus, letting go of a conventional parenthood story—something all couples who turn to ART must do. Their use of a donor embryo in our second attempt further revealed that their turn to surrogacy was never primarily about insuring bio-genetic continuity, but about having an opportunity to become parents at all.

Different surrogates will obviously evaluate their prospective IPs' reasons or proposed plans differently. In contrast to my attitude about my friends' use of donors other than me, it is reportedly an "important criterion" for other surrogates to assist only those IPs who would be transferring embryos related to both parents.[16] Some surrogates prefer to help intended mothers over gay male IPs because they have empathy for women struggling to become first-time moms given how important motherhood is to their own identities. Other surrogates prefer to help gay men over straight couples either because of their desire to support members of the LGBTQIA+ community or because they anticipate that a surrogacy journey with men would involve less power struggles than one involving an intended mother who may have unresolved feelings about her inability to gestate her own child. Surrogates might also vary in their willingness to help IPs who have not been successful with other surrogates or who might want to keep trying to use their "lower quality" embryos despite an unpromising prognosis. Surely surrogates as moral agents should examines themselves for their prejudices or implicit biases when discerning whether to help one set of prospective intended parents over others. Still, since it remains supererogatory to offer one's body to others to collaboratively bring forth new life, they should ultimately only assist prospective IPs with whom they feel comfortable.

Finally, prospective members of each surrogacy arrangement should consider whether they could foresee remaining in friendly, continued relationship with one another in the long-term. Given social scientific findings that ongoing contact with the surrogate is correlated with positive child outcomes, it would be best for the relationships to endure well beyond journey's end. As all these questions and issues are weighty, no part of this deliberative process should be rushed.

PRINCIPLE 2: COVENANT BEFORE CONTRACT

In turning now to the formal agreement between surrogate and IPs, my Reformed heritage inclines me toward using the language of covenant. Just as God is faithful to all creation through promise-keeping over time, this principle encourages the parent hopefuls and surrogate to remain faithful to one another by following through with their promises. "Covenant before Contract" not only engages surrogacy's moral and legal dimensions, but also includes the future child as a member of the covenant to whom the adults will bear special obligations after having jointly brought them to life.

Covenantal Commitments

The specifics of each arrangement should be worked out over a series of frank conversations. Beyond pledging to maintain trust and care for one another as their vulnerabilities or concerns might shift over time, the covenanting partners should agree on the following questions:

- How many IVF-HET cycles would they attempt if the first were not successful, given known limitations of time, resources, and other considerations?

- How many embryos would they transfer in one setting in light of the current, obstetrical standard of care and other best practices pertaining to potential risks and gains for all parties?

- What behavioral modifications, medical interventions, and prenatal screening or diagnostic tests would the surrogate willingly undergo once pregnant?

- What would they want to see happen in the event of a multifetal pregnancy or diagnosis of a serious fetal abnormality in light of the projected impact raising a child with disabilities might have on them, given the support (or lack thereof) available?

- What kind of relationship would they seek to cultivate during the long and uncertain path ahead and how might they envision their relationship changing at journey's end?

- How would they handle worst-case scenarios?

- What mechanism would they have in place to discuss unanticipated changes in feelings or courses of action about their plans?

- What would they do with any "excess" embryos? Far from being only a private IP matter, the surrogate might be (or else might feel) morally implicated for praise or blame depending on what ultimately became of them, particularly if the IPs created them only after she came on board.

The covenanting parties' views on some matters should affect their decision-making in others. As per my opening anecdote, if the IPs know or surmise they would not want their surrogate to carry a fetus with a certain gene mutation or congenital anomality to term, they should seriously consider PGT. These preimplantation genetic tests would not only spare them of having to wait until after the surrogate were pregnant to find out the results of any prenatal screening or diagnostic test, but they would also allow them to do something less difficult if those tests proved positive: not transfer the "affected" embryo(s) versus ask their surrogate to undergo an abortion. Alternatively, if the IPs were covenanting with a surrogate who would want human embryonic life to be treated with the same dignity and respect as born human beings, the IPs should go against the grain of standard IVF practice to avoid making their surrogate complicit in their actions from her point of view: they should only create one embryo at a time or as many as they would be willing to transfer, only transfer as many embryos in one procedure as they would be willing to bring to term without selective reduction, and give all embryos a chance to be born through themselves or through other prospective parents following embryo donation to them. The alternative, of course, would be for the IPs to partner with someone whose convictions about embryos more closely matches their own and vice versa.

In addition, each surrogate should covenantally undergo all aspects of prenatal care as advised by their doctors and as conscientiously as if they were carrying their own child. Each surrogate should also share regular updates about the pregnancy and hand over the IPs' baby at the prearranged time without incident. In turn, the IPs should support them in all pledged ways and assume parentage post-birth even if they do not end up with a "perfect baby"—something nearly all intended parents do. The parent's covenant with the future child, to be discussed further below in principle 5, should include disclosing their unconventional birth circumstances in age-appropriate ways and in helping them process whatever questions or feelings they might have about them. Each surrogate should also vow to remain indefinitely in the child's life not as a third parent, but to heed what has been learned from the adoption literature about ongoing contact centered on the needs and wishes of the child yielding better psychological outcomes for all parties.

Both Covenant and Contract

Astute observers will recognize the overlap between questions for covenant conversations and standard provisions in surrogacy contracts. The latter typically provide for "parental rights, custody issues, location of delivery, future contact between the parties . . . insurance (both health and life) . . . control over medical decisions during the pregnancy, payment of medical bills, lia-bility for medical complications, availability of medical history and personal medical information on the gestational carrier . . . the intended parents' pres-ence during doctor's visits and at the delivery" and the surrogate's expenses including "lost wages, legal fees, child care and maternity clothes."[17] The wisdom in formalizing covenantal conversations in contracts or signed pre-conception agreements lies in their jointly deciding *in advance* how they will manage possible future difficulties instead of naively presuming their good-will and intentions would prove sufficient to handle them should those trying scenarios come to pass.

"Covenant" should nevertheless precede "contract" as opposed to be *re-placed* by it for three key reasons: First, so the motivation to follow through with their promises would be connected to the principles of fidelity and in-tegrity, not to fears of being found in breach of contract. Second, to identify the future child as the third member of the covenant to whom both the IPs and the surrogate would bear special responsibilities, since the child cannot be a signatory even if the contract is ostensibly centered on their creation. Third, because there would be no binding obligations beyond those formally specified in the agreement if the surrogacy were understood as a purely con-tractual, not also covenantal, matter. Contracts—however detailed—may thus ultimately require less from a moral point of view than the covenant I envision the surrogacy triad maintaining over time.

My Experience Moving from Covenant to Contract

There were certain portions of the contract stage that were awkward for my friends and me. In one of the worst-case scenarios we were asked to consider—*what should happen if I were to become incapacitated or suffer a life-threatening injury while pregnant?*—I agreed to remain or to be placed anew on life support to continue to gestate their unborn child at least until the point of viability. While that provision was not difficult for me to agree on, a stranger "what if?" scenario was what reasonable compensation should I receive if I were to lose my reproductive capabilities in the process. I found that question odd because my husband and I did not want any more children and thus my reproductive capacities were of no value to me personally. Our attorney, however, insisted it was necessary to specify some credible amount.

Like other surrogates who report similar experiences in discussion forums and support groups, I reacted negatively to provisions in the draft contract

I found to be overly controlling. There were, for instance, clauses mandating that I refrain from using fingernail polish when pregnant and to limit my "exposure to radiation (i.e., cell phones, laptops, microwaves)." Fingernail polish I could do without, even though I thought the ban overzealous. But as I normally spend hours at a time in front of my laptop every day, the latter constraint was not workable, which is why I had my attorney delete it.

One especially bothersome clause was a provision stating I was not permitted to travel outside of the U.S. or even California unless I first obtained prior written approval from my reproductive endocrinologist or ob/gyn. My problem with it was not so much my two upcoming international trips and four out-of-state ones for work my friends and I had already discussed—and I had thought—settled. Nor was it my growing apprehension that our psychologist might have been right when she told Nathaniel and me that it is common for IPs to agree orally to whatever terms their surrogate requests out of their desperation for a child, with the contract stage being the time when their true colors would show. Rather, what irked me most was the draft contract's implication that many ordinary activities were dangerous for pregnant persons—a view I already found tiresome in American popular culture—and its treatment of surrogates as flight risks. Of course I understood why contracts were written in that way: IPs want assurances that the person gestating their unborn child would be taking precautions with their body. They also want to avoid scenarios where their surrogate would end up giving birth in a jurisdiction hostile to surrogacy or where their rights as intended parents would be less secure than the birth mother's. Still, since our contract was between us two couples who were close friends—not between parties previously unknown to one another as in many commercial arrangements—I insisted they change the default so I was expressly free to travel wherever and whenever *unless* my IVF physician or ob/gyn specifically advised against it.

Over several tense conversations where my husband and I pointed out to the IPs provisions in the draft contract that contradicted our oral agreements, we realized the four of us had been approaching the contract stage differently. I had entered into our discussions with an understanding that surrogates, not IPs, are the more vulnerable party in contract negotiations. Nathaniel and I were thus keen to ensure I would not be pressured into surrendering more control over my body than what was reasonable for anyone in my situation to yield. My friends explained they had been viewing the contract as a legal formality—something we just had to "get through" so I could finally begin my IVF meds protocol. They added they had been eager to rush for *my* sake as well, since I had previously told them a summertime (not an academic school year) delivery would have less of an impact on my professional responsibilities. Thus, to move the process along as quickly as possible, they largely accepted the first draft of the contract their attorney had prepared "as is," since they believed the many things we had agreed to orally would carry more weight in cases of conflict than would the words printed on a piece of paper. My husband and me as an attorney and ethicist, respectively, did not share their same view of the contract being of little practical consequence. Beyond wanting to do what we contractually represented we would do as matters of integrity, we also understood that a worst-case scenario might freakishly come to pass and thus an authorized person in the unlikely event of their incapacity or death would look to our contract as an expression of their last wishes about how to proceed.

The tension and awkwardness we experienced during our contract stage led me to analogize from our situation to what couples on the cusp of marriage might feel if and when they draw up a prenuptial agreement. In either situation, persons of goodwill must transform their voluntary commitments into a legally binding decision; they must also determine in advance what should happen if certain catastrophes were to befall them, including if their relationships later were to dissolve. Our experience revealed my IPs were acting as if our informal covenant would and should supersede our contract. The framework for surrogacy being proposed here, however, emphasizes the importance of both, in addition to the commitments expressed in the one to be essentially the same as those made in the other.

What about Breaking Covenantal or Contractual Commitments?

A final matter worth addressing is what should happen if one party reneges on their covenantal or contractual commitments. Should a surrogate be held morally or legally responsible for parenting her surro-baby in the highly unlikely event where the IPs refuse or otherwise prove unable to assume parentage? Television personality and former co-host of talk show *The View*, Sherri Shepherd, infamously attempted to walk away from her obligations as an intended mother after splitting from her husband, the baby's genetic and intended father, while their surrogate was pregnant (n.b., the child's genetic mother was a non-identified donor, and their arrangement was commercial). In cases where there are legally enforceable contracts and where IPs become the legal parents at the child's birth with all rights and responsibilities thereof, IPs who have a change of heart would still be legally required to live with the consequences of their commitments. Morally, their obligations should hold steady as well.

What if the IPs' failure to assume parentage were due more to tragic circumstances beyond their control than an abdication of responsibility, such as the IPs' sudden incapacity or deaths? Such scenarios would also ideally already have been covered in the parties' pre-conception agreement or contract, as it was in ours and is in most others, with the designated person(s) then assuming legal guardianship. Should those measures fall through, I would encourage the surrogate to take temporary custody of the child assuming it were in the child's best interests (i.e., there were no capable relatives, close friends, or godparents of the IPs who could step in, and the surrogate had the capacity to provide temporary care), until or unless other suitable arrangements could be made.

As discussed in chapter 3, it is statistically rare for a surrogate to attempt or even wish to keep the child for herself, though there are outliers. Legally, a surrogate mother may well be in her right to do so if the arrangement occurs in a jurisdiction where the person giving birth is automatically recognized as the child's legal mother (as does the U.K.),[18] or if her jurisdiction otherwise recognizes her right for a period of time not to relinquish (as does Virginia). As both an ethicist and former surrogate, however, I could not countenance such a decision and would urge the surrogate to seek counseling or other forms of support in lieu of breaking her covenantal commitments to the IPs and to their future child.

Principles to Guide Surrogacy Arrangements and Relationships

Three additional principles should guide a surrogacy journey as it enfolds. "Empathy, care, stewardship" turns on the recognition of one another's particular concerns and vulnerabilities. "Medical self-determination" first requires everyone to have frank and honest conversations with one another well before any embryo transfer(s) about prenatal care while unequivocally affirming the surrogate's right to make all medical decisions related to her body. "Disclosure, not secrecy" encourages the parents to tell their surrogate-born children early and often the circumstances surrounding their birth.

PRINCIPLE 3: EMPATHY, CARE, AND STEWARDSHIP

This principle starts with acknowledging the possibility of hurt, disappointment, and mistreatment occurring in all relationships, including those begun with good intentions. Covenantal relationships should be grounded in a mutual recognition of one another's vulnerabilities, a pledge to reciprocal care, and an understanding that the words and actions of one party have the power to affect others in either productive or damaging ways. As social worker Ellen Glazer has observed, misunderstanding is possible and quite likely at times given the different life experiences the adults involved in a collaborative reproduction ordinarily bring to the table. A surrogate, particularly a first-time one, typically assumes the surrogacy will go smoothly in light of her own fertility track record—that the first embryo transfer (ET) will prove successful, that her pregnancy will not end in a miscarriage, and that she will deliver a healthy child at full term vaginally without complications. The IPs, in contrast, will likely have faced years of reproductive loss if heterosexual or disbelief they could ever have their life partner and possibly also a biogenetically related child with them if same-sex and thus tend to be more guarded and less confident since their personal history has not primed them to expect a happy ending.[19]

Complex Feelings and Relational Dynamics

These very different starting points can create complex relational dynamics. Since many surrogates unconsciously expect "their own fertility would transfer to their IPs," many find themselves shocked if or when setbacks occur. Others can find their IPs' caution or negativity difficult to bear as they feel the IPs are "waiting for the other shoe to drop" and thus cannot share in the excitement of each step of the surro-pregnancy with them.[20] That is, while the surrogate could be thoroughly invested in the journey, the IPs might be emotionally holding themselves back as a way to psychologically prepare for unknown calamities that might yet befall them, as they may be struggling to believe they will finally become parents of a child at the end of this long process with no guarantees.

Though not to the extent some other surrogates have reported in the surrogacy literature, I believe my friends and I experienced a version of this phenomenon. Along with potential termination or selective reduction scenarios, I wanted to thoroughly discuss—and settle months in advance—all other major scenarios we could foreseeably face. A major one was how they wanted their baby girl to be fed moments after delivery. I cared about this matter greatly because I would be involved in two of the options we were considering: my breastfeeding their child directly or my attempting to express colostrum for her prior to childbirth (a more physically difficult prospect) until my milk came in, at which point I would switch to exclusive pumping for a season of time. Beyond the question of their daughter's first meal, I had also wanted to know in advance what their plan was for her nutrition after I were to stop expressing breastmilk, as it didn't feel right for me to stop until they had one. But in these and in other matters, my IPs only wanted to resolve the immediate question at hand due in part to a personality difference of their not wanting to foreclose options until the time a decision had to be made (i.e., their Myers-Briggs Personality type P to my J) and in part to their apparent ambivalence about formula. While what I interpreted as their punting and indecision for months before their child was born and then for months after childbirth was extremely frustrating to me, particularly since I repeatedly ask them about it in person, through texts, and through emails, I have learned over the course of researching this book that my IPs were no different than many other would-be parents in their position. Clinicians report that many IPs and prospective adoptive parents only have the capacity to focus on the concrete aspects of the immediate decision at hand such as "timing and cost" and thus bracket how their decisions will "affect the life of their family in the long term" because they "just can't think that far out; we've had so many disappointments" or only want to "cross that bridge when [they] come to it."[21]

Intended mothers (IMs) are also apt to experience a mixture of complex feelings toward the person standing in their place. Surrogates have biological capital, leaving many IMs to feel simultaneously grateful *and* envious about their substitute's ability to do things they cannot do—especially activities so conventionally tied to femininity and motherhood as carrying a child in one's womb and giving birth are. In addition, because nursing has been characterized by many cultures as a quintessential motherhood experience and "breast is best" public health campaigns have emphasized the nutritional value of breastmilk, these mixed feelings of appreciation and jealousy can compound when the surrogate also provides breastmilk to her surro-baby for some time if it is part of their arrangement, as it was in ours. In short, infertile intended mothers must have incredible resolve to watch their surrogate perform maternal functions that she cannot. Here, it is worth noting that gay male intended parents do not typically report having ambivalent feelings of gratitude and resentment as some of their intended mother counterparts do, which is one of the reasons why some surrogates prefer helping them. Regardless, it is not uncommon for disagreements and even power struggles about prenatal care or the birth plan to occur, as prospective parents (whether straight or same-sex) who turn to ART still commonly desire to assert some control in an ultimately uncontrollable situation. When these difficulties surface, the parties should do what they can to work through areas of tension.

The Intended Parents' Responsibilities

The surrogate's self-gift of her body necessarily involves her whole self: her body, of course, given the various pregnancy-related behavioral restrictions she commits to following, but also the discipline to complete her rigorous IVF regimen, since some medications need to be taken at timed intervals throughout each day and others several times per week. The IPs should thus exercise responsible stewardship by remembering she is not simply a means to their end: she is a person in her own right—not simply a fetal incubator or vessel. They should ensure she receives appropriate prenatal care for optimal health according to current obstetrical best practices—neither excessive check-ups (e.g., blood tests or ultrasounds beyond the standard of care) just so the IPs can continue to monitor their unborn child's progress, nor a reduction in appointments just so the IPs can save money when they are paying out-of-pocket for the pregnancy. They should neither request for her to curtail her ordinary activities unless medically indicated just to appease their anxieties, nor should they schedule an induction or C-section to ensure they will be present at their baby's planned birth unless it would not increase risks to their surrogate or baby in so doing.

Even as the new parents adjust to the exciting demands of raising their child, they should make a concerted effort to continue to demonstrate care for the person who helped to make their expanded family possible. Ongoing contact, even if it decreases in frequency and intensity, is advisable given the social scientific literature showing surrogates feeling sad and hurt if their once close relationship with their IPs abruptly ends following childbirth. The IPs should also be aware of the statistical probability of some pregnant persons experiencing mood swings or "baby blues" as they adjust hormonally to their body's changed state, with this period typically lasting either only a few hours or up to one to two weeks. In the event their surrogate is part of the statistical minority who experiences postpartum depression or other adjustment problems at journey's end, the IPs should check in with her in regular intervals (even if the time between them gradually increases) to prevent abrupt cut-off and also help arrange for her to receive other assistance as needed.

I will never forget the love and care I felt when my IPs intentionally stayed at the hospital for hours longer than was required after their baby had already been cleared to leave. They were concerned about the more difficult recovery ahead of me following my emergency C-section and my being mostly alone for several more days, since Nathaniel and I had decided it would be better for him to stay primarily at home with our young kids and not bring them to see me until my postpartum swelling decreased and I could be disconnected from most of my tubes (lest I scare them). My IPs were also lovely about making a one-hour roundtrip commute to visit regularly for months after I was discharged: at least one of them would come, usually with delicious food for my whole family, and I would then give them my latest batch of expressed breastmilk.

The Surrogate's Responsibilities

The surrogate, too, should exercise due care of her IPs. She should not take advantage of them monetarily, knowing they will be covering all of her pregnancy-related expenses. She should also provide timely updates of her progress and allow them to experience a pregnancy-by-proxy while preserving her sense of privacy. As many other surrogates do, I invited Katie and Steven to accompany me to whatever medical appointments they wanted to attend, so we scheduled these at mutually convenient times. Katie came to most of the ones involving an ultrasound and would usually start talking to her baby girl in utero whenever she would see her image on the screen, which was endearing for me to witness. A surrogate's hospitality on this score, including by granting occasional permission for the IPs to place their hands on her stomach to feel the baby move post-quickening, could help deepen the IPs' embodied connection to the surrogate-pregnancy. It could also facilitate early bonding between the IPs and their developing child and additionally help to heal an IM's residual pain of infertility (if any) by permitting her to experience the pregnancy secondhand.

Being a surrogate requires wisdom to know what news, feelings, or physical changes to share and what to withhold. As reported in surrogacy discussion forums, surrogates are commonly of two minds about whether they should tell their IPs the results of the many home pregnancy tests they are prone to taking during the anxiety-filled "two week wait" and whether they should minimize their reporting of any pregnancy discomfort or inconveniences as they arise. The reasons for indecision on the former should be obvious; the reason for concealment in the latter would be to avoid making the parent hopefuls feel even more indebted to them than they already likely feel and to remain sensitive to an IM's (if one is present) sadness she could not be the one experiencing the various aches—and glories—of pregnancy. I elected to disclose the results of my home pregnancy tests to prepare Katie and Steven for our fertility clinic's official results (which were accurate both times) and opted for selective disclosure in the other matter. I reasoned nothing would be gained if I shared everything, but I would be supplying a false picture of pregnancy if I consistently downplayed such information and thus would not ultimately be serving either myself or them well. Other surrogates might decide to share everything instead, "even the most visceral bodily functions, such as vomiting, dizziness, and physical pain." As one Israeli surrogate recounted

> I really tried to pass her all sorts of feelings so that she could, so to speak, feel like she was pregnant. . . . [I]f I had a headache, or I didn't sleep at night, or the fetus was kicking, moving. . . . I would call her and say, "she kicked me and it hurts." Then she would say, "okay, now which side hurts." I said "left. Say it hurts you too." And she would yell, "ay, ay, ay," on the phone . . . in the beginning when I had dizziness and vomiting, I could call her and say, "I feel yucky," and she would say, "I will go vomit instead of you." And she really felt like it belonged to her. Like she was pregnant. Because I shared everything with her.[22]

Surrogates would be wise to turn to in-person or online support groups to help them discern such matters before saying or doing something that could not be unsaid or undone. In general, I would recommend more, not less, explicit communication of news, wants, or needs, particularly if presented at appropriate times and in tactful ways. For instance, I conveyed to my friends I would likely cry at childbirth because of the hormones and my tendency to cry in moments of exuberance or exhaustion. I felt it important to do so in advance so they would not wrongly misinterpret my anticipated tears when the time came as sadness about needing to part with their baby girl. Because we had had these conversations in the months prior, I did not feel like I had to self-censor when the waterworks came in the surgical room both before and after my ob/gyn made the incision.

Dealing with Reproductive Loss

Finally, empathy among covenant members will be essential when dealing with reproductive loss. The ethnographic research shows that surrogates who may be experiencing unsuccessful transfers, chemical pregnancies, miscarriages, and stillbirths—usually for the first time ever—are often flummoxed by these events. The IPs will likely be distraught by the news, though not surprised. Some surrogates take reproductive failure or loss personally and feel guilty about it (for the record, I did not), given their sympathy for the IPs and the personal responsibility they may have assumed to overcome their plight. If the surrogate-pregnancy ends in termination, all are likely to find the scenario extremely difficult, even if everyone agreed with the decision to abort. The particular relationship might also come to an end after implantation failure, miscarriage, abortion, or stillbirth if the members will not be making another attempt—or at least not with one another. This parting of ways, too, should be acknowledged and mourned given their heavy investments to collectively bring a child to life. In these scenarios of reproductive loss, the parties should ideally find ways to comfort themselves and one another without minimizing, gaslighting, or assigning blame where none is warranted.[23]

Ongoing Psychological Care

For the sake of psychological health and the strength of the relationships, I recommend the new parents and surrogate scheduling at least one individual and one group therapy appointment between six weeks and three months following childbirth. Why that time period? In the U.S., it is standard for persons who have given birth to be examined for physical healing after six weeks and for healthcare providers to also check then for signs of postpartum depression. Given the collaborative reproduction, this postpartum psychological check-up would allow members to touch base with one another, as their relationships may well have changed in intensity and in frequency of contact in the days and weeks following childbirth. The parties might especially benefit from having the same psychologist who evaluated them at the start of their arrangement to do so again, as this mental health professional should have notes about their earlier concerns and thus be in a position to assess how the parties have dealt with them. Finally, this therapist might be well-positioned to advise any of the parties to seek ongoing therapy if needed as each continues to adjust to a significant change in their status and circumstances.

While this postpartum psychological check-up is only a recommendation, it is worth noting some jurisdictions legally mandate it. For example, the State of Louisiana might not be a paragon for surrogacy legislation given its highly restrictive laws, but I find commendable their requirement for all parties in a gestational surrogacy contract to agree to a minimum of one post-birth counseling session to commence within six months of the child's birth.[24]

PRINCIPLE 4: MEDICAL SELF-DETERMINATION

If the parties have done a thorough job discerning with one another, they will have had many conversations about their envisioned hopes for how each step of the collaborative reproduction would ideally proceed. They will have extensively discussed whether the IPs would want their surrogate either to selectively reduce in the case of multiples or terminate the pregnancy following a diagnosis of a serious fetal anomaly or some other problem, such as a serious risk to the surrogate's health or life. Their plans for labor and delivery should also include what pain management the surrogate intends to undergo, which guest(s) will be permitted in the birthing room and how they should station themselves relative to her, whether the taking of photos or video will be allowed and shared, including by posting on social media, and other details of importance to them. Everyone needs to know where they themselves and others in their arrangement stand on matters like this big and small.

Because overlapping agreement is essential, prospective surrogate-IP pairs who discover irreducible incompatibility on matters they deem nonnegotiable should *not* go through with their plans, however much they might be aligned on other matters. A parting of ways after high hopes would likely be painful, but the goal would be to prevent an even larger calamity from coming to pass. To illustrate, if the IPs were to request a selective reduction or an abortion for reasons the surrogate found objectionable and she were to refuse, the IPs would then have to assume parentage for a child (or children) they would not have wanted to bring to term unless they arranged for an adoption; pay the higher than anticipated medical costs associated with multiple gestation, such as the surrogate's bed rest (as needed) or infant care in the NICU (if relevant); and also provide long-term care for any children born with severe disabilities or medical needs.[25] Alternatively, the surrogate might in some jurisdictions find herself legally responsible for a child she would otherwise have relinquished at journey's end if the IPs, in response to her refusal to abort or selectively reduce, were to refuse parentage of some or all of the (born) children in retaliation for her refusal. In another disaster scenario, if the surrogate were to object to carrying multiples and opted for a selective reduction against the parents' wishes, the IPs who would have warmly welcomed them all would obviously be distraught.

The Surrogate's Prerogative

What if the members were in agreement with one another about hypothetical scenarios at the start of their journey, but later encountered uncertainty or outright conflict in a real situation? Studies indicate the above scenario is more than a remote possibility. A review of eleven empirical studies published in English conducted in seven countries across one decade found the decision to abort in the face of a Down syndrome (DS) diagnosis varied depending on "whether participants were prospective parents recruited from the general population (23%–33% would terminate), pregnant women at increased risk for having a child with DS (46%–86% would terminate), or women who received a positive diagnosis of DS during the prenatal period (87%–97% terminated)."[26] These findings suggest either social desirability bias—people are not willing to acknowledge publicly their willingness to abort—or else they are poor predictors of their own future behavior. Whatever the explanation, expectant parents receiving news of a fetal anomaly would often be facing real-time constraints to decide possible next steps. While detection is possible in the first trimester (e.g., chorionic villus sampling [CVS] is usually performed between ten and thirteen weeks), many expectant persons only find out about serious fetal anomalies in the second trimester when their pregnancy is well under way; for reference, an amniocentesis is generally done between fifteen and twenty weeks. In addition, a vast majority of states in the U.S. prohibit abortions after a certain point in pregnancy, including more than a third restricting the procedure after twenty weeks.[27]

In the event where deliberations about next steps result in a standstill, ultimate moral and legal decision-making prerogative *must* rest with the gestator. The reproductive justice framework denounces a coerced abortion (or coerced fetal reduction) just as much as it decries a coerced pregnancy under its core human rights commitments for every person to decide whether to have a child and whether not to have a child. Every pregnant person's right to termination also finds support in what the Human Rights Committee interpreted as entailed by the ICCPR's Art. 6 provision of the "inherent right to life."[28] Philosophers Ruth Walker and Liezl Van Zyl eloquently specifically defend a pregnant person's right to abort even in cases when they originally became pregnant for others:

> The right to decide whether to terminate a pregnancy does not depend on a genetic relationship between mother and fetus, nor is it based in the intention or duty to raise that child. Rather, it is grounded in the right to bodily integrity. Hence, in non-surrogate pregnancies, a woman's spouse or partner does not have a right to demand or prevent abortion, even if he is the genetic and would-be social parent. In the same way, the surrogate's right to decide whether to undergo an abortion is based on her status as a pregnant woman, regardless of the genetic or (intended) social relationship to the fetus.[29]

While the persons involved should come to some prior understanding about what they might do in hypothetical scenarios, their surrogacy arrangement should *not* be interpreted as any surrogate waiving their authority over medical self-determination. Believing otherwise, in the words of an earlier committee opinion of the American College of Obstetricians and Gynecologists (ACOG), would be tantamount to allowing surrogacy contracts to "institute contractual slavery."[30]

Thus, as the American Society for Reproductive Medicine (ASRM) instructs, all parties to a surrogacy agreement should receive counseling about the gestational carrier's "right to make choices for her body."[31] In a clinical context, knowledge that the locus of medical decision-making resides with the surrogate should prevent doctors from incorrectly "look[ing] for input from the intended parent(s) when medical decisions are being made during pregnancy, labor, or delivery."[32] While the persons involved should talk through as many foreseeable scenarios as possible and document their mutual understanding in their signed pre-conception agreement or contract, only the pregnant person—the true patient in every pregnancy—should be recognized as the party ultimately responsible for determining the course of her prenatal care.

Legal Matters

Might a court of law ever compel a surrogate against her will to remain pregnant or to terminate to enforce contract compliance? Recall from chapter 2 that some feminists fear surrogacy as a social practice will erode women's reproductive autonomy and abortion rights.

To be sure, some states do have provisions specifically protecting each surrogate's right to handle matters pertaining to selective reduction or pregnancy termination. Where the law is unclear, clauses in surrogacy contracts covering selective reduction or pregnancy termination in the U.S. have not generally been interpreted as legally enforceable. Judith Daar, chairman of the ASRM Ethics Committee and dean of the Samuel P. Chase College of Law at Northern Kentucky University, acknowledges the existence of a legal gray area but does not believe a U.S. court would ever direct a surrogate to undergo the procedure without her consent. Even as some reproductive law attorneys continue to insert abortion clauses into these contracts, most understand that "a remedy for breach, if any" would rest in "monetary damages rather than specific performance."[33] Daar adds that in California and elsewhere where pre-birth parentage orders can be filed, IPs could not coerce a surrogate into selectively reducing or aborting by threatening to leave her legally responsible for parentage post-birth so long as there were a valid contract between them. What remains uncertain is whether a surrogate who refused to abort or selectively reduce would be liable for damages, or—in the case of commercial contracts—would have to forfeit her fee.[34]

The Good *versus the* Right

A surrogate's retention of the *right* to medical decision-making in her pregnancy intended for others says nothing about how she should go about it. While she may be acting within her moral and legal rights to terminate the pregnancy or selectively reduce in the event of multiples, her reasons to do so might be morally suspect if she were to abort for a congenital anomaly against the IPs wishes and therein substitute her unwillingness to parent such a child for theirs, or if she were to fail to discuss with her IPs why she no longer wished to continue with the pregnancy. More controversially, if a surrogate earlier conveyed she would be willing to selectively reduce or abort under certain scenarios but then balked at doing so when the time came, I would still affirm her legal prerogative but disapprove of her refusal to follow through with her earlier representations. Her fault would lie in either having misrepresented to the IPs her willingness to perform certain actions when a real situation presented itself, or having failed to examine these matters as conscientiously as she should have as evidenced by a change of heart in such a short time period.

In light of the parties' mutual discernment and commitments, the surrogate's default should be to follow through with what she earlier conveyed she would do unless she is presented with genuinely new and unforeseen information or circumstances. If the latter occurs, she should factor into her decision-making the risks of multiples (for herself and the babies if born) and the impact they would have on the IPs in the event of multiple gestation. Following a potential diagnosis of a serious fetal abnormality, she should also consider the IPs' convictions, capacities, resources, and support system (or lack thereof) to raise a child with the projected long-term medical needs. Still, neither surrogates nor IPs should assume the future of persons predicted to have disabling conditions will necessarily be a poor one full of lifelong suffering.

Maintaining Patient Autonomy

All told, the principles of patient autonomy, bodily integrity, and reproductive justice ground the surrogate's retention of medical decision-making power in her pregnancy, particularly but not exclusively in matters pertaining to selective reduction, abortion, and pain management during labor and delivery. While outsiders might censure a surrogate's projected or actual decision, their assessment of its real or perceived wrongness would still be insufficient to undercut her right to decide accordingly. What this means is that surrogates like me cannot be let off the moral hook by allowing the IPs to make these decisions for us—we cannot avoid taking responsibility for actions we make in this arena even if we think we are just following our IPs' wishes. Likewise, the principle of medical self-determination should impress upon the parent hopefuls how much risk they would be assuming when they transfer their embryo(s) to another person's uterus: they would be "entrusting the surrogate with the fate of the fetus that may or may not become their child."[35]

Beyond seeking to assuage feminist fears about surrogacy undermining women's rights to determine what to do with their own bodies, this principle is also born from reflecting on how the specter of abortion figured in my own surrogacy journey. What has niggled at me—even years after the fact—is the inadequate counsel I received from my reproductive law attorney and various staffers at our fertility clinic. Prior to setting the terms of our contract, the two main questions these fertility professionals asked me about were (1) whether I understood the statistical odds and risks of multiples (particularly in light of our planned double embryo transfer) and (2) who would be the party responsible for deciding whether to selectively reduce or abort: me or the IPs. No one—not even the attorney paid to represent my interests—ever referred me to ACOG's or ASRM's positions on the matter or told me of my legal rights, and I had not thought to check on my own.

It was only a year following childbirth while conducting research for an academic presentation upon which this book expands when I realized I had never legally waived my rights to medical self-determination even though I had been operating as if I had. My mistaken belief that the decision to abort or not was legally out of my hands because of my contract, coupled with my IPs' reticence to disclose what they would want me to do in the event of fetal abnormalities, led me to feel almost regretful about prioritizing my friends' agency in the ways I had. All told, the misinformation I received from those fertility specialists and legal counsel, even if through omission and not deliberate deception, and the anxiety I felt when the prospect of abortion loomed after my positive first trimester screen remain painful parts of my surrogacy. It has also led me to feel concern for other prospective surrogates who may have been—or still might be—provided with similarly inadequate counsel. I cannot help but think if I as a professional ethicist with a doctorate and even an attorney husband could have been confused about my rights to patient autonomy on this score, other surrogates with fewer resources and less formal education at their disposal could have been or could still be similarly misinformed as well.

PRINCIPLE 5: DISCLOSURE, NOT SECRECY

I take it as axiomatic that Christian support for surrogacy must be premised upon the parents telling their surrogate-born child, and others more selectively, the truth about how that child came into the world even though temptations toward nondisclosure would be understandable. Some gay parents might conceal the genetic father's identity to others to avoid contributing to the societal misperceptions that only of them is the "real dad" and to promote the idea that "love makes a family."[36] Some straight couples might avoid disclosure to others due to ongoing shame about their infertility, difficulty accepting their child's surrogate birth or donor-conception, dread about broaching the topic or their inability to answer follow-up questions about the other biological parent (if they used a non-identified donor), or a desire to evade social criticism for their choices. Whether gay or straight, such parents also commonly cite child-centered reasons for concealment. They fear their children might handle the news poorly, reject the non-genetic or non-gestational parent as not their "true" mother or father, be teased by their peers if their birth circumstances became known to them, or not be fully accepted by extended family members if the latter were to discover biogenetic unrelatedness in the case of donor-conception.[37] According to writer Nancy Hess who herself used a surrogate and an egg donor, the "lure of the lie" tempts many parents to be secretive, evasive, or otherwise not forthcoming about their turn to ART, as they prefer not having to explain their child's origins when people unknowingly comment about physical resemblance or lack thereof or wonder how an "older" woman even came to be a mom.[38]

Why Disclose?

The progressive Christian framework for surrogacy I advance is committed to the parents' truth-telling—to themselves, to their child, and to selective others—for several reasons. First, as a practical matter, secrecy is psychologically and practically difficult to maintain. As confirmed by our psychologist in our group evaluation, the standard professional advice for parents who do not plan on disclosing to their children their adoption, donor conception, or surrogate-birth is for them to conceal the truth *from everyone else* to prevent possible disclosure from others. However, most persons who are adopting or using third-party reproduction will have already shared their plans with some friends, co-workers, or relatives who likely will have asked them how they will come to be parents if neither of them will undergo a pregnancy, particularly if they are a gay couple. That a handful of people would already know about the parents' use of ART prior to the child's birth would thus put in jeopardy the surrogacy staying a secret for the duration of the child's life. Still, in very rare cases, some intended mothers are so committed to concealing the truth due to unresolved feelings about their own infertility and/or fear of social disapproval by others that they feign an entire pregnancy, complete with prosthetic bellies matching the expanding sizes of their (hidden) surrogate's real "baby bump" and even faux trips to the doctor's office for medical check-ups.[39]

Second, parents who create an atmosphere of concealment, evasion, or even deception can inadvertently create a situation where those in whom they have confided come to feel burdened by their secret. Writer Dani Shapiro, for instance, reports feeling uncomfortable around her friends' donor-conceived children who were not aware of their own genetic parentage: she marveled at the unfairness of her "kn[owing] something so fundamental about them that they didn't know themselves" and wondered how the parents could possibly "believe this was for the best."[40] At discrete times during my surrogacy-pregnancy and in moments during the early years of their daughter's life, I, too, wondered about my intended parents' handling of certain matters pertaining to disclosure. I even felt awkward at times around their daughter and our mutual friends, since only some of them knew the full circumstances surrounding her birth. Still, I knew it was not my place, but their responsibility and prerogative, to tell. In sum, social scientific studies have shown that concealment about the truth can impair community by interfering with "reciprocal relationship[s] of trust" and by creating "boundaries between those who know and those who do not."[41]

A third reason for disclosure is the child's inability to form a true understanding of their identity, including from whence they come, if they are kept ignorant of their origins. Children who are prevented from knowing who their surro-mom is obviously could not be in a truthful relationship with her. The literature on adopted or donor-conceived children shows that it is not uncommon for them to seek out information about their birth circumstances and sometimes even personal contact with their biological parents and other relatives to obtain a more complete picture of who they are.[42] For writer Dani Shapiro, it was psychologically disorienting to have discovered at the age of fifty-four, after having taken a DNA test on a lark and investigated further, that her father had not been her biological one and that she had been conceived instead by non-identified donor insemination. Most tellingly, it was not her "unorthodox" conception which most floored her, but that her parents had hid "the truth even from themselves"—even as she still intuited from early childhood a sense of her "own otherness" and even blamed herself for it while suspecting all along something significant was being kept from her.[43] Of course, one need not reach middle-age like Shapiro did to be shocked by the truth upon discovering it. Even teenagers in one Australian study designed to study possible reactions to first learning of their donor conception showed nearly "100% agreement in their response to delayed disclosure: They urged parents to respect the importance of this information for children, and speak to them at an earlier age."[44]

As in the case of many donor-conceived children who finally find out the truth about their origins, adopted children also typically report feeling like a missing "piece of the puzzle" has been found after either learning crucial details of their adoption story or making contact with their first family. While gestational surrogates would obviously not be of genetic interest to their surro-children, it is reasonable to assume the latter would still want to avoid feeling shocked or betrayed if they were to find out later in life that they came into the world in a very different way from what they had been led to believe for years was the case.[45]

A fourth reason for disclosure would be to preempt surrogate-born children from discovering the truth in other ways, since parental decisions to withhold rather than to reveal cannot guarantee the children will be kept ignorant about it in perpetuity. The truth could be revealed through inadvertent disclosure by others, children overhearing the parents or others talk about it, or children someday finding paperwork, court documents, or other medical records or legal files to this effect. Accidental disclosure would also likely prove more damaging to both the child and to family intimacy than a planned and intentional disclosure, where the parents could have properly contextualized the information. When surrogacy is bundled with gamete donation, all parties should know that the widespread availability of comparatively low-cost, recreational DNA testing and sites such as the Donor Sibling Registry has led to the exposure of long-held secrets, lies, and cover-ups, with adolescent or adult children learning of their or their family members' births from illicit or extramarital affairs, adoption, conception via sperm or egg donor, or of their ethnic origins being other than what they had been told all their lives was the case.[46]

For these and other reasons, parental disclosure to children about their biological parents is now recommended by many professional societies and is even being claimed as a human right. While "never tell" may once have been the standard advice for both adoption and donor-conception to protect parties from the stigma of illegitimacy, out-of-wedlock births, or infertility, a massive cultural shift has taken place in the direction of "always tell." Virtually all U.S.-based adoption agencies today recommend disclosure. Several U.S. states and foreign countries in recent decades have also been more accommodating of requests by adult adoptees to open sealed adoption records and original birth certificates. The British-based Nuffield Council on Bioethics likewise recommends early disclosure of donor-conception by parents, particularly since the law was changed in the U.K. in 2005 prohibiting non-identified donation and since research has shown it is more difficult for older or adult children to process the information and its implications than it is for younger ones. Among other human rights bodies, the European Court of Human Rights (ECHR) has interpreted Article 8 of the European Convention on Human Rights covering the "right to respect for private and family life" as providing for the right of children to know the identity of their genetic parents. UNICEF has also interpreted the definition of "parents" a child has a right "to know and be cared for" in Article 7.1 of the Convention on the Rights of the Child (CRC) to include "genetic parents," "birth parents," and "psycho-logical parents" (the latter are "those who cared for the child for significant periods during infancy and childhood").[47]

Finally, Christians can ground additional support for disclosure on a bib-lical understanding that all human beings—however they came or come into this world—bear the image of God. As theologian Ted Peters has correctly observed, attempts by the parents to conceal their use of ART connote "a sense of embarrassment or shame," which would be detrimental to the child's self-esteem. But if the parents were to combine the theological conviction that every child is beloved by God, together with "the Herculean effort" they ex-erted to bring their child to life, there should be no reason for them to hide the truth.[48] Even now as IVF-HET allows for a child to have as many as five par-ents (the genetic mother, the genetic father, the gestational mother, and two social parents)—I share Peters's conclusion that such a scenario should still be a cause for celebration.[49] In the precocious words of thirteen-year-old Alice Kirkman, Australia's first surrogate-born child who understands herself as a daughter of "six parents but one Mum and Dad" (n.b., Alice was gestated by her aunt with her mother's egg and counts the wife of the sperm donor whom she knows as the sixth parent):

> Some people are born though IVF; some people are born because a man and a woman get very drunk; or when a man and a woman love each other; or when a man and a woman hire a scientist. There are different ways of being conceived. Mine was just one of them. . . .
>
> I think that we need to face up to the fact that it's not [Australian Prime Minister] John Howard's idealized, conservative world of the '50s . . . . It's the Noughties, and same-sex parents, single parents, IVF children, and conven-tional families should all be allowed to exist in peace. Alice's Wonderland is becoming more common. So don't be Tweedle Dum and Tweedle Dee about it. Let's join the tea party![50]

When and How to Disclose?

There is wisdom in parents disclosing to their children progressively in stages. They might begin by telling a simplified version of their birth at a very early age so there would never be a time when the information would register as news. Early disclosure would also allow the child to absorb the information gradually and eventually take the initiative to ask their parents more questions about it. *How* the parents share might be as important as *whether* they do at all, since parents who disclose but only grudgingly, with anxiety, or by insisting their child keep it a secret may be conveying there is something shameful or embarrassing about them. A team of British psychologists found that children who were aware of their birth circumstances and whose mothers remained "distressed" about their use of ART showed "greater adjustment difficulties," presumably because such children "felt less secure when faced with their mother's emotional problems."[51] This is to say parents do not only owe their children the truth, but also therapeutic resolution about their use of collaborative reproduction: parents owe it to their children not to pass down any lingering insecurities or shame.

Fortunately, disclosure rates about surrogacy are thus far promising. In one British longitudinal study of forty-two families created by surrogacy, 91% had disclosed their child's birth via another woman by the age of ten, with approximately half disclosing before age three and the other half disclosing between three and seven. Surrogate-born children whose parents told them at an early age seem to be able to integrate this information in their evolving sense of self. Most children who knew by age seven could understand the rudiments of surrogacy, as my children at ages six and eight could when we explained it to them, and the majority of surrogate-born children still in contact with their surro-mom at age ten reported liking her and thinking either positively or indifferently about their birth.[52]

Adolescent children, whether or not they are naturally conceived, are often curious about their parents' lifestyle and choices. My (naturally conceived) children, for instance, have asked me about my choice of profession and about falling in love and marrying their father who is of a different race. The parents of surrogate-born children should be prepared for the possibility of their child asking them someday about their use of ART. As social worker and adoption and infertility life coach Robin Allen observes from her clinical experience, a donor-conceived child might eventually press her parents on why they did not adopt instead. Like their adoptive or donor-conceived counterparts, surrogate-born children might wish to ascertain which parts of them are due to their biogenetics ("nature") and what parts are due to their upbringing ("nurture"), what motivated their surro-mom to carry them, and if there are half-siblings from a gamete donor (if used) or other children to whom their surro-mom has given birth they could meet. Parents should not be surprised if their children want to determine for themselves the type of relationship or amount of contact they would like to have with these persons—including possible attempts to find them if they are not currently in contact.[53]

In late adolescence to adulthood or as their understanding of reproduction deepens, surrogate-born children might express a desire to know about other sensitive matters. Their curiosity may involve why the parents did not seek out a donor who was willing to be contacted if the parents pursued non-identified donation or why they selected them at the embryonic stage to be transferred and what ultimately happened with the other, unselected embryos—were they donated to others, used for research, destroyed or left to die, or perhaps are still in cryopreserved storage to this day? They may want to hear more about how their parents chose the person who ultimately bore them, particularly if they are not someone with whom their parents were already in a close relationship. Parents of surrogate-born children would do well to prepare themselves for these questions as their child matures and also consider them at the very start of their surrogacy journey. Since it is reasonable to imagine surrogate-born children one day asking their parents to account for some key decisions culminating in their birth, prospective IPs who would be unwilling to reveal or stand behind them would be advised *not* to pursue ART from the start.

As many psychologists and social workers have acknowledged, whether and how the parents initiate these discussions, explain their children's birth, and respond to follow-up questions will influence how the children themselves will come to feel about their origins. Fortunately, the published track record thus far on the well-being of surrogate-born children is promising. In the U.K., studies have suggested most children born through national (i.e., not cross-border) surrogacy arrangements have "fare[d] well and are well cared for" and have a "full understanding of their conception, their other 'mother' and why they were conceived in this way."[54]

Public-Facing Principles Concerning Surrogacy

The final two principles in my constructive framework for surrogacy—"social justice" and "trust women"—are public-facing in dealing more with the ideal posture outsiders to any surrogacy arrangement ought to take toward the practice than on guiding members of surrogacy triads in their relationships with one another.

PRINCIPLE 6: "TRUST WOMEN"[55]

This principle takes seriously the importance of empowering and believing in women and others capable of pregnancy to make informed decisions about their own fertility. Against outsiders who paternalistically seek to protect them from surrogacy through prohibition or other strong disincentives, "trust women" recognizes both the human right and good of allowing each person to conscientiously determine how best to exercise their reproductive capacities through the development of their moral agency. Against those surrogacy opponents who presume women couldn't possibly know what they would be getting themselves into and thus would invariably come to regret bearing and relinquishing a child for someone else, "trust women" finds significant that persons who have successfully born children before—a near-universal surrogacy prerequisite—already know what pregnancy and childbirth is generally like for them and thus have the capacity to imagine what it would be like to undertake one for someone else. As I have previously shared, after my two childbirth experiences, it was not difficult for me to engage in a thought experiment of what being pregnant for another would be like after one friend, a recent breast cancer survivor (Melissa), shared with me her hopes of someday having a child via surrogacy and, some months later, a different friend (Katie) asked if I would serve as her and her husband's surrogate. In fact, the social scientific research reveals that in altruistic arrangements between IPs and surrogates who already know and care for one another, it is the (future) surrogate herself who commonly *initiates* the prospect of surrogacy and therein volunteers her body in service to that end—it is not that she needed to have been asked or persuaded to do it.[56]

According to philosophers L. A. Paul and Fiona Woollard, pregnancy among other life events such as fighting in a war is an "epistemically transformative experience"—it provides the holders of these experiences with a kind of knowledge that would have been impossible to acquire without it.[57] As Woollard describes, the experiences of pregnancy include "(1) multiple unexpected bodily sensations and physical changes to one's body; (2) having what will become another person growing inside one's body; (3) changes to one's relation to oneself and one's body resulting from (1) and (2)."[58] Knowledge of what pregnancy is like is extremely difficult to grasp if one has not had the experience oneself, and this knowledge differential across persons should be recognized as relevant to ethical assessments of pregnancy-related matters. For instance, someone who has been pregnant before and thus has experiential awareness of how different aspects or stages of pregnancy were inconvenient, difficult, or pleasant for them will normally be in a better position than someone who has never been pregnant before to understand "what it is to ask someone to remain pregnant against their will" in the abortion debate.[59] This does not mean those who have never experienced pregnancy firsthand will lack standing to engage in moral reasoning about sustaining or ending a pregnancy. It does, however, mean that the community of inquirers will need to work out how to engage in such discussions when all relevant pieces of information are not "fully accessible to all." Woollard suggests those who lack the relevant epistemically transformative experience should augment their partial understanding of pregnancy by engaging the narrative literature to try to grasp secondhand what pregnancy may be like.

My "trust women" principle in surrogacy combines Paul's and Woollard's concept of "transformative experiences" with the long-standing account of experience as the fourth, traditional source of moral wisdom for Christians. It is of normative significance to my framework that prospective surrogacy candidates who have already bore children before know whether pregnancy itself can be enjoyable for them, which may be contrary to conventional wisdom that pregnancy is either something that must be endured, or only enjoyed for its hoped-for outcome: the birth of one's child. Prospective surrogates in discernment with trusted others would also normally be better positioned than outsiders to judge whether the projected inconveniences, pains, and risks associated with a higher-risk pregnancy, childbirth, or postpartum recovery might be too much for them to handle (principle 1). Finally, persons with previous experiences of pregnancy and childbirth would generally know better than anyone else whether popular beliefs about the invariability of the maternal instinct or maternal-fetal attachment hold true in their own case, with surrogacy then posing a psychological risk for them, as it did not for me. As the first intended mother in Australia, Maggie Kirkman recounts that her sister Linda who bore her child knew she would not be able to "bear to give away a baby who looked back at me with my brown eyes," though would gladly serve as her gestational surrogate. In contrast her other sister, Cynthia, "knew that she could not give birth to a baby for someone else" though generously offered to donate eggs to her if needed. As Maggie summarized the matter: "For Cynthia, the origins of motherhood lie more in gestating a baby than in genetic connection; for Linda, the pattern is reversed. This encapsulates the individual differences that co-exist within the cultural meanings of motherhood."[60] Just as countless women told me upon learning of my surrogacy "wow, I could never do *that*" and only a handful disclosed how they had seriously entertained bearing a child for a loved one, most mature adults can discern what they are and aren't capable of doing on this front. To recall some of the central findings from the surrogacy literature presented earlier in chapter 2, the vast majority of surrogates in the U.S., U.K., Canada, and Australia voluntarily bear children for others precisely because they *like* being pregnant (or at least don't mind it) and helping others. They also typically "give the baby back" post-childbirth with a joyful sense of accomplishment—not trauma—and feel good about their surrogacy journey(s) even many years after the fact. As Olga B. A. van den Akker concludes from both her own studies in the UK context and from her review of the findings of others:

> Most surrogates report their experience as providing them with an enormous amount of satisfaction at having been instrumental in fulfilling a dream of a most desired baby for their commissioning couple. Some were so happy with their role as surrogate mother that they were willing to do it a second or third time for the same or other couples; others were happy that they met commissioning couples [if they didn't know them already] and became their friends.[61]

Importantly, even as the research on surrogacy families suggests noncommercial surrogacy arrangements typically end well, "trust women" as a principle is not premised on the assumption that all women and others capable of pregnancy will make procreative decisions they will ultimately judge to have been in their or others' best interests. It does, however, recognize that the risk of regretting one's reproductive behaviors or outcomes is not unique to surrogate motherhood—and thus should not be treated as if it were. I personally know some women who regret having had unprotected sex with a particular partner at a particular time in their life and having gotten pregnant. Or who regret having waited "too long" to start trying to have kids and then experienced infertility which was likely exacerbated by their old(er) age. Or some who regret either having delayed beginning infertility treatments or who regret staying on the "infertility treadmill" for as long as they did with their spouse or partner before making what they now regard was the better decision to have adopted their child. Or some who regret their birth experiences or the way their child came into the world (e.g., an unmedicated natural birth with lots of pain, a C-section despite their ardent desire for a vaginal delivery). Or some who live with "abortion regret," though, for the record, I know significantly more women friends who have had abortions and still believe many years after the fact that they acted wisely.[62] When we "trust women" to make informed decisions about their own fertility, we do so with foreknowledge that not all of them will make choices they themselves will ultimately affirm as the best.

In addition to that caveat, "trust women" as a principle is also neither premised upon notions of unlimited individual procreative liberty, nor that individuals have unfettered rights to do with their bodies or spend their money as they please. As feminist Catholic Maura Ryan has persuasively argued, birthing a child into the world is both an "inherently *relational*" act in establishing new relationships between parent(s) and child and an "inherently *social*" one in introducing a new member into society whose "potential needs and capacities have social implications."[63] Moreover, to the extent private or public insurance is paying for some or all of the IVF or prenatal care involved in a surrogacy arrangement, all beneficiaries and payers of those insurance plans are sharing in the costs. "Trust women" as a principle is thus not about immunizing one's choices from critical scrutiny out of a mistaken belief that surrogacy is a purely "private" affair among just the participants of the collaborative reproduction as it is about combatting paternalistic attitudes about women's abilities to assess what it is their best interests to do in matters pertaining to pregnancy. Given the conditions under which our initial assessment of surrogacy is based, my framework takes seriously that surrogates are persons who have entered into a pre-conception agreement or contract with others without the possibility of financial inducements encouraging them to do something they would not ordinarily have done without compensation. Of course, some close friends or relatives might feel social pressure to help an involuntarily childless couple become parents (for the record, I did not in the slightest), just as some close friends or relatives of patients with renal failure have reported a strong sense of family obligation to donate their kidney to them. But we recognize the prospect of interpersonal pressure does not mean informed and uncoerced consent is impossible. When we "trust women" to make reproductive decisions most suitable for them, we neither create social expectations for anyone capable of pregnancy to bear a child for someone else. Nor do we block the generosity of those willing to demonstrate radical hospitality to couples with a medical need for surrogacy by helping them realize their parenting hopes and dreams.

PRINCIPLE 7: SOCIAL JUSTICE

As with feminist Catholic ethicist Margaret Farley's reflections on social justice in her framework for Christian sexual ethics,[64] my social justice principle covers "big picture" considerations. Given the public's stakes in the broader issues surrounding this method of ART—how families are defined and permitted to be expanded, how children will be raised and by whom, and what individuals can and cannot be legally allowed to do with their bodies with respect to pregnancy—the norm of social justice should both matter to us all.

Structural Inequities in Surrogacy and Other Potential Problems

Reproductive justice (RJ) requires us to transcend the narrow focus on individual choice when attending to the social conditions shaping reproduction. The progressive Christian and RJ commitments undergirding my approach to surrogacy therein prompts us to identify practices or policies that have the potential to adversely affect vulnerable communities. While this question is especially important in commercial and/or cross-border surrogacies, even altruistic arrangements might raise social justice concerns if persons who bear children for others were routinely receiving better or worse prenatal care than when pregnant for themselves.[65] Or if we had reason to suspect surrogate-born children were at a greater risk of physical or psychological harm than their non-surrogate-born counterparts, even though research on surrogate-born children thus far has raised no red flags. Or if women of color were disproportionately serving as surrogates since pregnancies among this demographic are already higher risk. Or if the intended parents were primarily white due to ART being disproportionately out of reach for particular communities of color.

The answers to these questions, of course, might well be contextual. Surrogacy in one context might advance social justice by increasing opportunities for a historically oppressed group—for example, members of the LGBTQIA+ community—to become parents and therein realize an important life goal.[66] But local surrogacy practices in another context might be exacerbating group tensions, compromising women's health, or producing other social harms.

Healthcare Costs and Resource Allocation

Since intended parents and their surrogates tend to be drawn from the same demographic group in the non-commercial gift arrangements under consideration here, the demographic breakdown warranting greater scrutiny may not be between the commissioning parents and their surrogates, but between differentially positioned parent hopefuls: those who can afford the typically high costs of fertility services and those who cannot. The average surrogacy journey in the U.S. is estimated at $150,000 at the time of this writing.[67] As the National Council of Churches has acknowledged when commenting generally about the "fruits of the new and emerging biotechnologies" but not specifically about ART, the Christian community's stewardship of creation should lead us to interrogate global inequities in access to goods. Progressive Christians should examine scenarios where the ability to benefit from biotechnology depends upon the contingencies of social status or societal income.[68]

Infertility is not something afflicting only white, middle- to upper-class women, despite common misperceptions or caricatures to this effect. The World Health Organization (WHO) regards infertility as a "global health issue" affecting 15% of reproductive-aged couples worldwide and reports that the "availability, access, and quality of interventions to address infertility remain a challenge in most countries," with ART "still largely unaffordable in many parts of the world."[69] Even in the U.K., only approximately 40% of all IVF treatment cycles are funded by the NHS (the remaining 60% are privately funded), and some persons, including women in same-sex couplings, are "less likely to receive NHS funding for their treatment."[70] In the U.S., a founding foremother of the reproductive justice framework, Dr. Toni M. Bond, has acknowledged that some elite Black women including former First Lady Michele Obama and actress Gabrielle Union-Wade have been able to afford infertility treatments, but the vast majority of Black women in the U.S. cannot. This lack of accessibility is doubly problematic from a social justice perspective because Black women are also more likely to experience difficulty becoming pregnant and sustaining a pregnancy than non-Hispanic white women, including by having a higher incidence of uterine fibroids and at a younger age.[71] The popular downplaying of fertility problems among Black and other women of color not only misrepresents their experiences and needs, but also might play into classicist, and potentially even eugenicist, beliefs about them being "hyperfertile" or "closer to fertile nature than white women" and thus needing to be discouraged from (not assisted in) having children.[72]

This divide between those who have and those who lack genuine access to reproductive medicine should lead anyone committed to social justice to question the extent to which any given society should subsidize (in full or in part) ART and if so, for whom. Should only the medically infertile be eligible for public assistance if available or should it be anyone hoping to bear a biogenetically related child? The answer will partially depend on what social good society believes ART facilitates or provides, with possibilities including a cure or treatment for a medical problem, an expression of one's reproductive autonomy or potential, or a way to realize one's human right to found a family. To be sure, infertility due to a diagnosable medical condition or impairment is regarded as a disability under the Americans with Disabilities Act (ADA) and could fall under UN Convention on the Rights of Persons with Disabilities given the Convention's understanding that "disability is an evolving concept."[73] Some jurisdictions including in the U.S and the U.K. and some private health insurance companies have accordingly been subsidizing ART.

My progressive Christian framework of surrogacy applauds these and other efforts to provide assisted reproductive services for the infertile. Still, infertility as a minimum threshold for eligibility for assistance may prove wanting from the progressive Christian vision of social justice being advanced here because a diagnosis of medical infertility requires a demonstration of an inability to conceive over a specific period of time (normally twelve months or more) and thus is biased in favor of male-female couples and against same-sex ones.[74] Just as Israel's highest court finally struck down in 2020 a law blocking single men and gay couples from turning to surrogacy to have children, national health insurance plans or private employee benefits need not continue to privilege heterosexuals. For instance, Starbucks Coffee since 2019 has been providing coverage for fertility services including IVF (up to $25,000) and related medications (up to $10,000) for their eligible employees, including part-timers, in addition to offering "family expansion reimbursements" of up to $10,000 per adoption, surrogacy, or intrauterine insemination for eligible same-sex partners.[75]

While it lies beyond the scope of this book to provide a full account of just resource distribution, social justice would require each society to provide a fair, equitable, and transparent rationale for which family expansion plans and medical services, including for reproduction, it will subsidize and which it will not in light of their comprehensive healthcare priorities, limitations, and other values. A society struggling to provide basic public health measures such as antibiotics or vaccinations for preventable diseases will not normally be in a position to provide high-technology services to extend the life of older patients (e.g., organ transplantation or dialysis for renal failure, sustained artificial hydration and nutrition), even though all individuals have a "right to life."[76] These same societies might justifiably elect to prioritize basic healthcare needs over advancements in reproductive medicine or at least ration the amount of ART assistance any eligible person could receive even though the right to "marry" and "found a family" is also recognized in international human rights law (Art. 23, ICESR; Art. 16, UDHR). This is to say many societies might only be in a position to recognize the right to found a family in negative terms, meaning they will not block individuals from attempting to bear children or become parents, but will not positively assist them in their efforts due to a lack of resources.

What I do not find convincing is an argument sometimes made or implied in progressive circles: the cost-prohibitive nature of IVF and gestational surrogacy for most people should count as a sufficient reason against *anyone* resorting to it. That ART is out of reach for more than three-quarters of the world because of insufficient fertility clinics, structural support, or personal finances is empirically true but not a necessary feature of the world, since some jurisdictions or health insurance plans could treat ART as a public good depending on their priorities and available resources. As noted previously, Israel has heavily subsidized both IVF treatments and surrogacy due to their pronatalism, just as my denomination, the Presbyterian Church (U.S.A.) covers several rounds of ART for their employees and does not exclude surrogacy in its maternity coverage due to the particularity of their commitments. My point is that those with the economic means to pursue ART need not refrain from doing so just to stand in solidarity with their less privileged neighbors, just as straight couples who live in jurisdictions prohibiting same-sex marriage need not remain unmarried (if they wish to wed) to avoid capitalizing on their heterosexual privilege just to remain in solidarity with their LGBTQIA+ siblings. Rather, in either case, such persons could advocate for greater access to these goods (marriage or ART) for those who currently lack access to them. Of course, nothing prohibits conscientious persons from electing to forego ART as a luxury and therein realizing any vocational call they might have to parenthood in other ways, but such a decision to go without should be regarded more as a matter of conscience than as a requirement to meet the moral minimum.

Surrogacy and the Law
Finally, a discussion of social justice and surrogacy will invariably lead us to legal matters. Beyond insisting on the necessity of each surrogate retaining medical decision-making power over her own body, it is beyond the scope of this book to resolve all relevant legal or policy-related questions. *How should*

*each jurisdiction define who the legal parents of a surrogate-born child are fol-
lowing birth and whose names must or should be included on the birth certificate? What process must the IPs undertake to be declared the legal parents
if pre-birth orders are not permitted and should that process mirror adoption
proceedings? What minimum eligibility criteria should be set for prospective
IPs or surrogates? How should courts enforce compliance of surrogacy contracts
or resolve custody disputes?* While I expand upon some of these matters in
the next chapter, my overall account supports legalization, decriminalization,
and reasonable pluralism in regulation, since surrogacy is not intrinsically
immoral or harmful, national bans have not effectively deterred persons from
flouting surrogacy laws at home or abroad to fulfill their ART needs, and a
strong regulatory framework has a better chance of protecting vulnerable
parties—the ostensible goal of many surrogacy bans today.

My progressive Christian vision for surrogacy assumes the principle of
social justice can be satisfied even with reasonable variation in local surrogacy
laws and policies. Some societies might not positively assist an individual's
plans to become parents via surrogacy for reasons of urgent priorities and
limited resources, even if these same societies offer tax credit or other incentives for all such persons to adopt because adoption might also assist in the
state's child welfare goals. Some societies might follow the British model in
declaring any person who gives birth the legal mother while others might
follow the Californian model in permitting the recognition of legal parentage
of the intended parents, regardless of genetic connection or lack thereof, on
the day of the child's birth. Some societies might require prospective IPs to
be permanent residents or citizens either because they want to prioritize their
own people benefitting from the reproductive technology infrastructure they
have built or because they have not been able to prevent systemic abuses or exploitation when they previously allowed reproductive tourism or exiles inside
their borders. These examples do not exhaust all possibilities.

What the principle of social justice insists upon is treating surrogacy in
any one jurisdiction in an equitable manner by treating like cases alike. A
progressive Christian standpoint would therein frown upon policies that discriminated against same-sex couples as the U.K. once did but later corrected
when expanding its 1990 law in 2008 to allow for more than only married
heterosexual IPs the right to become legal parents of surrogate-born children.
Of course, the law might allow for different configurations of IP-surrogate
pairings than what I have assumed above in my seven simplifying parameters;

for instance, the law might allow, as it does in California, a single individual or a set of persons not romantically involved to serve as the IPs. But this difference is to be expected and is not in itself a cause for concern, since questions regarding what should be legally permitted are not synonymous with what is ideal from a progressive Christian standpoint.

————

These seven principles—discernment without haste; covenant before contract; empathy, care, and stewardship; medical self-determination; disclosure not secrecy; "trust women," and social justice comprise my progressive Christian framework for surrogacy when the arrangements take place under certain constraints. How we might assess the ethics of surrogacy when those constraints no longer all hold is the subject of my next and final chapter.

6 ASSESSING THE ETHICS OF MORE COMPLEX SURROGACY ARRANGEMENTS

WHEN I WAS CARRYING A baby for my involuntarily childless friends, many well-wishers commended me for my selfless act—for manifesting "love and life" as our Methodist clergy friend put it during his prayer before the meal at Katie and Steven's grand baby shower. Some fellow ethicists conveyed similar sentiments when commenting that my surrogacy was for them a quintessential act of supererogation. While I have appreciated those affirmations, they have also made me uncomfortable. Yes, my actions went beyond the call of duty, but pregnancy has never been onerous for me, parting with the baby at journey's end was an emotionally satisfying (not distressing) affair, and I suffered no career set-backs through it all. Community praise of me as an "angel" or even "St. Grace" and the abundance of beautiful flowers and other gifts I received post-childbirth thus sometimes felt too much.

Physically speaking, to be clear, I'm not someone who just *loves* being pregnant. I knew if I were to help my friends I would be inconvenienced by things like first trimester fatigue, swollen feet, and nights of interrupted sleep in the third trimester. But I also anticipated reveling in other bodily changes, my favorite being that second trimester energy surge. Pregnancy is just something my body inexplicably does well. I'd never had any difficulty conceiving when my husband and I felt we were ready for kids, nor suffered a reproductive loss.

I'd never once felt nauseated from being "with child," much less vomited from it. I did experience a novel kind of all-encompassing pain from labor contractions, but still not any preterm or other harrowing labor or delivery complications in either of my two pregnancies. Even on the vanity front, I'd never developed stretch marks nor gained weight I couldn't eventually shed post-childbirth.[1] Both my husband and I thus believed a third pregnancy for Katie and Steven would be relatively easy apart from the unknown of how I would handle the IVF, the sacrifice of mandated abstinence from the start of IVF injectables to a confirmation of pregnancy (approximately six weeks in each of our two embryo transfer attempts), and the time I would need to spend at doctor's appointments—including commuting in L.A. traffic to get there and back.

It turns out we were right. This higher risk pregnancy even at my then-age of forty was largely no big deal for me on a day-to-day basis, though there were difficult parts of our journey.[2] It was also gratifying for me to give the baby back—and I also knew from the start I would not experience any remorse about it. When friends and other conversation partners have pressed me to account for how I could have been so confident of my future emotional state, I have told them I was sure any third pregnancy would resemble my first two in one other crucial area.

For reasons unbeknownst to me, I never bonded with either of my own children while carrying them in utero. Don't get me wrong: I was brimming with excitement when expecting both of them and was astounded when I first laid eyes on my newborn after hours of pushing, heard him cry, and cradled him skin-to-skin on my chest to nurse for the first time. Still, I felt something more akin to shock and wonder than instant love for this tiny being when he first emerged outside of my body: he was shockingly bluish-purple, quickly turned into a more expected pink color, and then proceeded to pee all over the nurse. It was then only through caring for him around the clock and becoming acquainted with his wants and needs over several weeks when I developed what I would categorize as maternal feelings. Even so, as the due date for my second baby approached two years later, I was genuinely unsure whether I would have the capacity to love another little one as fiercely as I had come to love my first—would my heart be large enough to accommodate them both? The answer was ultimately yes, but I only knew that to be true in the days and weeks after my second son made his debut.

Given my past two pregnancy experiences, our lack of desire to have a third child, and our joint wish to help our friends become first-time parents, we were certain I would not have to do any psychological work to stay de-tached if I were to become pregnant for the third time because there would never be any danger of my attaching to their baby to begin with. When one of the embryos successfully "stuck" after our second transfer attempt, I felt both elation and tremendous responsibility for this nascent life growing inside of me. As the weeks progressed, I became even more vigilant about my diet, exercise, and rest than I had been when carrying my own kids due to my consciousness about my "geriatric" pregnancy and my hopes for the prenatal period to go well for all of our sakes. I also celebrated reaching various preg-nancy milestones and enjoyed having my IPs and my own young kids feel with their own hands and see with their own eyes the baby kick and flutter about post-quickening. But none of these feelings of heightened responsibility and anticipation ever transformed into those of maternal love.

All told, I had calculated it would not be too costly—physically, emotion-ally, or professionally—for me to give this gift to my friends. But as our sur-rogacy was an altruistic, independent, and gestational arrangement in the State of California—a gift between friends who were even members of the same Christian small group—it was not immediately clear how our journey might be relevant to the surrogacies of others arranged in notably different ways. What of reproductive collaborations remunerated above and beyond expenses where the members would be, in typical cases, previously strangers to one another? Or of cross-border partnerships often involving more legal maneuvering and usually greater wealth disparities between the parent hope-fuls and any person they would hire to help them? Or what if the surro-mom would not just be nurturing a genetically unrelated fetus in her womb, but also ultimately parting with her own flesh and blood because she had also granted the intended parents the use of her eggs? How might my progressive vision and framework for surrogacy handle these more complex scenarios?

———

I consider below these three different types of surrogacy arrangements given the additional legal, practical, and ethical questions they pose while holding constant the other four simplifying conditions enumerated previously. That is, while surrogacies under investigation might now be (1) paid, (2) transnational, and/or (3) traditional (instead of uncompensated, intrastate, and gestational), they would still be undertaken for intended parents (4) who are married or in a committed relationship and (5) who must rely upon another person to gestate their child given their own medical limitations (i.e., they lack a suitable uterus between them) and the current state of ART. All parties would also (6) have access to high-quality healthcare and the ability to provide informed consent and (7) be partnering together under non-dystopian realities where anti-natalism does not hold.

When Surrogacy Arrangements Are Paid

The lion's share of objections to surrogacy have to do with paying persons to have children for others and therein exploiting their need for money while also commodifying pregnancy and children in the process.

THE CHARGE: SURROGACY EXPLOITS

Arguably the most common protest against commercial surrogacy is that the industry has created the very conditions for more affluent couples to induce— and therein exploit—poorer and less-educated persons to undertake significant medical and psychological risks on their behalf. The landmark cases in the 1980s which ended tragically—of Baby M in the U.S. and Baby Cotton in the U.K.—did much to cement in the public imaginary the belief that no woman would willingly become pregnant with a stranger by artificial insemination and then "give up" her own child unless she were pathological or desperate for money. It also crystalized the now commonplace assumption that the intended parents would be more privileged than any person they would hire, save for the latter's superior reproductive abilities. While gestational surrogacy has done much to allay the public's fear about incentivizing poor people to give up "their own" biological kin, gestational surrogates must still undergo a more cumbersome IVF-HET process and a higher-risk pregnancy to collect their fee. In having provided an estimate that a U.S.-based surrogate is typically paid $20,000 to $25,000, which "averages to approximately $3.00 per hour" that she is pregnant based on a "pregnancy of 266 days or 6384 hours [38 weeks]," the Southern Baptist Convention has disdainfully concluded "few women who have the financial means [would be] willing to undergo the pain, trauma, and grief of surrogacy for such low wages."[3]

Some opponents of commercial surrogacy bundle their consternation about class with race, particularly when they assume—as the public commonly does—the IPs would be primarily white (or from developed Western countries) and the persons they would hire would be disproportionately of color (or from the Global South). After noting the ways in which the concept of surrogacy—of a person or group taking on the responsibilities that belong to someone else—has been a "negative force in African American women's lives" through all of U.S. history from slavery up to the present time, pioneering womanist theologian Delores Williams expressed fears that (reproductive) surrogacy would inflame already tense race relations. In her words:

> Will the law legitimate surrogacy to the point that black women's ovaries are targeted for use by groups more powerful than poor black women? Will surrogacy become such a common practice in wealthy women's experience that laws are established to regulate it—laws that work to the advantage of the wealthy and the disadvantage of the poor?. . . . Will poverty pressure poor black women to rent their bodies out as incubators for wealthier women unable to birth children?. . . . Are American women stepping into an age of reproduction control so rigid that women will be set against each other like Hagar and Sarah? Will the operation of certain reproduction technologies, acting in white women's favor, put even more strain upon the already strained relation between black and white women?[4]

Williams is certainly not alone in suspecting that commercial surrogacy would be especially problematic for people of color. In a 2019 Open Letter to New York Governor Andrew Cuomo, feminist icon Gloria Steinem also warned of "socio-economic and racial inequalities" in her ultimately unsuccessful attempt to block New York from legalizing commercial surrogacy after decades of its criminalization.[5]

Finally, commentators who find surrogacy exploitative sometimes also direct their concern for the involuntarily childless. Such critics view the fertility industry as doubly predatory—as exploiting gamete donors' and surrogates' economic precarity while capitalizing on the intended parents' unmet yearning for a child—especially a biogenetically related one—by selling the latter the possible realization of that dream for a steep price.

THE CHARGE: SURROGACY COMMODIFIES

One way to address this concern would be for surrogates to receive more compensation for their efforts or for IPs to have to pay less for reproductive care—perhaps by private or publicly funded healthcare absorbing more of the total costs. To wit: when labor activists decry abuses in the workplace and campaign for better working conditions, chief among their demands are higher wages. Similarly, when housing or college costs soar exponentially in ways that price out low-income or even middle-class families, activists usually call for more pathways for access (e.g., housing subsidies or loans, more educational scholarships or financial aid, debt or loan forgiveness).

With surrogacy, however, many opponents are not primarily incensed about individuals being underpaid for their reproductive labor or parent hopefuls being overcharged for ART. Rather, they find problematic the matter of payment being introduced at all into the equation. Thus, their deeper issue is with commodification—the treatment of pregnancy, parental rights, or children as fungible goods that can be bought and sold.

Commodifying Bodies and Reproduction

The charge of commodification in surrogacy can take several forms. In one, public outrage centers on putting human bodies, specifically their reproductive capacities, on the market and therein transforming persons who agree to become pregnant for others for pay into "baby-machines" or "reproductive prostitutes."[6] Just as many commentators believe sex for payment degrades sex and debases the persons trading it for money or otherwise facilitating payment ("pimps"), so comparing commercial surrogacy to sex work is intended to imply the sullying of pregnancy and the persons leasing out their wombs. According to bioethicist and former Society of Christian Ethics president Allen Verhey, ART practices such as surrogacy not only "reduc[e] women to their reproductive utility," but they also "demea[n] the 'good' exchanged . . . corrupt[t] the community of parent and child . . . and . . . distor[t] the way we think and talk about children and about ourselves" by encouraging women to engage in "acts of begetting . . . void of an intention to care for one's child."[7]

This combined commodification and exploitation charge is also the view held by the European Parliament. Since passing a nonbinding resolution in 2015, the European Union's only directly elected institution has supported the prohibition of commercial surrogacy on the grounds that it "undermines the human dignity of the woman" to treat "her body and its reproductive functions . . . as a commodity."[8] When commenting upon the war's impact on women following Russia's invasion of Ukraine on February 24, 2022, the European Parliament acknowledged the special difficulties facing Ukrainian surrogate mothers and the surrogate-born children unable to be cared for by their foreign (intended) parents before once again condemning surrogacy as an institution for "expos[ing] women around the world to exploitation, in particular those who are poorer and are in situations of vulnerability."[9]

Commodifying Children

A different part of the commodification critique centers on the sale of children—a practice every civilized society should have long abandoned. Treating surrogate-born children as the products of a contractual exchange would not only violate their inherent dignity and rights, but also potentially cause other children to fear they, too, could someday become traded away if the social practice of commercial surrogacy were to establish precedence for parents to "sell" their child (or their parental rights to them) if and when it is in their interests to do so. Since slavery has been universally condemned in both ethics and the law, what is being contested is not the moral permissibility of human trafficking per se, but whether commercial surrogacy constitutes a proper instance of it.

Some surrogacy opponents have responded yes. In the State of Louisiana for instance, anyone caught forming a gestational surrogacy contract outside of its strict parameters, including paying surrogates for anything beyond reimbursements for a specified list of pregnancy-related expenses, will be charged with the "sale of minor children" to be punishable by a fine not exceeding $50,000 or imprisonment for not more than ten years or both.[10] When presenting a thematic report to the U.N. General Assembly in October 2019 on safeguards for the protection of the rights of children born from surrogacy arrangements, the Special Rapporteur on the sale and sexual exploitation of children similarly concluded "commercial surrogacy as currently practised usually constitutes sale of children as defined under international human rights law," including the Optional Protocol to the Convention on the Rights of the Child on the Sale of Children, Child Prostitution, and Child Pornography.[11]

DEFENDING THE GOOD OF COMPENSATED SURROGACIES WHEN STRUCTURED ETHICALLY

In responding to charges that commercial surrogacy is exploitative, commodifying, and especially dangerous for poor women of color, I begin with two concessions. The first is that compensated surrogacies between persons who were previously strangers to one another does create conditions not normally present in altruistic or unremunerated surrogacies between family members or friends. The offering of financial inducements by a comparatively wealthier couple might entice the person they were hoping to commission to enter into an arrangement with known risks they might otherwise not have undertaken, with the lure of economic gain leading them to dismiss or minimize the real medical, social, and/or emotional costs of a pregnancy for others they and their loved ones might incur to earn it. Thus, the greater need any person or their family has for money, particularly if they have few to no other opportunities to make a comparable sum, the more likely they will agree to do something as unconventional and socially stigmatizing in some quarters as what radical feminists have derisively called a "contract pregnancy" to improve their economic situation. While none of this should be denied, there is fortunately little evidence in the U.S. that indigent persons are being recruited to become pregnant for others. This is because fertility clinics regularly screen out individuals on welfare or public assistance, a known correlation exists between poverty and poor health (rendering underprivileged persons undesirable candidates for surrogate motherhood), and because IPs do not want to feel like they must support the surrogate financially.[12] Of course, screening norms will vary from clinic to clinic and across contexts, so what is generally true in the U.S. does not invariably hold elsewhere.

The second concession we must make is that we cannot conclusively verify or put to rest the public's fears that surrogacy perpetuates racial inequities or exacerbates racial tensions. This is because there are no federal or international reporting requirements about the racial or socioeconomic status of the adults involved, fertility clinics only selectively self-report the demographics of their clients, and many "indy" arrangements are formed outside of any third-party mediation. I will consider cross-border surrogacies in the second section of this chapter as I examine popular stereotypes of white wealthy "reproductive tourists" from the Global North traveling to the largely non-white Global South to "outsource" pregnancy. However, in many empirical studies on *intrastate* surrogacy arrangements in several Western contexts including the U.S., U.K., Australia, and Canada, white people are overrepresented on *both* sides of the collaborative reproduction equation—as parent hopefuls and as surro-moms, while Black people are largely absent in either role.[13] Racially binary assumptions about mostly white intended parents hiring mostly Black women to bear their children might not only be distorting our perception of the persons normally involved in assisted reproduction, but also potentially failing to capture other important racial dynamics. For instance as I have written about elsewhere, Asian Americans have the highest rates of ART utilization in comparison to other racial-ethnic groups according to some studies, and growing numbers of foreign Chinese IPs prefer to hire white American surrogates—a pattern reversing the popular image of the race of the prospective parents and the race of the women they commission.[14]

Having acknowledged these points, I now pass to explaining why surrogate compensation might be morally permissible and even good when judged from the standards of my progressive Christian vision and framework for surrogacy. I then suggest ways to structure (intrastate) compensated arrangements so they can meet the moral baseline.

The Good of Offering Surrogate Compensation
The Co-existence of Altruism with Self-Love

One key reason why surrogate compensation is not in principle morally objectionable is my feminist Christian understanding that one can simultaneously seek to assist others and serve oneself in the process.[15] Not only do the women across the world who undertake pregnancies for others often report a mixture of self- and other-regarding motives (a point I shall elaborate upon below), but there is no reason to believe the presence of self-interest in accepting compensation invariably taints the beauty of their offering an intimate form of hospitality to others. We accept, for instance, the comingling of other-regard and self-regard in other lines of work: for instance, most people believe that good public school teachers should be paid a decent wage and that they might have selected teaching as their profession because they enjoy working with children, educating others about their subject, and/or empowering next generations. Most people in our society can also accept that persons in occupations including firefighting or lifeguarding exhibit genuine concern for others and even heroism at times without believing that if they were to be paid for their efforts (which they generally are), they would no longer be motivated to come to the aid of others for reasons other than for money. Why then does a popular characterization persist that persons who would bear children for others *with* pay would only or primarily be doing so *for* profit?

When we examine the literature on surrogate motivations as I have repeatedly encouraged us to do, we find that surro-moms consistently provide a combination of self- and other-regarding reasons for their actions. In the U.S., for instance, surrogates typically report being moved by the pain and sadness of others' involuntary childlessness, find their own identities as mothers important to them, either enjoy pregnancy or at least do not find it difficult or cumbersome, believe they could put the money they would earn to good use, and thus want to help others become parents, too.[16] While accepting financial compensation for their efforts, they also firmly believe that children are literally priceless. As Zsuzsa Berend has captured the phenomenon in both the U.S. and the U.K., the latter where surrogacy cannot be commercialized though surrogates can still receive some compensation above and beyond reimbursement:

> Surrogacy most often is a hybrid of contractual and gift relationship, and gift relationships are not terminated in the same way that contractual relations are: at the last payment. Surrogates generally believe that surrogacy creates a bond that is not dissolved by payment and that intended parents' appreciation and friendship is the best reward for what they have done for the couple. The best way to show appreciation and friendship is to stay in touch. Accordingly, surrogates generally want to know how the family is doing, and that they enjoy the fruit of the surrogate's labour. . . . *Even though surrogates are paid for carrying babies for others, they call it "giving the gift of life."* This is not simply a gloss over starker realities; most US and UK surrogates appreciate the money, and *most would not do it without the money, but no one thinks that children or pregnancies are commodities to be bought and sold.* (emphasis added)[17]

That said, some ethnographic studies have shown how surrogates themselves in the U.S. sometimes express discomfort about receiving payment. Heather Jacobson found in her study of Texas- and California-based surrogates that many of her subjects deliberately sought to obscure the profit motive by either suggesting they would have done it without pay but it was their partner or husband who insisted upon compensation, or by minimizing the amount they received by using the language of work—they were paid "what a part-time job would be for a year" without any vacation, sick days, or days off, or that they ended up earning "less than minimum wage."[18] Cultural anthropologist Helene Ragoné who produced the first ethnographic study of surrogate motherhood in the early 1990s of U.S. surrogates who received approximately $10,000–$15,00 similarly found remuneration to be the "most problematic" part for them: they recognized financial compensation detracted from "the idealized cultural image of women/mothers as selfless, nurturant, and altruistic" that they themselves affirmed and thus did not want to "lose the sense that theirs is a gift that transcends all monetary compensation"—even as they accepted money for their services.[19] Ragoné found significant that the women in her study rarely spent the money they earned on themselves: most spent it on their children such as by contributing to their family funds while others "spen[t] it on home improvement, gifts for their husbands, a family vacation, or simply to pay off 'family debts.'"[20] Jacobson's surrogates similarly often thought of money as a way to compensate their family members who endured their share of sacrifices in the process: to pay family bills, buy a car, or splurge on something like a trip to Disney or to start a college fund.[21]

In having acknowledged this tendency among U.S.-based surrogates to downplay the financial part of their motivational scheme, it is also important to recognize that there may be culturally specific, white middle-class American values at play that do not invariably hold constant across all contexts.[22] A study conducted among Thai surrogates in 2010 found that most participants freely "responded in economic terms when asked" about their willingness to offer their services as a surrogate, with most also emphasizing their compassion for infertile couples and their "love of being pregnant." Some even referenced the idea of *tan-bun* (merit-making)—the Buddhist idea of doing meritorious deeds to "counterbalance demerits accumulated through sinful and bad deeds and ensure the alleviation of suffering in this or the next life."[23] Sociologist Amrita Pande who performed fieldwork in 2006 and 2008 in Anand in the western Indian state of Gujarat found her poor rural women subjects did something different while still mixing self- with other-regard in their narratives: they "highlight[ed] their mothering role within surrogacy . . . [while] actively deny[ing] the labor aspects" by insisting it was not "choice" but their sense of "*majboori* [a compulsion]" when linking their "economic desperation . . . to their need to fulfill their motherly duties," such as providing for their children's education or marriage.[24] While Pande herself has encouraged us to view commercial surrogacy in India as a particular kind of labor, the "striking absence of surrogacy as work" in the surrogates' own narratives suggests to her that they "do not resist this image of . . . selfless dutiful women whose primary role is to serve the family" and that they are "overcompensating for their (temporary) role as breadwinners" in a culturally gendered way as they simultaneously defend their husband's moral worth.[25] To provide a third example of this mixture of motives without attempting to obfuscate their hope for financial gain, the Israeli surrogates in Elly Teman's study who are necessarily unmarried and raising children on their own (as per Israeli regulations) articulated many of the same motives as U.S. and British surrogates, "such as love of pregnancy, empathy for childless couples, and the desire to make a unique contribution." In contrast to them, however, they were "unapologetic, honest, and upfront about money being their primary goal in pursuing surrogacy," whether their economic goals were to pay off debts, provide for their children's needs, or to save money for the future.[26]

Again, Let's "Trust Women" (Principle 6)
It is not simply my feminist Christian conviction that self- and other-regarding motives can coexist which leads me to support the provision of surrogate compensation if sought, but also my understanding that people can conscientiously and ethically consent to work under risky or hazardous conditions for monetary compensation. This is already the case with workers in the logging or commercial fishing industries (among others) which consistently rank among the most dangerous jobs in the U.S., or when persons rigorously train for and then work in careers as professional athletes or dancers while knowing they will most likely experience injuries along the way, including one that could be career-ending. Analogously, people can willingly undertake work with socially undesirable elements, such as janitorial services, housecleaning, or various service industry jobs if they believe the compensation and other benefits they would receive would be, all things considered, "worth it"—their best option among the range of possibilities open to them. Thus, to the extent a critic is arguing that a poor or working-class person cannot reasonably consent to surrogacy because it is their lower economic status or need for money that is driving their decision, they must conclude they cannot reasonably consent to work at *any* other job either.[27] Surely persons who are genuinely informed of the higher risks of an IVF pregnancy (in gestational arrangements) and are not duped into signing agreements they do not understand should be trusted to weigh the benefits a collaborative reproduction might yield (as measured in financial compensation, the deepening of relationships, the satisfaction of bringing a child into the world) against the projected costs, sacrifices, and disadvantages of serving in such a capacity, particularly if they first engage in a period of serious and unrushed discernment (as per my principle 1).

To conclude this point as feminist Lori Andrews argued decades ago, we should recognize the implicit sexism in the paternalistic assumption that individuals who become surrogates in part for financial gain—for their children's education or to help pay off family debts—are invariably being taken advantage of when society would most likely hail a husband or male partner taking on a second job to do the same as a responsible parent. In her words: it "undercuts the legitimacy of women's role in the workforce to assume they are being exploited if they plan to use their money for serious purchases. It seems to harken back to a notion that women work (and should work) only for pin money (a stereotype that is the basis for firing women in times of economic crisis)."[28]

Avoiding the Tyranny of the Gift

A third reason why surrogate compensation might be appropriate would be to help intended parents ameliorate what has been called the "tyranny of the gift"—a phenomenon experienced by persons who have received a much-needed organ from a living donor who is a family member or friend and then feel—or are made to feel—endlessly indebted to them because of it.[29] As Renée Fox and Judith Swazey described the phenomenon: "The gift the recipient has received from the donor is so extraordinary that it is inherently unreciprocal. It has no physical or symbolic equivalent. As a consequence, the giver, the receiver, and the families may find themselves locked in a creditor-debtor-vise that binds them to each other in a mutually fettering way."[30] In my own case, I experienced Katie and Steven taking every opportunity they could while I was going through IVF, pregnant with their child, or recovering in the months following childbirth while providing breastmilk for their child to shower me with gifts to express their gratitude. At some point I had to tell them to please stop—that they needn't feel like they were "on the hook" until their child left for college (!) and that this is just one of the things that could never properly be reciprocated—and that they needed to be okay with that. Katie, to be sure, is naturally a generous person, and one of her "love languages" is giving gifts, so I didn't interpret her actions as her trying to work off some imaginary, unpayable debt.[31] Still, my experience of being on the receiving end of copious gifts has given me some insight into the real desire among intended parents I have read about in the surrogacy literature and discussion groups: the IPs want to try to equalize the exchange, so they feel like the surrogate is not just endlessly giving but also receiving something substantial from them in return.[32] In short, payment if and when permitted would allow the parents to have another way to express their gratitude for the tremendous efforts their surrogate has expended on their behalf.

Meeting the Standards of Fairness and Justice

A final reason why paid surrogacy arrangements ought to be permitted is to meet the standards of fairness and justice in contexts where persons involved in other aspects of assisted reproduction are already entitled to receive compensation. As several commentators have noted, the distinction between altruistic and commercial surrogacy is ultimately misleading not only because many commercial surrogates report a combination of self-interested economic and other-regarding motives as discussed above, but also because uncompensated surrogacy arrangements regularly take place *inside* the commercial landscape of the broader fertility industry. In my non-remunerated surrogacy, for instance, everyone was paid for their services except for me: the attorneys who drew up our contracts, the psychologist who was hired to evaluate us, and the reproductive endocrinologists and staff at our fertility clinic, among others. While I did not seek payment from Katie and Steven, it is *not* because I philosophically support drawing the line at compensating persons to become pregnant for others, particularly when gestational surrogacy is a lengthier and more arduous process than sperm or egg donation and the law in my context (and elsewhere) permits financial remuneration in those cases.

So understood, a jurisdiction which legally permits both compensated and uncompensated surrogacy arrangements would be one in which persons willing to become pregnant for others could decide whether or not to seek or receive compensation. Some would—and have—accepted payment because they believe it is appropriate for them (and their families) to be compensated for their reproductive labor and service. Others like me would not (and did not) so we could provide our reproductive hospitality as a gift to a loved one.[33] Recall that some commentators, including Catholic moral theologian John Berkman in conformity with Congregation for the Doctrine of the Faith's *Donum Vitae*, oppose all types of surrogacy whether or not the surrogate is paid, while others, like feminist attorney Susan L. Bender and psychologist Phyllis Chesler, reserve their harsh judgment only for commercial arrangements.[34] However, the moral condemnation and call for legal prohibition of *all* surrogacies actually makes more sense to me, since persons who take issue only with commercial arrangements are basically saying they would rather those persons incur all the risks, inconveniences, and sacrifices of pregnancy for free.

How to Compensate Surrogates Ethically

Having presented reasons for supporting surrogate compensation when requested or desired, let us now pass to the question of how to provide it ethically by underscoring two key points.

First, all parties should be clear on what payment would and would not be for—to compensate surrogates for their "time, inconvenience and risk associated with embryo transfer, pregnancy, and delivery" on analogy to the way individuals who participate in medical research are normally compensated for their "time, stress, physical effort, and risk."[35] Surrogate compensation should not be premised upon achieving a particular pregnancy outcome, including delivery of a healthy child. In contrast, to harken back to an earlier example in the Baby M scandal of the mid-1980s, Mary Beth Whitehead was to be paid $10,000 after birth and relinquishment, but only $1,000 if she either miscarried after the fifth month or bore a stillborn and nothing if she miscarried before that. Critics were not wrong to allege the differential pay scheme revealed she was being paid to produce and hand over a child, not simply to provide reproductive labor (i.e., her genetic material, gestation, and labor and delivery), because her time and reproductive contributions would have been the same whether her pregnancy had ended with a stillborn or live birth.

One way to provide clarity about surrogate compensation and also avoid commodifying the child in the process would be for the IPs to provide the same flat fee regardless of the result of the pregnancy (i.e., miscarriage, stillbirth, premature birth, child born with congenital abnormalities, child born in good health).[36] While maintaining the surrogate's right to selective reduction and abortion, the parties would ideally work out in advance what should happen to payment should those hypothetical scenarios come to pass (e.g., the surrogate keeps her fee if the abortion is for an agreed upon reason such as to save her life or because the IPs do not wish to bring to term a baby projected to have a particular medical condition). In the rare case where a surrogate changes her mind and wishes to keep the child at journey's end (as it is her legal right to do so in the U.K. and elsewhere), she would forfeit her fee and pay back all reimbursements she has already received for pregnancy-related expenses because she ultimately would have incurred them for her own (not the IPs') sake.

The U.N. Special Rapporteur on the sale and sexual exploitation of children has offered additional helpful recommendations to prevent the sale of children in surrogacy. One is to ensure all payments would be made to the surrogate "prior to any legal or physical transfer of the child" and would be "non-reimbursable (except in cases of fraud)."[37] Another is to insist that all courts or competent legal authorities entrusted in making parentage decisions would be guided by a "best interests of the child" analysis. A third is for jurisdictions to either prohibit surrogacy until and unless "properly regulated systems are put in place" or to strictly regulate both commercial and altruistic arrangements, the latter by ensuring all reimbursements and payments are reasonable and "subject to oversight by a court or other competent authority."[38] I will return to other U.N. Special Rapporteur recommendations I affirm, such as to "protect the rights of all surrogate-born children, regardless of the legal status of the arrangement under national or international law," when I discuss cross-border arrangements in the next section.

Second, financial compensation to surrogates should not be understood as absolving the IPs' debt of gratitude to her or their duty to maintain relational ties. There are cases in the surrogacy literature of intended parents who felt this way—they believed payment removed any residual obligations they had to their surrogate, with some always envisioning a purely business relationship that would end at the birth and return of the child.[39] However, as per my framework's second principle, "covenant before contract," covenantal relationships and responsibilities should be understood to endure well before and even long after all contractual obligations have been met.

The social scientific literature on surrogates across several cultural contexts has shown how relational cut-off is painful even for surrogates who have been compensated monetarily for their service. U.S. surrogates reportedly experience it as an interpersonal betrayal since the arrangement was always for them a journey of "shared love"—not simply a terminal "business transaction."[40] For Israeli surrogates, the IPs' remaining in touch after the birth of the baby "constituted an acknowledgment that the IPs valued the surrogate's contribution . . . and she herself as a person."[41] As noted previously in chapter 2, Thai surrogates formed expectations that their compassionate service to the infertile couples would be reciprocated both financially and by a "lasting personal relationship" with "special treatment" during the surrogacy and after.[42] Finally, poor Indian women who served as surrogates during the heyday of India's commercial surrogacy enterprise have resisted the ways the industry has treated them as "disposable" by highlighting the special bonds or special connections they have forged with the couple and baby. When subsequently calling for fair trade principles of transparency in surrogacy and criticizing the ways the "relationships emerging in and through these markets are often abruptly terminated with the contract," Amrita Pande has encouraged an "open acknowledgement of these relationships" to show an "appreciation of the complex and demanding nature of service provided by gestational surrogates."[43] It should be clear that most surrogates' emotional and relational needs for enduring connection are not exhausted by their receipt of payment;

prospective IPs who hire women to perform reproductive labor for them would be wise to know this beforehand and respond accordingly.

When Surrogacy Arrangements Cross Borders

While waiting for one of my earliest appointments in the lobby of the Los Angeles–based fertility clinic we had used for me to become pregnant through science, I remember noticing I was surrounded by Mandarin speakers who looked East Asian like me. There were non-Asians present, too, but more than I would have expected were either conversing in non-American English or in another language. That the composition of people at our clinic that day was not a fluke but a repeated occurrence led me to discover something I had not yet known: California is by many accounts the surrogacy industry epicenter of the globe. While I'll never know for sure since Americans, too, speak Mandarin, a portion of those Mandarin speakers who regularly turned up in my fertility clinic may well have been foreign. In fact, some California-based surrogacy agencies report large numbers of foreign Chinese clients, with the drop head of an article in a popular magazine explaining why: "Top Fertility Agencies Scramble to Meet Foreign Demand for the State's Surrogate Moms as New Wealth and the End of One-Child Laws Bring Baby Seekers Willing to Spend $200,000."[44]

As per my anecdotal observations, patients seeking assisted reproduction are not invariably white. In addition, persons engaging in intercountry arrangements do not all fit the reproductive tourist stereotype of wealthy Westerners going abroad to an "exotic" locale in the two-thirds world to commission less privileged and likely non-white women to bear their children. As with my example in chapter 1 of gay male Israeli couples who commissioned mostly Indian surrogates in Nepal, a segment of reproductive travelers might be more properly termed reproductive exiles: persons who would prefer to stay put to expand their families but cannot either because they are blocked from receiving ART treatments at home (due to illegality, unavailability, ineligibility, or unaffordability), their legal rights as parents would be insecure there, and/or adoption might be foreclosed to them for similar reasons.[45] Of course, some foreign IPs might be a combination of reproductive tourist and reproductive exile. As alluded to earlier, the aftermath of China's long-standing (but since repealed) one-child policy and the legal gray area surrounding surrogacy in China has pushed many Chinese IPs to go abroad, while California's surrogacy-friendly laws, abundance of agencies and clinics catering to international clients, ethnic enclaves, and the lure of U.S. birthright citizenship has likely attracted many of them to the Golden State.

Whether transnational surrogacy involves the movement of persons from high- or upper-middle income countries to lower-middle or low-income countries, movement in the reverse direction, or something in between, there are additional risks and questions to be considered. As a general principle, when collaborative reproduction takes place under conditions of economic or other situational precarity, there is a greater chance the interests and well-being of persons in lower income countries might be subordinated to those of the wealthier prospective parents in higher income countries who have hired them. Still, my overall position is that cross-border surrogacy arrangements are *not* in principle morally problematic just as intrastate altruistic arrangements are not invariably morally good, though either could pass or fail ethical muster depending on how they are conducted within the broader social context in which they occur.

THE RISKS AND ETHICAL QUESTIONS OF CROSS-BORDER SURROGACY

There are several additional risks for persons contemplating an interstate, especially an intercountry, surrogacy arrangement. As such, the need for serious discernment and competent legal counsel increases because of them.

Greater Legal Precarity

Cross-border surrogacies are more legally complex—and thus often more precarious—than intrastate ones particularly when transnational. IPs seeking cross-border reproductive care are more likely to be unfamiliar with the laws and customs of the different jurisdiction with which they may have no previous ties and thus might have to rely more on surrogacy brokers or others to provide them with accurate information about how to proceed. In the remote chance where things were to go horribly wrong, reproductive travelers will often lack recourse to a higher tribunal to which to appeal beyond potentially a regional human rights court, as there are no internationally recognized conventions as there are for adoption. In addition, cross-border checks concerning the suitability of prospective surrogates or intended parents are not routinely performed, leaving parties susceptible to the statistically rare but possible disaster of one party working with another with a criminal background, as per the much-publicized "baby Gammy" controversy involving a Thai surrogate and an Australian white-Asian couple, the husband of which turned out to be a convicted sex offender who had served time for child molestation.

One of the less dramatic but more common risks in intercountry surrogacies is one or more parties running afoul of the law and facing adverse consequences. Since a portion of reproductive travelers seek foreign fertility services precisely because they are legally barred from doing so at home, they may be liable to criminal sanctions of varying degrees of severity if they are caught and prosecuted. Their hoped-for child might also suffer real harm if the interaction between two or more legal regimes creates a scenario where they are placed in legal limbo for weeks to even years in worst-case scenarios before being resolved. While rare, there are documented cases of cross-border surrogacy arrangements resulting in *stateless* children when the IPs' home country bans surrogacy and refuses to extend citizenship to the foreign, surrogate-born children of their nationals when the parents have attempted to bring them back and the destination country also does not recognize them as citizens either.[46] There have also been rare cases of surrogate-born children being rendered legally *parentless*, such as when the destination country recognizes the IPs as the legal parents, but the IPs' home country recognizes the "birth mother" as the legal mother and thus the child is unable to obtain a passport to leave the country until resolution years later.[47]

Still, other difficulties might yet befall families with a child from transnational surrogacy. For instance in the U.K., an estimated majority of parents never properly register their surrogate-born children (whether from a domestic or cross-border arrangement) and therein create what a high court judge in the family division has called a "legal ticking time bomb." Because any birth mother in the U.K. will remain the child's legal mother until and unless a court order formally extinguishes her maternal rights and responsibilities, the child will "retai[n] a claim on the estate of the birth mother—even if she was abroad" if the parents fail to complete all paperwork and court proceedings and might later encounter testamentary (inheritance) issues upon their parents' death.[48] Here, it is worth noting a speculated reason why many British parents fail to register their surrogate-born children: they have provided more surrogate compensation above expenses than what they think might be approved and thus would rather "fly under the radar" than risk becoming caught.

Children's fundamental human rights would be violated should some of these worst-case scenarios come to pass. International human rights law recognizes every child's right to be cared for by his or her parents, to acquire a nationality, and to be registered immediately after birth.[49] If a child were to be denied citizenship and its benefits such as healthcare and education or potentially face separation from their parents for a prolonged period of time, they would arguably become reproductive exiles, too. Thus, any cross-border arrangement where there is a high chance of the parents being removed from their children for flouting surrogacy laws (and perhaps the children being placed in foster homes, as has occurred), or where children are otherwise likely to bear the brunt of the consequences of their parents' decisions such as have an unclear immigration status, falls outside of what could be considered good by my progressive Christian vision for surrogacy.

Beyond advising reproductive care seekers to avoid arrangements where these catastrophes have a greater likelihood of occurring, a structural response would be to call for the legalization of surrogacy everywhere and concomitantly reduce some of the very reasons why people cross borders for reproductive healthcare, the social stigma surrounding use of assisted reproduction, and the vulnerabilities of parties currently involved in or directly affected by unregulated interstate or intercountry arrangements.[50] While I support such a proposal but lack the space to fully defend here, it is clear that the worldwide trend is toward greater, not lesser, restrictions on surrogacy, with national bans showing no signs of abating. Even in a such a world, however, we might still seek ways to reduce the legal uncertainties and thus vulnerabilities of members of the surrogacy triad by "regulat[ing] the legal implications of surrogacy (i.e., legal parenthood) without making surrogacy itself legal" where it is not.[51] France, for instance, continues to maintain its decades-long prohibition against surrogacy but a judgment of the European Court of Human Rights in 2014 and evolving French case law since 2015 has moved the country increasingly in the direction of recognizing the children of French parents born in surrogacy arrangements outside of France as the parent's legal children—and also with French citizenship if certain conditions are met.[52] Indeed, as the U.N. Special Rapporteur on the sale and sexual exploitation of children has recommended, all member states regardless of the legal status of surrogacy under domestic or international law should "protect the rights of all surrogate-born children . . . including by protecting the best interests of the child, protecting rights to identity and to access to origins, and cooperating internationally to avoid statelessness."[53] Since 2011, the Permanent Bureau of the Hague Conference on Private International Law has also been considering questions of legal parentage and the citizenship of surrogate-born children in cases of intercountry surrogacy with prohibitive laws.[54] Though it would "likely take years to develop and potentially decades to implement," my progressive Christian account of surrogacy joins the chorus of persons calling for a regulatory framework by an intercountry surrogacy agreement that is developed and adopted by Hague Convention countries, perhaps in an analogous way the Hague Convention of Intercountry Adoption governs adoptions for member states.[55]

What the Covid-19 Pandemic Has Taught Us

A final point about the greater legal precarity of transnational surrogacies worth underscoring is that even in cross-border arrangements where there are no attempts to break or circumvent the law (because surrogacy is lawful in both jurisdictions), reproductive travelers and the persons who bear their children could still be at the mercy of public officials in the other country who might restrict travel, deny visas, or fail to issue passports in a timely fashion.

The world witnessed global examples of these very phenomena due to Covid-19, particularly in the months after the World Health Organization declared the havoc caused by the novel coronavirus a "public health emergency" on January 31, 2020, and then a "pandemic" on March 11, 2020. By July 2020, up to 1,000 babies that had been born to Russian surrogates since February had been unable to meet their parents due to pandemic-related border closures. Surrogacy program caseworkers, former surrogates, and sometimes the surrogates themselves who had just given birth in Russia as well as elsewhere, such as the Ukraine, were thus called upon to care for these children as attorneys scrambled to file temporary custody and guardianship agreements.[56] To provide another example of massive disruption, while foreign intended parents in the U.S. are normally able to receive an expected U.S. passport for their surrogate-born child and return to their home country several days after childbirth, the Department of State's ceasing of normal operations on March 20, 2020, and limiting the issuing of U.S. passports to only those with a life or death emergency stranded numerous foreign parents of surrogate-born children for weeks. Those unanticipated delays caused tremendous stress and upheaval in the lives of the persons affected, "financial drain on these families [since they "typically do not have health insurance that covers medical care provided in the States"] and on [U.S.] health care resources," and even danger for those families given the then-high Covid-19 infection rates in the U.S.[57]

In light of those unprecedented challenges, the American Society of Reproductive Medicine (ASRM) formed its Covid-19 Task Force on March 13, 2020, and has issued updates and recommendations for best practices throughout the pandemic, with some principles applicable beyond public health crises. One principle stresses the importance of retaining separate legal counsel for the IPs and for the surrogate not because their relationship will necessarily be adversarial, but because their different interests will need to be represented and protected. A second best practice is to specify the provisions of care *in the destination country* should the parents be unable to be present at the time of their child's birth (due to death, incapacity, or a sudden inability to travel). This recommendation if implemented would represent a change in how arrangements pre-Covid 19 were ordinarily made, since in standard contracts the person(s) the intended parents usually selected to take custody in worst-case scenarios resided *in their same country* (as per my contract with Katie and Steven) and this same-country pattern would obviously not have solved emergency custody issues of the type that arose during the pandemic.[58]

To be sure, all parties should recognize that even designating a temporary custodian in the destination country might not be enough to forestall an unexpected crisis. For instance, when Russia invaded Ukraine on February 24, 2022, some foreign intended parents in Ukraine were stuck in the country with their newborns while other Ukrainian surrogates were tasked to care for their newly delivered surro-babies (while their foreign IPs remained in their own countries) at the same time they were seeking safe passage for themselves and their own children.[59] The point of highlighting possible disastrous outcomes in cross-border arrangements is neither for parties to assume they will happen, nor to give the false impression that altruistic, intrastate arrangements such as the one I had with Katie and Steven would invariably be crisis-free. It is, however, to underscore some distinctive risks to persons engaged in cross-border as opposed to intrastate arrangements.

Geographic, Cultural, or Linguistic Challenges

In addition to various challenges posed by the law, persons engaged in cross-border surrogacy arrangements must deal with the physical distance, cultural differences, and possible language barriers among them. What kind of relationship could the adults realistically develop during the journey ahead of them and could those affective ties endure post-childbirth? These are important questions to consider given my framework's exhortation for the surrogate and IPs to be covenanting with one another prior to any formal contract between them (principle 2), recognizing and caring for one another's needs and vulnerabilities during the partnership (principle 3), and maintaining friendly contact over the long haul for the good of all members, particularly for the child to have an accurate understanding of their biological origins (principle 5). As a research study found involving sixteen Israeli gay men who were in the process of becoming fathers through mostly Indian surrogates (fourteen out of the sixteen), geographical distance and, specifically, the IPs' "lack of physical and direct contact with the surrogate and the developing child" can lead parent hopefuls to feel more anxious, frustrated, and out of control.[60]

Of course, whether any given intercountry arrangement would require greater travel or more negotiation of cultural or linguistic differences than what might be involved in intrastate arrangements are contingent, not necessary, matters. To illustrate, a set of English- or Mandarin-speaking Hong Kongers could partner with a culturally competent English- or Mandarin-speaking Canadian who would bear their child, and the adults could develop a close relationship through telecommunication in all its forms; the exchanging of photos, letters, and cards; and occasional in-person visits. Even so, some empirical studies suggest that the quantity and quality of contact between surrogates and their IPs may have less to do with cultural homogeneity or geographical proximity and more with cultural expectations about how the parties ought to be relating to one another. In one study of thirty gay Italian men who became fathers through Californian or Canadian surrogates, all revealed the "surrogate played an essential role in making them feel emotionally connected to their developing child"; all wished for her to "always be [a] part of their lives" with many calling her "auntie" to reflect her emotional closeness to them and their child; and most sought surrogates in those locations precisely to foster a "long-lasting relationship" given cultural expectations for them in contrast to other popular surrogacy destinations at the time such as "India, where creating an ongoing connection with the surrogate [was] very difficult and rare."[61] Sociologist Zsuzsa Berend has corroborated this finding from the perspective of U.S. surrogates who likewise expect "real friendship" to form with their IPs. When geographical distance has prevented them being able to attend their surrogate's doctors' appointments, these U.S. surrogates would send "ultrasound images and the fetus' tape-recorded heartbeat," call their IPs and "put their cell phone close to the monitor so that the couple could hear it in real time" and/or share "their journals of 'the IPs' pregnancy,'" and "play IPs' voice-recorded stories to the fetus so that it would 'know its parents'" to help the IPs experience a vicarious pregnancy and therein deepen the bonds between them.[62]

Though India no longer permits transnational or commercial surrogacy, these studies help to demonstrate how some transnational arrangements could be better or worse at cultivating close relationships, given differing cultural norms or desires for them. My progressive Christian framework for surrogacy accordingly frowns upon cross-border arrangements where contact between IPs and surrogates is not direct but channeled through intermediaries or where the surrogates would remain veiled to the commissioning parents themselves. Both scenarios would not only carry a greater likelihood for the IPs to view their surrogate as simply a means to their end and not a person in her own right, but it would also render it virtually impossible for the surrogacy triad to maintain friendships over the long haul. The responsibility thus falls upon both parties—especially intended parents given their typically greater power relative to hers—to discern in advance whether a contemplated arrangement has the potential to be more than simply a business transaction. If the answer is no, they should take that as a compelling reason to decline.

Social Justice, Reproductive Justice, and Cross-Border Reproductive Care

Two other concerns about cross-border arrangements merit attention here given the reproductive justice movement's concern about inequities between and among social groups, particularly in access to healthcare.

The first involves elaborating upon a point raised in our earlier discussion of social justice (principle 7) as it pertains to questions of fairness in the distribution of opportunities and resources for persons to decide how and when to make or expand one's family. Legitimate social and reproductive justice considerations could be raised if the medical expertise and the fertility clinics of one country were disproportionately being used by reproductive travelers (be they tourists or exiles) and not by the country's own nationals and other residents whose taxes and other collective efforts have been supporting that very infrastructure. While the U.S. may be the only nation in the world that is both a sending and a destination country, most other nations are either one or the other. Thus, if the surrogacy industry in a particular context only or primarily serves *foreign* intended parents, not local residents, and if the maternal care offered to the persons hired by them were qualitatively superior to what they would receive if pregnant for or with their own children, course corrections might be in order for the sake of distributive and social justice.

A related social and reproductive justice concern would arise if local surrogacy agencies or fertility clinics were operating in such a way as to privilege the interests of their foreign IP clients at the expense of the surrogates in the destination country. An anthology on transnational surrogacy edited by a women's and human rights' activist chronicles how surrogates in some parts of the world, including India, Mexico, and Nepal, nearly always had scheduled C-sections to accommodate the commissioning parents desire for advanced planning given their need to travel, though these women were sometimes misleadingly told that the C-sections were in their own best interests.[63] This example shows how surrogates might have access to the standard of care, but the providers intentionally prioritize the intended parents' convenience over the women's health and well-being. My principle of "medical self-determination" (principle 4), however, would insist upon a reversal of priorities since the true patient in any pregnancy—even in a pregnancy for others—is the pregnant person.

Beyond the particular issue of scheduling C-sections out of convenience to benefit the IPs, there is a broader concern about arrangements where the wealth gap would be especially pronounced between the intended parents drawn from one jurisdiction and surrogates drawn from another. In a variant of the "surrogacy exploits" objection discussed above, the oft-expressed concern here is that poor women in the Global South might have no other alternatives to improve their economic situation, save to lease their bodies to others. They might also lack the ability to provide truly informed consent to the surrogacy contract either because of their poverty or their generally low(er) educational attainment. How are we to regard these cases?

Even as we acknowledge that the potential for exploitation is greater when the arrangement takes place under such conditions, I concur with a host of postcolonial scholars and reproductive justice activists who have warned against characterizing such women as always "powerless victims in need of aid."[64] Some qualitative researchers who conducted studies in three Indian cities (Mumbai, New Delhi, and Chennai) in 2013–2014 have found the majority of their subjects who were previously in "wage-paid employment" *preferred* surrogacy to their previous job: it was better paid, had better working conditions since "working late and reaching home late [in other jobs is] . . . frowned upon in their neighborhood and lead to harassment or a bad reputation," and might even be less harmful than "other wage labor available for women in India." Their empirical data thus failed to "sustain the hypothesis that it is an economic non-choice for surrogates"; rather surrogacy "thus appears as a strategic and thoughtful choice to improve living conditions."[65]

Feminist anthropologists who have studied the once multibillion-dollar transnational surrogacy industry in India have observed that while the women have been facing "stratified reproduction" and sometimes a "lack of transparency and power in negotiating contracts," they have not been helpless: they have "expressed resistance and agency within the context of structural factors that limit [their] opportunities."[66] For instance, some women have persuaded their husbands to permit them to become pregnant for others, thus "contradicting some concerns that Indian women were being forced into surrogacy by their husbands against their will" while also creating a new balance of power within the marriage with the "significant incomes their wives earned as surrogates."[67]

Feminist New Testament scholar Sharon Jacob who describes herself as an "Indian immigrant living in the United States" has compared the Indian women who transgress traditional patriarchal and sexual norms by participating in surrogacy—an act of "irregular conception"—to the biblical character of Ruth as well as other "scandalous women" in Matthew's genealogy of Jesus.[68] While likewise rejecting a simplistic and colonialist reading of these biblical or contemporary women as powerless victims, she sees a kind of complex agency at work: they all perform reproductive labor so "they can exploit the societies that exploit them" in their hopes for a better future.[69] In the words of sociologist Amrita Pande who has conducted ethnographic studies in Indian surrogacy clinics for a decade: "Unarguably the limited range of Indian women's alternative economic opportunities undermines the voluntary nature of this labour. But instead of dismissing the labour market as inherently oppressive and the women involved as subjects of this oppressive structure, it makes sense to recognize, validate and systematically evaluate the choices that women make in order to participate in that market."[70] Her work likewise contains examples of Indian women advocating for themselves in the midst of their limiting circumstances: one surrogate successfully lobbied for the intended mother to pay her while she rested for six months at the clinic following childbirth since in previous pregnancies she had to resume work nearly the next day but wanted things to be different for her in this one.[71] Pande ultimately judges national bans on surrogacy in India (or elsewhere) not only practically ineffective as a deterrent, but also morally "undesirable" for pushing surrogacy "underground, further stigmatizing the profession and the women and involved and undermining their rights as workers."[72] What women and prospective surrogates need in her judgment is not legal prohibitions against the practice, but a strong, regulatory framework recognizing surrogacy as work that is guided by fair trade principles such as transparency and dialogue in the structuring of payments, in the explanation of medical processes and provision of medical care, and in the fostering of relationships.

In sum, not all reasons for pursuing cross-border surrogacy should be regarded as equally good or morally commendable. If intended parents were to seek out a foreign destination primarily for reasons of reduced costs, we might interrogate the global and local distribution of resources while cautioning the parent hopefuls to remember the remote but catastrophic possibility of ending up stuck in a legal quagmire and perhaps "spending more money rescuing the situation" than if they had initially invested a greater amount in a domestic arrangement (assuming they could have) when the laws have suddenly changed or when a natural or man-made disaster potentially upends their best-laid plans.[73] If intended parents were to go abroad to find a clinic with less oversight on maternity care, their motives would be comparable to a transnational corporation moving their factories overseas to avoid having to comply with more stringent worker's rights laws at home. If a queer couple were to be shut out of accessing infertility services at home that was otherwise available to their heterosexual counterparts (as was the case in Israel prior to 2022), we could understand their actions as a work-around to a reproductive injustice while continue to advocate institutionally for an end to the discrimination. If a couple were to be traveling abroad not just for surrogacy, but also to do preimplantation genetic diagnosis for the purposes of nonmedical sex selection to be able to bear male heirs, my progressive Christian framework for surrogacy could not celebrate their choices while conceding it would be difficult for the law or even healthcare providers to prevent or even detect their true motives given the ease with which they could conceal them.[74] Obviously cases of cross-border surrogacy involving human trafficking would be beyond the moral pale, with the responsibility falling among multiple parties (including law enforcement, nongovernmental agencies, surrogacy brokers, healthcare providers) to prevent such violations from happening. It is ultimately impossible to generalize or evaluate the propriety of a cross-border surrogacy arrangement without knowing the particulars. But as feminists and activists in the reproductive justice movement have taught us, our inability to generalize should be expected—not mourned—given the importance of re-maining sensitive to context.

When Surrogacy Arrangements Are Traditional

Even as gestational surrogacy remains controversial—whether it is altruistic or commercial, intrastate or cross-border—societal disapproval about tradi-tional surrogacy is even greater. Not only was there massive social and legal fallout following the landmark (traditional) surrogacy cases in the 1980s in the U.S. and the U.K. which ended tragically, but traditional surrogacy in some cultural contexts also connotes adultery or at least inappropriate in-timacy between the father and the "other woman." As cultural anthropolo-gist Helene Ragoné reports in a (traditional) surrogate's writing to the *San Diego Tribune* in 1986: "The general public think I went to bed with the father; people consider this adultery because of lack of knowledge. The public needs to be educated."[75] The general public also typically presumes traditional sur-rogates would become even more attached to the child—and thus anguished upon relinquishment—than their gestational counterparts would since the former would presumably be "giving away" or even "selling" her own flesh and blood at journey's end for a price.[76] When we also factor in the fewer legal protections for traditional surrogacy in many jurisdictions, it is not difficult to appreciate why traditional surrogacy today is rare: most intended parents opt for gestational over traditional arrangements even when both types are legally permitted and even when they must still rely upon use of donor eggs as well.

Given these considerations, is there space in my progressive Christian vision and framework for surrogacy to support traditional arrangements as well? My answer is a qualified yes where not legally prohibited and when the covenanting parties not only take pains to mitigate the possible greater risks involved, but also abide by the same seven guiding principles for the forma-tion of ethical relationships.

WHAT ARE THE GREATER RISKS?

There could be additional risks for those who undergo traditional over gestational surrogacy involving the law, psychological well-being, and partial disclosure.

The Law

The first potentially greater risk of traditional over gestational surrogacy has to do with the law. In the U.S., even when traditional surrogacy is not officially proscribed, many states either have no governing statutes or more restrictions on who can enter into traditional surrogacy contracts. For instance in Nevada, traditional surrogacy is neither included in their statute on "gestational agreements," nor in existing case law, while in Maine, traditional surrogacy is permitted only if the surrogate and intended parents are family members.[77] Whether in the U.S. or abroad, intended parents might also need to undergo a more onerous process to become recognized as the legal parents. They might also be more likely to lose in a rare case of a custody dispute if the traditional surro-mom were either to lay claim upon the child or refuse to consent to the adoption court orders because of a breakdown between them.[78] Prospective surrogates and intended parents will therefore need competent legal counsel and other trusted advisors to guide them in their discernment process.

Greater Attachment and Thus, Psychological Maladjustment?

The second potential risk has to do with the widespread assumption that traditional surrogates would face an even higher likelihood of bonding with the child they are carrying for others and thus endure more psychological distress post-handover. Social scientists who research surrogacy families sometimes incorporate this belief into their working hypotheses when conducting studies to assess the overall welfare of the surrogacy triad. In one U.K. study where the majority of the surrogates were traditional (56%), more women reported "some" or "moderate" difficulties initially at the handover (32%) and still one year after (6%) than in other studies where the majority of the subjects were gestational surrogates.[79] However, in a later U.K. study of 34 surrogates who had completed 102 total surrogacy arrangements that also had more traditional (61) than gestational (41) arrangements, "no significant difference was found between whether a surrogate's overall experience . . . had been positive or not, and the type of surrogacy carried out."[80]

Even as the social scientific literature contains mixed findings on this question, a progressive Christian account of surrogacy should still encourage society to "trust women" (principle 6) who are operating under genuine conditions of informed consent and in contexts where the standard of care can be met to know what they can and cannot handle in matters pertaining to pregnancy, given their previous epistemically transformative experiences of pregnancy and childbirth.[81] For instance, the gestational surrogates in Heather Jacobson's California- and Texas-based study did not see themselves as willing or even capable of relinquishing a genetically related child since they believed genetic parentage to represent the truest form of family connection. In the words of Dawn Rudge, a two-time surrogate: "I would never be a traditional surrogate. I would never use my own eggs. I can separate actually having a child for somebody else, because it's not my genetic makeup. . . . [T]hat would be a piece of me out there in the world and . . . I can't. Some people can be egg donors and donate their eggs. And some people can carry. And some people can do neither."[82] The Israeli surrogates Elly Teman studied were likewise "nearly all horrified by the idea of traditional surrogacy, which they believe would be 'giving away my own child.'" They understood themselves instead as carrying the IP's baby and "genetic lineage"—and thereby providing a "'continuing generation' [*dor hemshech*] for their couple" given the particularity of Jewish-Israeli pronatalism, the "Israeli nation's struggle for survival, the reality of war, the biblical imperative, and the collective calling to make up for the murder of six million Jews in the Holocaust."[83] In contrast, the traditional surrogates in Zsuzsa Berend's online ethnography of the largest, mediated public surrogacy website in the U.S., www.surromomsonline .com, collectively believe that intentionality—a "desire for children coupled with the acts of parenting" is a "firmer basis of parenthood" than either genes or gestation. In similarly resisting identifying themselves as their surro-baby's true mother, many describe themselves as the "'egg donor and gestational surrogate in one,'" with one "fairly typical account" reading as follows:

> This child in my womb is NOT mine. I am nurturing him or her for the time being, but upon birth, he or she will go to their parents where they belong. I am of the belief that the egg used in conceiving this baby was meant for my IPs from before we even knew we'd do this surrogacy. I just don't want anyone thinking this is my baby, I guess I shouldn't care what anyone thinks, as I KNOW what is true.[84]

In my own case, beyond Katie and Steven wanting to create embryos without my (genetic) involvement, I knew even if I had been a good candidate for traditional surrogacy (I was not—recall I was then forty), I did not have to seriously entertain it since my parents would have considered any child with my genes as their grandchild, thus breaking their heart even more than I knew my planned gestational surrogacy would have already upset them. In short, my reasoning, that of the surrogates in Jacobsen's study, the Israeli surrogates in Teman's study, and the traditional surrogates observed in Berend's study all corroborate what British psychologist Olga B. A. van den Akker has found in her own study of traditional and gestational surrogates: "All surrogates knew before commencing surrogacy what type . . . would be acceptable to them. Significantly, those who opted to be gestational surrogates considered a genetic link to be important to them, hence they used the intended couple's egg. Those who used their own genetic material, believed a genetic link was not important to them."[85]

Partial Disclosure

The third potentially greater risk of traditional surrogacy has to do with partial disclosure, as some studies suggest intended parents tend to be less than fully truthful about their child's biological origins. While most parents tend to disclose to their children at an early age their use of a surrogate in ways parents of (only) donor-conceived children do not of their use of a gamete donor, it is not uncommon for these same parents to omit revealing that their surrogate is *also* their child's genetic mother, including in cases where the child and surro-mom remain in contact. One U.K. study of surrogate-born children at age seven suggests there may be self-deception involved: "although the parents considered themselves to have been open, they had not in fact told about the donor conception," therein creating a potentially difficult situation when the parents believe they have disclosed but "their children do not yet know the full story and remain unaware of the absence of a genetic link between themselves and their mother."[86] As the researchers themselves theorize, the parents' apparent "unwillingness" to tell their children the full truth about their biological origins may "sugges[t] that the IPs find it more difficult to disclose the use of third party gametes than the use of third-party gestation."[87]

Partial disclosure can compromise trust and intimacy between the parents and their surrogate-born child as well as prevent the child from being in a truthful relationship with their "tummy mummy." Other problems include the parents needing to perpetuate the lie every time others assume the child to be biologically the mom's ("your daughter has your nose!"), every time their child comments upon family resemblance or lack thereof about traits they assume were inherited by their mother, and every time the parents fill out their child's medical forms. Were a child to be without accurate medical history, they may end up worrying needlessly or undergoing diagnostic testing about heritable medical conditions for which they were not statistically at risk. I would add that to the extent silence and secrecy surrounding the gamete donation part of the surrogacy were connected to the parents' ongoing shame or discomfort about their break in genetic linkage to their child, they would be reinforcing the problematic idea from a Christian perspective that it is ultimately biogenetic connection—not love, intimacy, care, and commitment—that makes a family. Given my encouragement toward "disclosure, not secrecy" in my constructive framework for surrogacy (principle 5), I could neither countenance parental self-deception nor only partial disclosure when bundled with an intention never to disclose the child's full biogenetic history. I would thus urge all prospective parents contemplating traditional surrogacy to be aware of greater temptations toward these modes of operating.

WHY TRADITIONAL SURROGACY MIGHT BE PREFERRABLE

While for a host of reasons gestational surrogacy is likely to remain the more popular option, it is worth noting several possible upsides to traditional, rather than gestational, surrogacy that prospective intended parents might consider in their discernment process (principle 1). The usual method of impregnation (insemination) would be less expensive, less medically complicated and risky while requiring fewer decisions than what is involved in gestational surrogacy's IVF-HET, in addition to being more likely to result in a live birth.[88] To buttress these points, upon providing a "feminist-health-informed" review of five memoirs of gay men who became fathers through surrogacy, the anthropologist and reproductive sociology researcher Linda Layne observed that there was "significant maternal morbidity" in each of the gestational surrogacies and "none with traditional surrogacy." While acknowledging hers was not a systemic comparison, she was left puzzling why more couples don't choose traditional surrogacy given the known health risks to women who donate their eggs because of "overstimulation with hormones to maximize yield" and the memoirists' own descriptions of their gestational surrogates' suffering (e.g., multiple gestation in all four gestational surrogate-pregnancies, C-sections for all four, placenta previa and medical bed rest for some). As she saw it, traditional surrogacy "especially if undertaken by younger women" would decrease costs for the men and would also "greatly reduce the risks to the women who are willing to help them achieve their dreams."[89]

Beyond these real or potential advantages, we could imagine other carefully circumscribed scenarios where traditional surrogacy might be preferrable to gestational surrogacy.

One scenario would be when gestational surrogacy is not a live option for a couple because IVF-HET is inaccessible for reasons of cost or is otherwise ill-advised, such as the poor quality of healthcare. The person would also be a good candidate for traditional surrogacy when assessed under standard markers (i.e., they would be able to clear medical and psychological screening) and also ideally someone the intended parents already trusted. The couple, in turn, would feel confident that they would not exert themself in their child's life post-childbirth in ways beyond the role they were comfortable with their surrogate assuming.

Another scenario would involve all of the aforementioned parameters with the exception of the first: the couple would select traditional surrogacy not because its alternative is not feasible, but because they are actively seeking to build upon the long-standing bonds of intimacy and trust they have with someone else who is now willing to help in intimate, embodied ways their family expansion dreams come true. They have also concluded it would be of benefit to them to neither have to secure, nor negotiate the presence of, an additional third party—the egg donor—in their family-building plans.

Whether in the first or second scenarios, it is reasonable to believe the surrogacy triad would be even more likely to keep in long-term contact because of their preexisting relationships and trust. Once again, the maintenance of friendly ties would be a desideratum from the child's perspective since the surrogate is likely to be of genetic interest to them (as birth parents often are to children they have placed for adoption) and because ongoing relationships are correlated with better psychological outcomes for all in the surrogacy triad. While it is possible that this scenario might lead to an intended mother in a heterosexual couple feeling even more ambivalent about the collaborative reproduction (i.e., grateful and resentful about one and the same person standing in her gestational and genetic place), these conflicted feelings might not be present in the case of a gay couple.[90]

In a third scenario as a variant of the first or second, the traditional surrogate would be an intended parent's sister and the prospective parents a gay male couple with the other partner the biogenetic father. In this case, the parents would have the additional advantage of *both* being biologically related to their child who they could also both physically resemble. Studies show that gay men who have turned to a sister to be their egg donor have generally been more open about biogenetic paternity when compared to their counterparts, likely because they feel less of a need to protect the details of their asymmetrical genetic parentage when there is biological relatedness in this other way.[91]

No doubt gestational surrogacy will likely continue to be the preferred option for most couples who turn to surrogacy for many good and valid reasons. Provided that persons contemplating surrogacy educate themselves of the potential risks of pursuing a traditional instead of a gestational arrangement where both are lawful and commit to mitigating them, there may be no need for a principled objection to traditional surrogacy provided a grounding in the aforementioned principles for the formation of ethical surrogacy relationships.

Conclusion

As we have seen, surrogacy arrangements that are commercial, cross-border, or traditional arguably can pose additional risks and challenges than those that are not. Persons pursuing them should accordingly take extra precautions just as ethicists, public-policy makers, and others committed to reproductive justice should continue to advocate for the well-being of the social groups who might be more vulnerable to discrimination, disparities in power or access to resources, and other forms of mistreatment because of them. It must nonetheless be said that the vulnerabilities of those who become pregnant for others and the children they bear do not invariably increase if they partake in traditional versus gestational, commercial versus altruistic, or cross-border arrangements versus intrastate arrangements, since much will depend on the particularities of any given arrangement.

My progressive Christian framework for surrogacy recommends that any given surrogacy arrangement should only commence after a period of serious discernment, with the adults involved committing covenantally and contractually (where legal) to one another over the long haul while showing empathy, care, and stewardship toward one another as they fulfill their responsibilities to all members of the triad (principles 1–3). They should always remember who the true patient is in any pregnancy—the pregnant person—and the parents should commit to disclosing, ideally early and often, the truth of their child's biogenetic origins (principles 4–5). It is my hope that others outside of these arrangements ultimately "trust women" and others capable of pregnancy to make their own conscientious decisions about intimate reproductive matters when the conditions of informed consent and the standard of care have been met and that we collectively work toward a world where the social practice of one person bearing a child for another who cannot does not impede but in fact advances social justice (principles 6–7).

CONCLUSION

MORE THAN SIX YEARS HAVE passed since I gave birth for the third time under the unusual circumstances of surrogacy. Once raised, red, and prominent, the scar from my emergency C-section is now barely noticeable. Once nervous and excited about the many steps ahead of them in their turn to IVF and third-party reproduction, my friends have long settled into being nervous and excited about more ordinary questions facing first-time, middle-class parents in the U.S. Once only a dream who was then born into the world through a combination of love and science, the baby is now a well-adjusted, happy girl doing the things kids her age love to do.

One question I occasionally get asked by friends and colleagues is whether I would do it again. If what is meant is whether I would be willing to bear *another* surro-child, such as a sibling for Katie and Steven's daughter or a first child for a different set of intended parents, the answer is an easy no—my even older age now and need to spare my parents from stress and worry would be reasons enough for me to decline. But if the question is whether I would make the *same* decision again to serve as my friends' surro-mom if I could somehow turn back time, the answer is yes. That said, if we knew then at the beginning of our journey what we've since learned about ourselves and one another after going through the process, I'm sure we all would have changed certain aspects of our arrangement.

Another question I get asked with some frequency is whether I am still in touch with the family I helped. The visible shock in my interlocutors' faces, if not their explicit comments, betrays their surprise when I tell them yes. As I have intimated, many persons presume surro-moms would resemble a stereotypical birth mother in a closed adoption who, after the pain and agony of relinquishment, would not want to be reminded of—much less regularly face—the child they "gave up." One of the reasons why I have written this book and spoken or published about surrogacy elsewhere is precisely to correct these commonplace misperceptions about surrogate remorse for having to give the baby back. As my experience and more than four decades of research on surrogate mothers has shown, widespread fears about adverse psychological outcomes for women who become pregnant for others remain largely unsupported by the data. Though the public wouldn't know this from popular culture or from media headlines about surrogacies gone wrong, surrogates who regret their decisions or even have a difficult time separating from the child they bore for others, are the statistical exception, not the norm.

Surrogacy as a practice obviously disrupts conventional ways of thinking about childbearing and family formation. When judged by official statements and denominational resolutions, most mainline Protestant denominations have been growing more comfortable with the possible use of IVF by infertile married couples and with marriage between two men or two women, but they have not yet resolved what to make of third-party reproduction. The positive vision for surrogacy I have offered in these pages is one where willing women or other persons capable of pregnancy demonstrate reproductive solidarity and generosity toward others who have conscientiously discerned both a call to parenthood and the appropriateness of ART for themselves. The seven ethical principles in my framework have been constructed to guide the deliberations and relationships between and among the prospective members in any collaborative reproduction as well as the broader society's overall attitude toward the surrogacies of others. Finally, the ways I have adapted these same principles to cover even more complex cases where the collaboration is financially compensated, cross-border, and/or traditional acknowledges additional ways the reproductive partnership could go sideways without judging them to be beyond the moral pale.

Surrogacy is certainly not for everyone, nor need it be. I appreciate the reasons why surrogacy as an industry and practice remains controversial in the broader society even as I have arrived at a different conclusion about the goods the practice can facilitate when conscientiously undertaken under certain parameters. While I have found many feminist misgivings about surrogacy wanting, I support the ways feminists and womanists are principally committed to interrogating any practice with the potential to exploit, objectify, commodify, alienate, or control women's bodies or rights. While research thus far on surrogate-born children shows no major pathologies, I similarly applaud child advocates for continuing to prioritize children's well-being and identify potential areas of vulnerability or concern for them. Because surrogacy arrangements for profit arguably involve conditions more conducive to abuse or corruption, it makes sense to me why progressives would especially scrutinize local contexts where the potential to exploit persons commissioned to bear children for others is high or higher, such as when the pool of women recruited to serve as surrogates might not be able to meet the conditions of informed consent (e.g., the contracts are routinely written in a language or in a style the candidates cannot understand). Finally, while the progressive Christian judgments I render about family, sex, and reproduction differs markedly from those of my more conservative evangelical, Catholic, or Orthodox counterparts, I appreciate their good faith engagement of the topic and the other theological commitments we nonetheless share.

In having said yes to becoming a surrogate for my friends and in having constructed this positive vision and framework of guiding principles for surrogacy, I have clearly concluded that parenthood involves more than genes or gestation. While not every sincere and desperate desire for a child should be fulfilled, many parent hopefuls who have done the careful work of discernment and are prepared to follow the principles and recommendations in my framework for surrogacy should be afforded the support to at least try.

From Surrogacy to Other and New Frontiers

My firsthand experience with surrogacy has also led me to wonder about the ethics of other reproductive techniques or practices. Today, assisted reproductive technology not only allows women like me to birth genetically unrelated children for others via heterologous embryo transfer, but also postmenopausal women giving birth to their own biogenetic grandchildren. More irregularly, there are also women bearing children they first "adopted" as frozen embryos approximately their same chronological age due to those embryos' prior years in cryopreservation. There are also women, including transwomen, who are breastfeeding their children through induced lactation without having first undergone a pregnancy.[1] Ethicists today are also still debating what to make of both "three-person babies" (i.e., children born through IVF involving the genetic material of three persons through a mitochondrial DNA transfer) and uterine transplantation in women with uterine factor infertility (UFI), including in transgender women.[2] Depending on developments in reproductive technology and what ethics committee boards and public-policy makers will determine are advisable or even allowable, other techniques might eventually move from the realm of science fiction to reality. Perhaps someday babies will enter into the world from having been gestated in full in artificial wombs or "biobags" (ectogenesis).[3] Perhaps children will be born with only one genetic parent or two same-sex genetic parents if *in vitro gametogenesis* (IVF), where gametes can be created in a lab from adult cells, someday becomes possible in humans as it has already in mice.

My personal experience with, and positive argument for, surrogacy does not commit me to the view "anything goes" in the name of science or reproductive freedom. But my intimate knowledge of and firsthand experience with a medical technique so misunderstood and even shunned in many quarters does prompt me to call for thoughtful, deliberative discussion of these possibilities to critically assess them one by one instead of dismiss them outright for their deviation from the norm. Indeed, several of the aforementioned ART techniques might not be more strange, miraculous, and potentially awe-inspiring than the traditional biblical understanding of a God who "opens" or "closes" wombs and who otherwise "makes all things possible" (Mat 19:26). Surrogacy in particular and assisted reproductive technology more generally allow us human beings to transcend the limits of the natural. If the arguments of this book have been persuasive, progressive Christians should have reason to welcome this type of transcendence in the case of surrogacy for the scientific marvel that it is *and* for providing us an occasion to shout "Hallelujah!" as we collectively welcome new, precious life into the world.

NOTES

Introduction

1. Elizabeth Kane, *Birth Mother: The Story of America's First Legal Surrogate Mother* (San Diego, CA: Harcourt Brace Jovanovich, 1988), 124.

2. Five surveys in the U.S. since the 1980s show "most people do not approve of surrogacy, finding it the least acceptable route" to parenthood. See Heather Jacobson, *Labor of Love: Gestational Surrogacy and the Work of Making Babies* (New Brunswick, NJ: Rutgers University Press, 2016), 46. While a 2015 YouGov poll found a majority approve of surrogacy (71%), 50% believe couples who cannot conceive a child on their own should adopt, and only 15% say they should use a surrogate. See Peter Moore, "Americans Want Biological Children but Prefer Adoption to Surrogacy," YouGov America, Dec 2, 2015, https://today.yougov.com/topics/lifestyle/articles-reports/2015/12/02/americans-biological-children-adoption-surrogacy.

3. I will use pseudonyms throughout to protect the anonymity of the intended parents of the child I bore.

4. This term generally refers to a medically-assisted scenario where a child is born with the biological help of a third party: a gamete donor, a surrogate, and/or a couple who has donated their leftover embryo(s) to the parent(s).

5. See L. A. Paul, *Transformative Experiences* (New York: Oxford University Press, 2014) and Fiona Woollard, "Mother Knows Best: Pregnancy, Applied Ethics, and Epistemically Transformative Experiences," *Journal of Applied Philosophy* 38.1 (2021): 155–171.

6. See The Practice Committee of the American Society for Reproductive Medicine and the Practice Committee of the Society for Assisted Reproductive Technology, "Guidance Regarding Gamete and Embryo Donation," *Fertility and Sterility* 115.6 (2021): 1395–1410 at 1396 and Alex Pearlman, "Gamete Donor Anonymity Is a Myth: Q&A with Seema Mohapatra," Digital Symposium on *Consuming Genetics: Ethical*

and Legal Considerations of New Technologies, May 23, 2019, https://blog.petrieflom. law.harvard.edu/2019/05/23/gamete-donor-anonymity-is-a-myth-a-qa-with-seema -mohapatra/. For the Colorado "Donor-Conceived Persons and Families of Donor-Conceived Persons Protection Act," see Sam Tabachnik, "Colorado Becomes the First State to Ban Anonymous Sperm and Egg Donations," *Denver Post*, Jun 1, 2022, https:// www.denverpost.com/2022/06/01/colorado-donor-conceived-persons-protection -act/.

7. See Damien W. Riggs, "Transgender Men's Self-Representations of Bearing Children Post-Transition," in *Who's Your Daddy? And Other Writings on Queer Parenting*, ed. Rachel Epstein, 62–71 (Toronto, Canada: Sumach Press, 2009), and K. J. Surkan, "That Fat Man Is Giving Birth: Gender Identity, Reproduction and the Pregnant Body," in *Natal Signs: Cultural Representations of Pregnancy, Birth and Parenting*, ed. Nadya Burton, 58-72 (Bradford, Ontario, Canada: Demeter Press, 2015).

8. See "Ricky Martin Opens Up about Using a Surrogate," *Oprah Winfrey Show*, Nov. 2, 2010, http://www.oprah.com/own-oprahshow/ricky-martin-opens-up-about -using-a-surrogate and Jenny Desborough, "How Many Children Does Cristiano Ronaldo Have?" *Newsweek*, Oct 29, 2021, https://www.newsweek.com/how-many-chil dren-does-cristiano-ronaldo-have-girlfriend-georgina-rodriguez-relationship-164 3728.

9. Reciprocal IVF is an ART process that allows both female partners in a couple to participate biologically in their child's birth. One partner's eggs are retrieved and then fertilized with sperm from a known or non-identified donor. At least one resultant embryo is then transferred to the other partner for gestation and, eventually, childbirth if the embryo implants.

Chapter 1

1. According to the Centers for Disease Control and Prevention (CDC), embryo transfers into gestational surrogates in the U.S. increased from 2,589 in 2008 to 6,556 in 2017. While the number of international surrogacy arrangements are "impossible to determine," the Hague estimates an increase of nearly 1,000% between 2006 and 2010. See CDC, "2017 Assisted Reproductive Technology: National Summary Report," US Department of Health and Human Services, 2019, 12 and 19, https://www.cdc.gov/art/ pdf/2017-report/ART-2017-National-Summary-Figures_508.pdf; The Permanent Bureau of the Hague Conference on Private International Law, "A Preliminary Report on the Issues Arising from International Surrogacy Arrangements," Preliminary Doc. No. 10, Mar 2012, https://assets.hcch.net/docs/d4ff8ecd-f747-46da-86c3-61074e9b17fe .pdf (8).

2. See Bonnie Johnson, "And Baby Makes Four: For the First Time a Surrogate Bears a Child Genetically Not Her Own," *People*, May 4, 1987, https://people.com /archive/and-baby-makes-four-for-the-first-time-a-surrogate-bears-a-child-geneti cally-not-her-own-vol-27-no-18/ and "No More Test-Tube Babies, Surrogate Vows; Hospital Says It Was Misled," *Associated Press*, Apr 17, 1986, https://apnews.com /20914bdee91e48949eec4914f45dfe10. Reports of a successful embryo transfer to a sur-

rogate predate this, but did not result in a live birth. See Wulf H. Utian et al., "Successful Pregnancy After In Vitro Fertilization and Embryo Transfer from an Infertile Woman to a Surrogate," *New England Journal of Medicine* 313:21 (1985): 1351–1352.

3. There is no one definition of assisted reproductive technology. The CDC only includes those procedures to treat infertility wherein both egg and sperm are handled. I will use the term ART more expansively, such that it involves any treatment or procedure that aims to achieve a pregnancy outside of sexual intercourse. Thus, artificial insemination would not qualify as ART under the CDC's definition but would under my definition.

4. Patrick Sawyer, "Greek Grandmother Becomes World's Oldest Surrogate Mother," *The Telegraph*, Dec 23, 2016, https://www.telegraph.co.uk/news/2016/12/23/greek -grandmother-becomes-worlds-oldest-surrogate-mother/.

5. See Masayuki Kodama, "The Current State of Surrogate Conception in Japan and the Ethical Assessment of Dr. Yahiro Netsu: An Ethical Investigation of Japanese Reproductive Medicine (Surrogacy)," *Asian Bioethics Review* 6.1 (2014): 55–65 at 58–59 and Sachi Spaulding, "Surrogacy and Japan: A Case for Regulation," *Pacific Basin Law Journal* 38.1 (2021): 61–84 at 62.

6. Chisa Fujoka, "Japan's Surrogate Mothers Emerge from Shadows," *Reuters,* Mar 12, 2008; https://www.reuters.com/article/idUST35655.

7. By day three, the embryo consists of four to eight cells and is called a multicell or cleavage-stage embryo. By day five, the embryo, which is now a blastocyst, has approximately seventy to one hundred cells.

8. Some tout the benefits of acupuncture on the day of the transfer to relax the patient or improve blood flow to the uterus or both. However, studies on acupuncture's effect on IVF outcomes have yielded inconclusive or contradictory results. See, for example, Juan-Enrique Schwarze et al., "Does Acupuncture the Day of Embryo Transfer Affect the Clinical Pregnancy Rate? Systematic Review and Meta-Analysis, *JBRA Assisted Reproduction* 22.4 (2018): 363–368; Kehinde T. Eniola et al., "Does Acupuncture Therapy Improve Fertility Outcome in Women Undergoing IVF?" *Evidence- Based Practice* 23.3 (2020): 30–31; Alamtaj Samsami Dehghani et al., "The Effect of Acupuncture on the Day of Embryo Transfer on the In Vitro Fertilization Outcomes: An RCT," *International Journal of Reproductive Biomedicine* 18.3 (2020): 209–214.

9. Several subjects in Heather Jacobson's study of Texas and California-based surrogates were ordered to spend three or four days on bed rest following the embryo transfer due to "physicians' beliefs that it would aid pregnancy." See her *Labor of Love*: *Gestational Surrogacy and the Work of Making Babies* (New Brunswick, NJ: Rutgers University Press, 2016), 133. While bed rest has long been recommended for IVF patients, more recent studies suggest it does not improve pregnancy outcomes. See Mauro Cozzolino, Gianmarco Troiano, and Ecem Esencan, "Bed Rest after an Embryo Transfer: A Systematic Review and Meta-Analysis," *Archives of Gynecology and Obstetrics* 300.5 (2019): 1121–1130.

I had done some reading on the topic in 2015 and had concluded that post-ET bedrest was not medically necessary or even helpful. I thus presumed it was something designed to give both IVF patients a greater sense of control and the fertility clinic a way to preempt complaints of the type "you didn't tell me to rest afterward and I walked down a flight of stairs and that's probably why my embryo(s) didn't 'stick.'" I complied nevertheless because it was required by our fertility clinic and thus something my IPs wanted me to do. I felt then, as I do now, that it might have been my body resting, but the prescribed bedrest was not ultimately for *me*.

10. Dangers of multiple gestation for the pregnant person include increased risks of preeclampsia, premature rupture of the members, delivery by Caesarean section, and a greater likelihood of needing medical bed rest in the final weeks of pregnancy. Increased risks for the babies include premature birth, low birth weight, respiratory problems, jaundice, and a greater likelihood of requiring care in the neonatal intensive care unit (NICU). To reduce these risks, the Practice Committees of the American Society for Reproductive Medicine (ASRM) and the Society for Assisted Reproductive Technology (SART) call for elective single embryo transfer (eSET) as the standard of care for "patients with a favorable prognosis." See their "Guidance on the Limits to the Number of Embryos to Transfer: A Committee Opinion," *Fertility and Sterility* 116.3 (2021): 651–654.

11. See Ann M. Gronowski et al., "The Ethical Implications of Preimplantation Genetic Diagnosis," *Clinical Chemistry* 60.1 (2014): 25–28.

12. See Practice Committee of the American Society for Reproductive Medicine and Practice Committee of the Society for Assisted Reproductive Technology, "Recommendations for Practices Utilizing Gestational Carriers: A Committee Opinion," *Fertility and Sterility* 107. 2 (2017): e3-e10 at e3 and The Practice Committee of the American Society for Reproductive Medicine and the Practice Committee of the Society for Assisted Reproductive Technology, "Guidance Regarding Gamete and Embryo Donation," *Fertility and Sterility* 115.6 (2021): 1395–1410 at 1396.

13. American College of Obstetricians and Gynecologists, "Committee Opinion: Family Building through Surrogacy," No. 660, Mar 2016 (reaffirmed 2019); Olga B. A. van den Akker, *Surrogate Motherhood Families* (Cham, Switzerland: Palgrave Macmillan, 2017), 62.

14. Kodama, "The Current State of Surrogate Conception in Japan and the Ethical Assessment of Dr. Yahiro Netsu," 59.

15. Surrogacy UK, https://surrogacyuk.org/. As their homepage states: "Our ethos is 'surrogacy through friendship.' Through our organisation surrogates and intended parents can meet one another and form the friendships that can lead to dreams coming true. We are here to help and support you through all the stages of your surrogacy journey."

16. See Hammurabi's Code of Laws, especially numbers 144, 146, 147, https://avalon .law.yale.edu/ancient/hamframe.asp.

17. Following the discovery of the Nuzi tablets (ca. 1450–1350 BCE) in the twentieth century depicting similar Hurrian "children by proxy" practices, some scholars have contended that the cultural practices of surrogacy described in Genesis were authentic (not fictional). I thank Hebrew Bible scholar Gale Yee for this point and this refer-

ence: Bryant G. Wood, "Great Discoveries in Biblical Archaeology: The Nuzi Tablets," *Bible and Spade* (Winter 2005), https://biblearchaeology.org/research/patriarchal-era /3492-great-discoveries-in-biblical-archaeology-the-nuzi-tablets.

18. See Isadore Schmukler and Betsy P. Aigen, "The Terror of Surrogate Motherhood: Fantasies, Realities, and Viable Legislation," in *Gender in Transition: A New Frontier*, ed. J. Offerman-Zuckerberg, 235–248 (Boston: Springer, 1989) and Lawrence Van Gelder, "Noel Keane, 58, Lawyer in Surrogate Mother Cases, Is Dead," *New York Times*, Jan. 28, 1997, https://www.nytimes.com/1997/01/28/nyregion/noel-keane-58 -lawyer-in-surrogate-mother-cases-is-dead.html?_r=0.

19. See *In Re Baby M*, 109 N.J. 396, 537 A.2d 1227 (1988), "Who's Who in the Fight for Baby M," Apr 1, 1987, https://www.nytimes.com/1987/04/01/nyregion/who-s-who-in -the-fight-for-baby-m.html?searchResultPosition=1 and Robert Blank and Janna C. Merrick, *Human Reproduction, Emerging Technologies, and Conflicting Rights* (Washington, D.C.: Congressional Quarterly Inc., 1995), 122. The media depicted Mary Beth Whitehead as a high school dropout at fifteen, a two-time mother before nineteen, and someone who was in a shaky marriage with a sanitation worker with a drinking problem and an uneven employment history. They also had a joint annual income of $28,000 and were facing foreclosure on their house. In contrast, the media depicted the well-educated and upper-crust intended parents—a biochemist (William Stern) and a professor of pediatrics (Elizabeth Stern)—as having a joint annual income of more than $90,000 and as turning to surrogacy so William could preserve his family line as the last surviving member of his family (i.e., others had perished in the Holocaust) because Elizabeth had feared a pregnancy would aggravate her self-diagnosed case of multiple sclerosis.

20. In re Baby M, 537 A.2d 1227 (N.J. 1988).

21. For the statutes in question, see Annie Yau et al., "Medical and Mental Health Implications of Gestational Surrogates," *American Journal of Obstetrics and Gynecology* 225.3 (2021): 264–269 at 265 and the "U.S. Surrogacy Map" database by the Maryland-based Creative Family Connections, https://www.creativefamilyconnections .com/us-surrogacy-law-map/.

22. See especially California Family Code Section 7960–7962 (2013) and *Johnson v. Calvert*, 5 Cal.4th 84 19 Cal.Rptr. 494 (1993) and In Re Marriage of Buzzanca (Cal App. 4 Dist. 1998) 72 Cal. Rptr.2d 280, which were two cases cited in the "recitals" section of my surrogacy contract. See also the Creative Family Connections' "U.S. Surrogacy Map" database.

23. See Title 20, Chapter 9 §20-156-165 of the Virginia Code entitled "Status of Children of Assisted Conception," https://law.lis.virginia.gov/vacode/title20/chapter9/. The "reasonable medical and ancillary costs" eligible for reimbursement as follows: "The costs of the performance of assisted conception, the costs of prenatal maternal health care, the costs of maternal and child health care for a reasonable postpartum period, the reasonable costs for medications and maternity clothes, and additional and reasonable costs for housing and other living expenses attributable to the pregnancy" (§20–156).

24. See "Gestational Surrogacy in Tennessee," https://www.creativefamilyconnec tions.com/us-surrogacy-law-map/tennessee/ and Tennessee Code Ann. §36-1-102 (51) (A); In re Adoption of Male Child A.F.C, https://www.tncourts.gov/sites/default/files /inre.a.f.c.opn_.pdf.

25. Alex Finkelstein et al., "Surrogacy Law and Policy in the U.S.: National Conversation Informed by Global Lawmaking," Columbia Law School Sexuality and Gender Law Clinic (2016), 11.

26. Jérôme Courduriès, "At the Nation's Doorstep: The Fate of Children Born Via Surrogacy," *Reproductive BioMedicine and Society Online* (2018): 47–54 at 49.

27. To be clear, there is no legal definition of a "reasonable expense" and surrogates *can* receive more than expenses in the U.K. According to the nonprofit surrogacy agency Brilliant Beginnings, surrogacy teams in the U.K. have taken one of three approaches to handling expenses: reimburse along the way, estimate expenses in advance, or agree upon a reasonable figure (£12,000 to £20,000). See their "How Much Can a UK Surrogate Get Paid?" https://brilliantbeginnings.co.uk/how-much-can-a -uk-surrogate-get-paid/#:~:text=How%20much%20can%20a%20UK,compensation% 20of%20%2430%2C000%20to%20%2460%2C000).

28. An IP who is genetically related to the child can apply for a Parental Order (PO) after six weeks but within six months of the child's birth. If the IPs bear no genetic relation to the child, they must undergo an adoption proceeding. See https://www .legislation.gov.uk/ukpga/1985/49/contents for the Surrogacy Arrangements Act 1985 and https://www.legislation.gov.uk/ukpga/2008/22 for the Human Fertilisation and Embryology Act 2008.

29. Surrogacy Australia, "I Need a Surrogate, What's Next?" https://www.surroga cyaustralia.org/need-surrogate-whats-next/.

30. In Ukraine, IPs would immediately be recognized as the legal parents, with their names listed on the birth certificate, so long as they could demonstrate they had exhausted other ways of carrying a baby to term or a pregnancy would be contraindicated for the intended mother. Since Ukraine does not permit gay couples or singles to hire surrogates, IPs fitting those profiles have often turned to neighboring Russia. Foreign gay couples in Russia normally have just one parent sign the contract and the other adopt the child upon return to their home country. See Susan Dominus, "It's a Terrible Thing When a Grown Person Does Not Belong to Herself," *New York Times*, May 3, 2022, https://www.nytimes.com/2022/05/03/magazine/surrogates-ukraine .html.

31. The bill which passed nearly unanimously in its first reading, requires two more readings and a review by the upper house of Parliament before it can be signed into law by President Vladimir Putin. See "Russia Moves to Bar Foreigners from Using its Surrogate Mothers," *Reuters*, May 24, 2022, https://www.reuters.com/world/europe /russia-moves-bar-foreigners-using-its-surrogate-mothers-2022-05-24/.

32. See Neha Thirani Bagri/Anand, "A Controversial Ban on Commercial Surrogacy Could Leave Women in India with Even Fewer Choices," *Time,* Jun 30, 2021, https://time.com/6075971/commercial-surrogacy-ban-india/.

33. See Debra Kamin, "Israel Evacuates Surrogate Babies from Nepal but Leaves the Mothers Behind," *Time,* Apr 28, 2015, https://time.com/3838319/israel-nepal-surro gates/ and U.S. Embassy Kathmandu, "Surrogacy Services are Banned in Nepal," Jun 4, 2021, https://np.usembassy.gov/surrogacy-services-are-banned-in-nepal/#:~:text= The%20Supreme%20Court's%20final%20verdict,transgender%20couples%2C%20and %20foreign%20nationals.

34. See "Baby Gammy: Surrogacy Row Family Cleared of Abandoning Child with Down Syndrome in Thailand," *ABC News,* Apr 13, 2016, https://www.abc.net.au/news /2016-04-14/baby-gammy-twin-must-remain-with-family-wa-court-rules/7326196 and "David Farnell, Father of Baby Gammy and Convicted Sex Offender Dies," *ABC News,* Jul 16, 2020, https://www.news.com.au/lifestyle/real-life/news-life/david-far nell-father-of-baby-gammy-and-convicted-sex-offender-dies/news-story/5be57b2605 03c8445f18e168f6ab82e5.

35. *National Review* Interview, "Wombs for Rent," *National Review,* June 28, 2013, https://www.nationalreview.com/2013/06/wombs-rent-interview/.

36. Virginie Rozée, Sayeed Unisa, and Elise de La Rochebrochard, "The Social Para- doxes of Commercial Surrogacy in Developing Countries: India before the New Law of 2018," *BMC Women's Health* 20.234 (2020), https://doi.org/10.1186/s12905-020-01087-2.

37. "Help Wanted: As Demand for Surrogacy Soars, More Countries Are Trying to Ban It," May 13, 2017, *The Economist,* https://www.economist.com/international/2017 /05/13/as-demand-for-surrogacy-soars-more-countries-are-trying-to-ban-it.

38. Marcia C. Inhorn and Pasquale Patrizio, "Rethinking Reproductive 'Tourism' as Reproductive 'Exile,'" *Fertility and Sterility* 92.3 (2009): 904–906.

39. The number of ET transfers into surrogates increased from 2,649 in 2010 to 9,195 in 2019. Surrogacy also accounts for a higher percentage of ET transfers among patients using ART, from 2.1% of all cycles in 2010 to 5.4% in 2019. See CDC, "2019 Assisted Reproductive Technology: Fertility Clinic and National Summary Report," US Dept of Health and Human Services, 2021, 34, https://www.cdc.gov/art/reports /2019/pdf/2019-Report-ART-Fertility-Clinic-National-Summary-h.pdf.

40. Olivia Miller, "Number of Parents Using Surrogates in England and Wales Quadruples in 10 Years," University of Kent News Centre, Sep 22, 2021, https://www .kent.ac.uk/news/society/29777/number-of-parents-using-surrogates-in-england-and -wales-quadruples-in-10.

41. Hague Conference on Private International Law, "A Study of Legal Parentage and the Issues Arising from International Surrogacy Arrangements," Prel. Doc. No. 3 C of March 2014, https://assets.hcch.net/docs/bb90cfd2-a66a-4fe4-a05b-55f33b009cfc .pdf (§125, p. 56, n. 507; §130-§131, p. 58). The Hague Expert's Group has met every year since being commissioned by the Hague's Council on General Affairs and Policy (CGAP) in 2015 and is projected to submit its final report in 2023. See HCCH, "The Parentage/Surrogacy Project," https://www.hcch.net/en/projects/legislative-projects /parentage-surrogacy.

42. Éva Beaujouan and Tomás Sobotka, "Late Childbearing Continues to Increase in Developed Countries," *Population & Societies* 562.1 (2019): 1–4.

43. See CDC, "2016 Assisted Reproductive Technology: National Summary Report" (Atlanta: GA, US Department of Health and Human Services, 2018), 42, https://www .cdc.gov/art/pdf/2016-report/ART-2016-National-Summary-Report.pdf.

44. Nicola Carone, Roberto Baiocco, and Vittoro Lingiardi, "Single Fathers by Choice Using Surrogacy: Why Men Decide to Have a Child as a Single Parent," *Human Reproduction* 32.9 (2017): 1871–1879.

45. Marcin Smietana, Claris Thompson, and France Winddance Twine, "Making and Breaking Families—Reading Queer Reproductions, Stratified Reproduction and Reproductive Justice Together," *Reproductive BioMedicine and Society Online* 7 (2018): 112–130 at 114. Gender norms have "helped lesbian mothers draw on dominant scripts of femininity when fighting for parental rights," though those same norms have "sometimes intensified opposition to gay fatherhood" (114).

46. For the U.S. context, see chapter 3 of Jacobsen's *Labor of Love*. For the Thai context, see Yuri Hibino and Yosuke Shimazono, "Becoming a Surrogate Online: 'Message Board' Surrogacy in Thailand," *Asian Bioethics Review* 5.1 (2013): 56–72 at 59–66, and Yuri Hibino, "Non-Commercial Surrogacy in Thailand: Ethical, Legal, and Social Implications in Local and Global Contexts," *Asian Bioethics Review* 12.2 (2020): 135–147 at 138–139. For the Israeli context, see Elly Teman, *Birthing a Mother: The Surrogate Body and the Pregnant Self* (Los Angeles: University of California Press, 2010), 23 and Part 3. For the UK context, see van den Akker, *Surrogate Motherhood Families*, 83–90.

Chapter 2

1. Media coverage about fraud or scams has led some to conclude the entire multibillion-dollar industry is a dodgy, "buyer beware" enterprise. See Tamar Lewin, "A Surrogacy Agency That Delivered Heartache," *New York Times*, Jul 27, 2014, https: //www.nytimes.com/2014/07/28/us/surrogacy-agency-planet-hospital-delivered -heartache.html.

2. Elizabeth Kane, *Birth Mother: The Story of America's First Legal Surrogate Mother* (San Diego, CA: Harcourt Brace Jovanovich, 1988), 277–279.

3. See Kim Cotton and Denise Winn, *Baby Cotton: For Love and Money* (London: Dorling Kindersley, 1985) and Kim Cotton, "Selling My Fertility Changed the Law in Britain," *BBC News*, Mar 29, 2017, https://www.bbc.com/news/av/magazine-39416994.

4. Friends, "The One Hundredth," Episode 3, Season 5, 1998. This episode is referenced in Claire Shefchik, "A Short History of Surrogacy Shows How Much More We Have to Learn," *Romper*, Oct 31, 2016, https://www.romper.com/p/a-short-history-of -surrogacy-shows-how-much-more-we-have-to-learn-17612.

5. Susan Golombok et al., "Families Created through Surrogacy Arrangements: Parent-Child Relationships in the 1st Year of Life," *Developmental Psychology* 40.3 (2004): 400–411 at 401.

6. Golombok et al., "Families Created through Surrogacy Arrangements," 401.

7. Philosopher Kwame Anthony Appiah of the popular *New York Times* column "The Ethicist" addressed the matter of social disapproval on Feb 10, 2016 with this

question: "Is it Selfish for a Gay Couple to Have Kids via Surrogacy?" For challenges facing gay male intended parents, see Dean A. Murphy, *Gay Men Pursuing Parenthood via Surrogacy: Reconfiguring Kinship* (Sydney, Australia: University of North South Wales Press, 2015), 20–21.

8. Valory Mitchell and Robert-Jay Green, "Different Storks for Different Folks: Gay and Lesbian Parents' Experiences with Alternative Insemination and Surrogacy," *Journal of GLBT Family Studies* 3:2–3 (2007): 81–104 at 91; Deborah Dempsey, "Surrogacy, Gay Male Couples and the Significance of Biogenetic Paternity," *New Genetics and Society* 32.1 (2013): 37–53 at 48. Lesbian couples could face a parallel issue about deciding upon genetic motherhood if they used a (gestational) surrogate to expand their families, but I know of no studies or published stories about such cases. Heterosexual couples who have used one, but not two, gamete donors will also only have one parent genetically related to their child, though they may be able to conceal this fact from outsiders in ways queer couples typically cannot.

9. Kane's own traditional surrogacy not only exacerbated existing tensions between her husband and her, but also likely led to him being fired from his job given the ostracism he faced at work about her media-sensationalized arrangement. See Kane, *Birth Mother*, 163–165.

10. Heather Jacobson, *Labor of Love: Gestational Surrogacy and the Work of Making Babies* (New Brunswick, NJ: Rutgers University Press, 2016), 144.

11. Katha Pollitt, "The Strange Case of Baby M," *The Nation*, May 23, 1987, reprinted on Jan 2, 1998, https://www.thenation.com/article/archive/strange-case-baby-m/.

12. Jacobson, *Labor of Love*, 144.

13. Ironically, I bumped into the intended father's mother at my parents' church that same day who offered some encouraging words to me after I briefly told her what had happened. It was as if she, the future grandmother of the child I was carrying in my womb, served as a surrogate mother of sorts to me that Mother's Day morning.

14. It was only after my parents could see that no disaster (beyond the emergency C-section) had befallen me that they felt free to tell me that I had done a loving, beautiful thing for my friends and support me in other ways, such as bring our family multiple days' worth of food to eat for weeks on end when I was recovering from childbirth.

15. Amrita Pande, "Not an 'Angel', Not a 'Whore': Surrogates as 'Dirty' Workers in India," *Indian Journal of Gender Studies* 16:2 (2009): 141–173 at 154.

16. For a sampling of this literature, see Helena Ragoné, "Chasing the Blood Tie: Surrogate Mothers, Adoptive Mothers and Fathers," *American Ethnologist* 23.2 (1996): 352–365; Hazel Baslington, "The Social Organization of Surrogacy: Relinquishing a Baby and the Role of Payment in the Psychological Detachment Process," *Journal of Health Psychology* 7.1 (2002): 57–71; Vasanti Jadva et al., "Surrogacy: The Experiences of Surrogate Mothers," *Human Reproduction* 18.10 (2003): 2196–2204; Elly Teman, *Birthing a Mother: The Surrogate Body and the Pregnant Self* (Berkeley: University of California Press, 2010); and Olga B. A. van den Akker, *Surrogate Motherhood Families* (Cham, Switzerland: Palgrave Macmillan, 2017).

17. See Elly Teman, "The Social Construction of Surrogacy Research: An Anthropological Critique of the Psychological Scholarship on Surrogate Motherhood," *Social Science & Medicine* 67 (2008): 1104–1112 at 1104. ACOG has likewise found only in a "handful of cases" do parenting plans fall through—either where gestational surrogates seek to assert parental rights over the IPs' or where the IPs refuse to accept their parental obligations at journey's end. See ACOG Committee Opinion, "Family Building through Gestational Surrogacy," No. 660, March 2016 (reaffirmed 2019), 4, https://www.acog.org/clinical/clinical-guidance/committee-opinion/articles/2016/03/family-building-through-gestational-surrogacy.

18. Childlessness Overcome Through Surrogacy (COTS), https://www.surrogacy.org.uk/. Britain's second oldest surrogacy charity, Surrogacy UK, similarly reports it has seen zero cases of surrogates changing their mind and wanting to keep the baby for themselves since their organization's founding in 2002. See "Help Wanted: As Demand for Surrogacy Soars, More Countries Are Trying to Ban It," *The Economist*, May 13, 2017, https://www.economist.com/international/2017/05/13/as-demand-for-surrogacy-soars-more-countries-are-trying-to-ban-it.

19. See Surrogacy in Canada Online, "FAQ: How many gestational surrogate mothers have changed their mind and wanted to keep the baby?" https://surrogacy.ca/intended-parents/ip-faq.html#how-many-gestational-surrogate-mothers-have-changed-their-mind-and-wanted-to-keep-the-baby and Cynthia Vukets, "Surrogate Mother's Nightmare," *Toronto Star*, Sep 9, 2011, https://www.thestar.com/news/canada/2011/09/09/surrogate_mothers_nightmare.html.

20. Annie Yau et al., "Medical and Mental Health Implications of Gestational Surrogates," *American Journal of Obstetrics and Gynecology* 225.3 (2021): 264–269 at 267.

21. Jacobson, *Labor of Love*, 110.

22. Yuri Hibino, "Non-commercial Surrogacy in Thailand: Ethical, Legal, and Social Implications in Local and Global Contexts," *Asian Bioethics Review* 12 (2020): 135–147 at 140.

23. Hibino, "Non-commercial Surrogacy in Thailand," 139.

24. See Baslington, "The Social Organization of Surrogacy," 64–65.

25. Pollitt, "The Strange Case of Baby M."

26. The first two responses come from an Israeli surrogate (Rinat) and an anonymous American one in Elly Teman and Zsuzsa Berend, "Surrogate Non-Motherhood: Israeli and US Surrogates Speak about Kinship and Parenthood," *Anthropology & Medicine* 25.3 (2018): 296–310 at 299–300. Both report surrogates in their study "did not see themselves as the mother of this baby, and most were vocal about never having the emotions that they felt toward their 'own' child" (299). The third is from Zsuzsa Berend, "Surrogate Losses: Understandings of Pregnancy Loss and Assisted Reproduction among Surrogate Mothers," *Medical Anthropology Quarterly* 24.2 (2010): 240–262 at 242–243. The fourth is from Jacobson, *Labor of Love*, 58, with Jacobson also reporting all thirty-one of her U.S. surrogates expressed similar sentiments. The fifth is from Yuri Hibino and Yosuke Shimazono, "Becoming a Surrogate Online: 'Message Board' Surrogacy in Thailand," *Asian Bioethics Review* 5.1 (2013): 56–72 at 65, with the

authors finding all Thai subjects interviewed in Bangkok in 2010 were "confident" they could "control their emotions" and none reported pain or regret upon relinquishment (65).

27. Virginie Rozée, Sayeed Unisa, and Elise de La Rochebrochard, "The Social Paradoxes of Commercial Surrogacy in Developing Countries: India before the New Law of 2018," *BMC Women's Health* 20.234 (2020), https://doi.org/10.1186/S12905-020-01 087-2.

28. van den Akker, *Surrogate Motherhood Families*, 178.

29. Hibino and Shimazono, "Becoming a Surrogate Online," 67.

30. Ashley Padilla, quoted in Jacobson, *Labor of Love*,103.

31. See Vasanti Jadva et al. "Surrogacy Families 10 Years On: Relationship with the Surrogate, Decisions over Disclosure and Children's Understanding of Their Surrogacy Origins," *Human Reproduction* 27.10 (2012): 3008–14 at 3010–11.

32. See Helena Ragoné in *Surrogate Motherhood: Conception in the Heart* (New York: Routledge, 1994), 79, Teman, "The Social Construction of Surrogacy Research," 1109, and Zsuzsa Berend, "The Romance of Surrogacy," *Sociological Forum* 27.4 (2012): 913–936 at 926–928.

33. Teman, *Birthing a Mother*, 30.

34. Golombok et al., "Families Created through Surrogacy Arrangements," 403, 408.

35. See Susan Golombok et al., "Surrogacy Families: Parental Functioning, Parent–Child Relationships and Children's Psychological Development at Age 2," *Journal of Child Psychology & Psychiatry* 47.2 (2006): 213–222 at 219 and Susan Golombok et al., "Non-Genetic and Non-Gestational Parenthood: Consequences for Parent-Child Relationships and the Psychological Well-being of Mothers, Fathers and Children at Age 3," *Human Reproduction* 21.7 (2006): 1918–1924 at 1922–1923.

36. For analogous accounts of "living with uncertainty" when embarking on a surrogacy journey from the perspective of gay male couples and of the positive outcomes they experienced thereafter, see Samuel Sanabria, "When Adoption Is Not an Option: Counseling Implications Related to Surrogacy," *Journal of Gay and Lesbian Social Services* 25 (2013): 269–286 at 273 and Kim Bergman et al., "Gay Men Who Become Fathers via Surrogacy: The Transition to Parenthood," *Journal of GLBT Family Studies* 6.2 (2010): 111–141.

37. Quoted in Bergman et al., "Gay Men Who Become Fathers via Surrogacy," 125.

38. Mitchell and Green, "Different Storks for Different Folks," 89.

39. Mitchell and Green, 82.

40. One gay couple, Drew and Nico, worked out the matter thusly: Nico had a strong urge to become a biological father but Drew, who was also a known donor to a lesbian couple, did not personally care if he was biologically related to his kids and thus wanted to facilitate his partner's yearning. See Maura Ryan and Dana Berkowitz, "Constructing Gay and Lesbian Parent Families 'Beyond the Closet,'" *Qualitative Sociology* 32.2 (2009): 153–172 at 161–163.

41. Mitchell and Green, "Different Storks for Different Folks," 91.

42. Dempsey, "Surrogacy, Gay Male Couples and the Significance of Biogenetic Paternity," 45.

43. Dempsey, 45.

44. Dempsey, 47.

45. Another approach has been called the "gold standard" for gay couples: use *one* egg donor, fertilize half with one partner's sperm and the other half with the other's, transfer two embryos at a time (the "best quality" from each) into the same surrogate, and if both embryos implant and eventuate in live births, the twins would be biological half-siblings (due to use of the same egg donor) with both partners becoming fathers genetically related to their children at the same time. See Camisha Russell, "Rights-Holders or Refugees? Do Gay Men Need Reproductive Justice?" *Reproductive Biomedicine and Society Online* 7 (2018): 131–140 at 137. To be sure, the organization Men Having Babies discourages this option in their "Framework for Ethical Surrogacy for Intended Parents" because of the increased risks multiple gestation poses to the babies and the surrogate. See https://menhavingbabies.org/cms-data/depot/docs/MHB_Framework-for-Ethical-Surrogacy_2016_MHB-Handout.pdf. In chapter 6, I discuss another way both partners could be biologically related to their child: one partner is the genetic father and the other's sister is either their egg donor or traditional surrogate.

46. Mitchell and Green, "Different Storks for Different Folks," 89–91; Dempsey, "Surrogacy, Gay Male Couples and the Significance of Biogenetic Paternity," 46, 48–50. Murphy in *Gay Men Pursuing Parenthood* calls this "strategic silence" (219).

47. In this eponymous, 2010 Golden Globe–winning film, the lives of a queer family with teenagers suddenly change after they begin interacting with their genetic father who was previously a non-identified sperm donor at their grown children's instigation.

48. Susan Golombok and Fiona Tasker, "Socio-emotional Development in Changing Families," in *Handbook of Child Psychology and Developmental Science, vol. 3: Socioemotional Processes, 7th ed.*, ed. Richard R. Lerner 419-463 (Hoboken, New Jersey: Wiley, 2015).

49. Susan Golombok et al., "A Longitudinal Study of Families Formed Through Reproductive Donation: Parent-Adolescent Relationships and Adolescent Adjustment at Age 14," *Developmental Psychology* 53.10 (2017): 1966–1977.

50. Susan Golombok et al., "Parenting and the Adjustment of Children Born to Gay Fathers through Surrogacy," *Child Development* 89.4 (2018): 1223–1233 at 1228–1230.

51. Jadva et al., "Surrogacy Families 10 Years On," 3011–3012.

52. van den Akker, *Surrogate Motherhood Families*, 187.

53. Susan Golombok, "I've Spent Decades Studying How People Build Their Families. Here's What I've Learned Matters Most," *Time*, Oct 14, 2020, https://time.com/5899546/family-structures/.

54. Susan Golombok et al., "Children Born through Reproductive Donation: A Longitudinal Study of Psychological Development," *Journal of Child Psychology and Psychiatry* 54.6 (2013): 653–660 at 657.

55. Quoted in Jadva et al., "Surrogacy Families 10 Years On," 3011. In contrast, other studies have shown that even if the parents of donor-conceived children tell them about their genetic origins at the same age (7), few kids understand it. Researchers speculate that it is likely easier for young children to understand what is involved in gestational surrogacy since they can imagine being born to another person (other than their mother) than it is for them to understand other forms of donor-assisted reproduction, since the latter requires knowledge about gametes and fertilization. See Lucy Blake et al., "'Daddy Ran Out of Tadpoles': How Parents Tell Their Children That They Are Donor Conceived, and What Their 7-Year-Olds Understand," *Human Reproduction* 25. 10 (2010): 2527–2534 at 2532-2533.

56. Golombok et al., "Children Born through Reproductive Donation," 658 and Golombok et al., "A Longitudinal Study of Families Formed through Reproductive Donation," 1967, 1973-1974.

57. See Jadva et al., Surrogacy Families 10 Years On," 3012 and Golombok et al., "Non-Genetic and Non-Gestational Parenthood," 1922. Spanish psychologists have also concluded that "the well-being of the child seems to be associated with the maintenance of a relationship with the surrogate and the amount of contact with her" (189). See Nicolás Ruiz-Robledillo and Luis Moya-Albiol, "Gestational Surrogacy: Psychosocial Aspects," *Psychosocial Intervention* 25 (2016): 187–193.

58. An example of a neutral/different response to their feelings about their surrogate birth is the following: "Um, I feel fine. I don't feel bad or cross in anyway. It's just pretty much nature so I can't do anything about it. I wouldn't like to do anything about it." Jadva et al., "Surrogacy Families 10 Years On," 3012.

59. As one child said: "[She] was really kind about . . . carrying me in her tummy." See Jadva et al., "Surrogacy Families 10 Years On," 3011; van Den Akker, *Surrogate Motherhood Families*, 178.

60. Jacobson, *Labor of Love*, 66.

61. Berend, "Romance of Surrogacy," 923.

62. Vasanti Jadva and Susan Imrie, "Children of Surrogate Mothers: Psychological Well-Being, Family Relationships and Experiences of Surrogacy," *Human Reproduction* 29.1 (2014): 90–96 at 95. All thirty-six of the children interviewed were between twelve and twenty-five years of age whose mothers had been either a traditional or gestational surrogate five to fifteen years prior to the interview.

63. Jadva and Imrie, "Children of Surrogate Mothers," 93. There was one child out of the thirty-six interviewed who was coded as having "some difficulties" following the handover initially, a few months later, and currently. All others reported no difficulties at all with the handover.

64. The other 14% were coded as having "neutral/ambivalent" responses, such as the following from the child of a traditional surrogate: "Um, I don't have a problem with it, if mum wants to do it that's her prerogative" (Jadva and Imrie, 95).

65. Jacobson, *Labor of Love*, 143.

66. Jacobson, 152.

67. Van den Akker, *Surrogate Motherhood Families*, 93.

68. Jadva and Imrie, "Children of Surrogate Mothers," 95-96.

69. Sarah A. Phillips, *The Kangaroo Pouch: A Story about Surrogacy for Young Children*, 3rd ed. (Geneva, IL: Haven Stone Media, 2017 [2006]).

70. What we did not know, however, is how their classmates and friends would handle my news, since any explanation of how and why "PJ and KC's mom is pregnant with a child who won't become their baby sister" would involve rudimentary sex education. We thus talked to their elementary school teachers, Cub Scout den leaders, and some of their friends' parents about it in advance.

71. Linda Kirkman's 1999 statement, quoted in Maggie Kirkman, "Sister-to-Sister Gestational 'Surrogacy' 13 Years On: A Narrative of Parenthood," *Journal of Reproductive and Infant Psychology* 20.3 (2002): 135–147 at 138.

72. See Kirkman, "Sister-to-Sister Gestational 'Surrogacy' 13 Years On," 138.

73. See, for example, Corinne H. Rocca et al. "Emotions and Decision Rightness over Five Years Following an Abortion: An Examination of Decision Difficulty and Abortion Stigma," *Social Science & Medicine* 248 (2020), https://doi.org/10.1016/j.socscimed.2019.112704.

Chapter 3

1. Barbara Katz Rothman, "On Markens," *Sociological Forum* 26.1 (2011): 201–205 at 202.

2. Katha Pollit, "The Strange Case of Baby M," *The Nation*, May 23, 1987, reprinted on Jan 2, 1998, https://www.thenation.com/article/archive/strange-case-baby-m/.

3. Rosemarie Tong, "The Overdue Death of a Feminist Chameleon: Taking a Stand on Surrogacy," *Journal of Social Philosophy* 21–2.3 (1990): 40–56 at 40–41.

4. *MC. v. CM*, 138 S. Ct. 239 (2017) (*amici curiae* brief of Fifteen Feminist Academics and Advocates, at 10) (*cert. denied*). The brief is available here: https://www.thecassidylawfirm.com/global_pictures/Feminists_Amicus_Brief.pdf.

5. Pollitt, "The Strange Case of Baby M."

6. Gloria Steinem's open letter has been made available in a Jun 11, 2019 blog at the Center for Bioethics and Culture, https://cbc-network.org/2019/06/gloria-steinem-calls-to-not-legalize-commercial-surrogacy/.

7. See Suki Finn, "Metaphysics of Surrogacy" in *The Palgrave Handbook of Philosophy and Public Policy*, ed. David Boonin, 649–659 (Cham, Switzerland: Palgrave MacMillan/Springer International Publishing, 2018), Elselijn Kingma, "Were You Part of Your Mother?" *Mind* 128.511 (2019): 609–646, and Grace Kao, "Thinking Through the 'Metaphysics of Pregnancy' and Surrogacy," Roundtable on *Trust Women: A Progressive Christian Argument for Reproductive Justice* (Rebecca Todd Peters), Apr 24, 2019; https://syndicate.network/symposia/theology/trust-women/.

8. Sharon Jacob, *Reading Mary Alongside of Indian Surrogate Mothers: Violent Love, Oppressive Liberation, and Infancy Narratives* (New York: Palgrave Macmillan, 2015), 28.

9. Elly Teman, *Birthing a Mother: The Surrogate Body and the Pregnant Self* (Berkeley: University of California Press, 2010), 35.

10. Suki Finn, "Bun vs. Bump? Does the Mother Contain the Foetus or Is It Part of

Her?," *Aeon*, Jul 27, 2017, https://aeon.co/essays/is-the-mother-a-container-for-the
-foetus-or-is-it-part-of-her.

11. Phyllis Chesler and Susan L. Bender "Commercial Surrogacy Breeds False
Equality between Sperm, Egg and Nine Months of Pregnancy and Childbirth," *New
York Law Journal*, Mar 8, 2019.

12. Gena Corea, *The Mother Machine: Reproductive Technologies from Artificial
Insemination to Artificial Wombs* (New York: Harper Collins, 1985), 232.

13. Janice G. Raymond, *Women as Wombs: Reproductive Technologies and the
Battle over Women's Freedom* (San Francisco: HarperSanFrancisco, 1993), 57.

14. Lisa Sowle Cahill, *Sex, Gender, Christian Ethics* (New York: Cambridge University Press, 1996), 254, 243, 242, 245–246.

15. Ethics and Religious Liberty Commission of the Southern Baptist Convention,
"Issue Analysis: Surrogacy," Jul 10, 2014, https://erlc.com/resource-library/articles
/issue-analysis-surrogacy.

16. *Donum Vitae* IIA1. *Donum Vitae* continues Catholic social teaching on keeping
the unitive and procreative dimensions of marital intercourse conjoined and intact.
This trajectory includes Pope Paul VI's 1968 instruction in *Humanae Vitae* ("Of
Human Life") about the "inseparable connection" between union and procreation
(§11–12), Pope Pius XII's May 19, 1956, address to the Second World Congress on Fertility and Sterility condemning practices that sever the connection between conjugal
love and procreative possibilities, and Pope Pius XI's 1930 instruction in *Casti Connubii* ("On Christian Marriage") that the "conjugal act is destined primarily by nature
for the begetting of children," thus those who seek to "deliberately frustrate its natural
power and purpose sin against nature" (§54).

17. *Donum Vitae* IIA3.

18. John Berkman, "Gestating the Embryos of Others: Surrogacy? Adoption?
Rescue?" *National Catholic Bioethics Quarterly* 3.2 (2003): 309–329 at 312.

19. According to the Orthodox Church in America, married couples may licitly
"express their love in sexual union without always intending the conception of a
child" so long as their "means of controlling conception . . . do not harm a fetus already conceived." They may even use "medical means to enhance conception of their
common children," but are forbidden from using donor gametes to do so. See the
section entitled "The Procreation of Children," in the Orthodox Church in America's
Synodal Affirmations on Marriage, Family, Sexuality, and the Sanctity of Life, Jul
1992, https://www.oca.org/holy-synod/statements/holy-synod/synodal-affirmations
-on-marriage-family-sexuality-and-the-sanctity-of-life.

20. Russell Moore, "How Should Christians Think about Surrogacy?" *The Gospel
Coalition*, Jan 14, 2019, https://www.thegospelcoalition.org/video/russell-moore-sur
rogacy/.

21. See Scott B. Rae and D. Joy Riley, *Outside the Womb: Moral Guidance for Assisted Reproduction* (Chicago: Moody, 2011), 41.

22. Allen Verhey, *Reading the Bible in the Strange World of Medicine* (Grand Rapids,
MI: Wm. B. Eerdmans, 2003), 267, 281.

23. Verhey, *Reading the Bible in the Strange World of Medicine*, 279, 292–293.

24. Russian Orthodox Church, "The Basis of the Social Concept," Section XII Problems of Bioethics, §4, 2004, http://orthodoxrights.org/documents/the-basis-of -the-social-concept/xii.

25. The Ethics and Religious Liberty Commission of the Southern Baptist Convention, "Issue Analysis: Surrogacy."

26. Several contributors in the following volume hold this view, though not the co-editors: Sarah-Vaughan Brakman and Darlene Fozard Weaver, *The Ethics of Embryo Adoption and the Catholic Tradition: Moral Arguments, Economic Reality and Social Analysis* (New York: Springer, 2007), 144.

27. Mark E. Lones, "A Christian Ethical Perspective on Surrogacy," *Bioethics in Faith and Practice* 2.1 (2016), https://digitalcommons.cedarville.edu/bioethics_in_faith _and_practice/vol2/iss1/5 at 29–30.

28. *Donum Vitae* I.1.

29. Russian Orthodox Church, "The Basis of the Social Concept," Section XII: Problems of Bioethics, §2, §4.

30. Russell Moore, "Is Embryo Adoption Immoral?" Feb 22, 2010, https://www.rus sellmoore.com/2010/02/22/is-embryo-adoption-immoral/.

31. Rae and Riley, *Outside the Womb*, 152–154, 160–161. Matthew Arbo, the Director of the Center for Faith and Public Life at Oklahoma Baptist University and a Research Fellow in Christian Ethics for the SBC, has provided similar counsel for couples to only attempt to create one fertilized egg at a time. Should they fail to take his advice and end up with multiple embryos, he urges them to attempt to bring them all to life over a period of successive ET procedures, unless doing so would be impossible (e.g., the wife has undergone a hysterectomy or died), in which case they should allow others to "adopt" them. See his Matthew Arbo, *Walking Through Infertility: Biblical, Theological, and Moral Counsel for Those Who Are Struggling* (Wheaton, IL: Crossway, 2018), 89.

32. According to Christian ethicist Allen Verhey, both adoption ministries are grounded in the "adoptive love of God." Similarly, Russell Moore holds it would be entirely "Christ-like" for Christians to "ope[n] our hearts, and our homes, *and sometimes our wombs*, to the least of these," which is why he encourages those "called to adopt" these embryos not to fear becoming complicit in their wrongful "production" any more than parents who adopt children "from an unwed mother [should therein fear] endorsing fornication or adultery" (emphasis added). See Verhey, *Reading the Bible in the Strange World of Medicine*, 300 and Moore, "Should Christians Adopt Embryos?" Sep 20, 2012, https://www.russellmoore.com/2012/09/20/should-christians -adopt-embryos/. It is worth noting that his desire to save embryonic or fetal life from destruction is not absolute: he could imagine scenarios where couples could justifiably donate their "spare" embryos to research, and he also neither rules out some uses of preimplantation genetic diagnosis or screening (PGD/PGS) even if it leads to the couple not selecting the "affected" embryo for transfer, nor objects to some uses of prenatal testing even if it leads to an abortion (165–166, 187, 245–250, 299).

33. Berkman, "Gestating the Embryos of Others"; The Human Fertilisation and Embryology Act 1990 https://www.legislation.gov.uk/ukpga/1990/37/contents.

34. Among others, Catholic theologians Sarah-Vaughn Brakman and Darlene Fozard Weaver have argued "there is no more vulnerable than these early humans," which is why they advocate for the "morally praiseworthy" alternative of embryo adoption even after many Catholic commentators have interpreted *Dignitas Personae* (2008) as ruling out its permissibility. See their "Embryo Adoption before and after *Dignitatis Personae*: Defending an Argument of Limited Permissibility," in *Contemporary Controversies in Catholic Bioethics*, ed. Jason T. Eberl, 147–167 (Cham, Switzerland: Springer, 2017), 161, 149. See also Whitny Braun, "May You Live in Interesting Times: The Brave New World of Embryo Adoption," *Huffington Post*, Mar 20, 2017, https://www.huffpost.com/entry/may-you-live-in-interesti_1_b _9508690.

35. See Braun, "May You Live in Interesting Times" and Braun, "Embryo Adoptions: The Alternative That's on the Rise," Take Two, *KPCC*, May 18, 2016, https://www.scpr.org/programs/take-two/2016/05/18/48961/embryo-adoptions-the-alternative-that-s-on-the-ris/. See Nightlife Christian Adoption, "Why Choose Our Snowflakes Embryo Adoption Program?" https://www.nightlight.org/snowflakes-embryo-adoption-donation/embryo-adoption/.

36. To illustrate by way of Rae and Wiley's real-life example: a married couple had five embryos left from IVF but could no longer transfer them because of the wife's emergency hysterectomy following their tragic miscarriage of their IVF-conceived triplets. Surrogacy in their judgment would be "acceptable damage control to prevent the much more problematic discarding of embryos" while also facilitating the desired "continuity between procreation and parenting." Joe Carter of the SBC has reasoned similarly about a "rescue surrogacy" situation, when a woman "volunteers her womb to save an IVF-created embryo that has been frozen and is destined for destruction." See Rae and Riley, *Outside the Womb*, 51–52, and Joe Carter, "9 Things You Should Know About Surrogacy," *The Gospel Coalition*, Jun 6, 2014, https://www.thegospelcoalition.org/article/9-things-you-should-know-about-surrogacy/.

37. Bender and Chesler further suspect many IPs opt for surrogacy over adoption because of their "genetic narcissism," racism (since the majority of children available for adoption in the U.S. are racial-ethnic minorities), or "desire not to be investigated" since the state screens potential adoptive parents before children can be placed in their care in ways they do not typically in surrogacy. Susan L. Bender and Phyllis Chesler, "Handmaids for Hire: Should Commercial Surrogacy be Legalized in NYS?" *New York Law Journal*, Feb 21, 2019, https://www.law.com/newyorklawjournal/2019/02/22/handmaids-for-hire-should-commercial-surrogacy-be-legalized-in-nys/?slreturn=20190220230639. To be clear, they do not oppose uncompensated, altruistic surrogacy arrangements among friends or relatives.

38. An estimated 60–70% of all domestic adoptions in the U.S. are open. See "Adoption Statistics and Legal Trends," *FindLaw*, Oct 10, 2019, https://www.findlaw.com/family/adoption/adoption-statistics-and-legal-trends.html.

39. Mary Warnock, chair, *Report of the Committee of Inquiry into Human Fertilisation and Embryology* (London: Her Majesty's Stationery Office, 1984). Philosopher Bonnie Steinbock outlines Warnock's three other major moral objections to surro-

gacy: (1) it is against human dignity for a woman to use her uterus for profit, (2) surrogacy degrades because it amounts to child-selling, (3) women should not be asked to undergo surrogacy for profit given the risks of pregnancy. See Bonnie Steinbock, "Surrogate Motherhood as Prenatal Adoption," *Journal of Law, Medicine & Ethics* 16.1/2 (1988): 44–50 .

40. See, for example, Lisa Sowle Cahill, "Adoption: A Roman Catholic Perspective," in Timothy Jackson, *The Morality of Adoption: Social-Psychological, Theological, and Legal Perspectives,* 148–170 (Grand Rapids, MI: Eerdmans, 2005).

41. Cahill, *Sex, Gender, Christian Ethics,* 247.

42. Gilbert C. Meilander, *Not by Nature but by Grace: Forming Families through Adoption* (Notre Dame, IN: University of Notre Dame Press, 2016), 70–71.

43. To be sure, U.K. courts have ruled that even someone considered legally a man who gives birth must still be listed as "mother"—not "father" or "parent" on the child's birth certificate because of the child's right to know the biological circumstances surrounding their birth. See Robert Booth, "Trans Man Loses UK Legal Battle to Register as His Child's Father," *The Guardian,* Nov 16, 2020, https://www.theguardian.com /society/2020/nov/16/trans-man-loses-uk-legal-battle-to-register-as-his-childs-father.

44. See Gloria Steinem's Jun 11, 2019 Open Letter; https://cbc-network.org/2019/06 /gloria-steinem-calls-to-not-legalize-commercial-surrogacy/.

45. I will return to discussing what to make of unequal power dynamics in surrogacy arrangements in chapters 5–6.

46. Some states already mandate these protections. In Florida, IPs must contractually stipulate that the surrogate is "the sole source of consent with respect to clinical intervention and management of the pregnancy." The legislature of Indiana has similarly declared it to be "against public policy" to enforce the terms of a surrogacy agreement if the surrogate were contractually required to do one of several things, including "consent to undergo or undergo an abortion." In New York's "Gestational Surrogates' Bill of Rights," surrogates have the "right to make all health and welfare decisions regarding themselves and their pregnancy," including the decision to "continue or end the pregnancy" or to "keep or reduce the number of fetuses or embryos they are carrying." See Florida Statute §742.15 (3) (a), http://www.leg.state.fl.us/statutes/index.cfm ?App_mode=Display_Statute&URL=0700-0799/0742/0742.html, Indiana Code §31-20-1-1 (3), http://iga.in.gov/legislative/laws/2018/ic/titles/031#31-20-1-1, and the State of New York's Child Parent Security Act/Gestational Surrogacy, https://health.ny.gov /community/pregnancy/surrogacy/surrogate_bill_of_rights.htm.

47. As per philosopher Judith Jarvis Thompson's celebrated defense of abortion, any "right to life" a fetus might have still would not translate into an obligation for a pregnant person to do everything in their power to preserve it because they have something akin to a property right over their own body. See her "A Defense of Abortion," *Philosophy & Public Affairs* 1.1 (1971): 47–66.

48. Alex Kuczynski, "Her Body, My Baby," *New York Times Magazine,* Nov 28, 2008, https://www.nytimes.com/2008/11/30/magazine/30Surrogate-t.html.

49. See Victoria Ward, "Sir Elton John Boycotts Dolce & Gabbana after Row over

Same-Sex Families," *The Telegraph*, Mar 15, 2015, https://www.telegraph.co.uk/news /celebritynews/11473198/Sir-Elton-John-calls-for-Dolce-and-Gabbana-boycott-after -row-over-same-sex-families.html.

50. This is the essence of William May's argument for the moral permissibility of embryo adoption against those who hold HET necessarily involves marital infidelity. I also find telling that other Catholic moral theologians including John Berkman oppose surrogacy, but not because surrogacy represents adultery. See Brakman and Fozard Weaver, *The Ethics of Embryo Adoption and the Catholic Tradition*, 145.

51. *Humane Vitae*, §11, §12. My rejection of the "inseparability thesis" aligns me with the general stance taken by most Orthodox churches, most Protestant denominations today, and the Anglican Communion in holding that Christians can still take the "embodied and communal character of human begetting" seriously by keeping both "lovemaking and baby-making" generally in the context of marriage and family *without* requiring each and every unitive act to remain open to the creation of new life. See Verhey, *Reading the Bible in the Strange World of Medicine*, 165, 282; Stanley S. Harakas, "The Stand of the Orthodox Church on Controversial Issues," Greek Orthodox Archdiocese of America, Aug 2, 1985, https://www.goarch .org/-/the-stand-of-the-orthodox-church-on-controversial-issues; and Resolution 15 of The Lambeth Conference, 1930, Anglican Communion Office, 2005; https:// www.anglicancommunion.org/media/127734/1930.pdf.

To be sure, the *Magisterium*'s own teaching in *Humane Vitae* §16 that a married couple must avoid artificial contraception but can "take advantage of the natural cycles immanent in the reproductive system and engage in marital intercourse only during those times that are infertile" if they have "well-grounded reasons for spacing birth" appears to my non-Catholic sensibilities as ultimately a distinction without a moral difference, just as it strikes some dissident Catholics as problematic for its hyper "physicalism or biologism." See Charles E. Curran, "Roman Catholic Sexual Ethics: A Dissenting View," *Christian Century* Dec 16, 1987, 1139–1142. Reprinted in *Religion Online*, https://www.religion-online.org/article/roman-catholic-sexual-ethics-a-dis senting-view/.

52. The Religious Institute, "Religious Declaration on Sexual Morality, Justice, and Healing," Jan 2000, http://religiousinstitute.org/religious-declaration-on-sexual-mor ality-justice-and-healing/.

53. Margaret Farley, "Feminist Theology and Bioethics" in *Women's Consciousness, Women's Conscience: A Reader in Feminist Ethics*, ed. Barbara Hilkert Andolsen, Christine E. Gudorf, and Mary D. Pellauer, 285–305 (Minneapolis, MN: Winston Press, 1985), 301. Christian bioethicist Scott R. Paeth has also argued that IVF could still affirm the "embodied and communal dimensions" of childbearing even if the "clinical setting . . . removes the relationship between physical love and procreation" by allowing married couples to "express their love in the context of a family relationship" and accordingly "overcome[e] the encumbrance to parenthood caused by infertility." See his "Eight Is Enough? The Ethics of the California Octuplets Case," *Christian Bioethics* 18.3 (2012): 252–270 at 259.

54. Robert B. Allen and Michelle Hester, "Babies Grow Up," Apr 6, 2021, https://www.shadygrovefertility.com/emotional-support-articles/babies-grow.

55. David Dodge, "What I Spent to Adopt My Child," *New York Times*, Feb 11, 2020, https://www.nytimes.com/2020/02/11/parenting/adoption-costs.html.

56. Darlene Fozard Weaver, "Adoption, Social justice, and Catholic Tradition," *Journal of Catholic Social Thought* 13.2 (2016): 197–213. Importantly, Weaver draws our attention to the dangers in the clerical tendency to mention adoption primarily in response to infertility or when denouncing assisted reproductive technologies, abortion, or adoption by same-sex couples, since doing so ultimately "does a disserve to children and adoptive families" by "distorting the witness adoptive families provide" (207, 197).

57. Cf. "[R]esponsible parenthood is exercised by those who prudently and generously decide to have more children, and by those who, for serious reasons and with due respect to moral precepts, decide not to have additional children for either a certain or an indefinite period of time" (*Humane Vitae*, §10).

58. Maura A. Ryan, *Ethics and Economics of Assisted Reproduction: The Cost of Longing* (Washington, D.C.: Georgetown University Press, 2001), 57.

59. As clinical psychologist-psychoanalyst Freeman-Carroll has noted: "No matter what the merits of adoption may be (and they are many), for the couple that cannot conceive when and how they want to, this feels like a burden, a cost, or even a punishment for their infertility. In the privacy of my consulting room, I hear the sorrow, outrage and discomfort aroused by such suggestions, and the corresponding worry about the social consequences for use of assisted reproduction" (46). See Nancy Freeman-Carroll, "The Possibilities and Pitfalls of Talking about Conception with Donor Egg: Why Parents Struggle and How Clinicians Can Help," *Journal of Infant, Child, and Adolescent Psychotherapy* 15:1 (2016): 40–50. For separate reasons, Maura A. Ryan likewise challenges the commonplace presentation of adoption as superior in all ways when it, too, is influenced by "market values." See her *Ethics and Economics of Assisted Reproduction*, 65 at n30.

60. Some adult adoptees have been challenging the dominant "adoption as child rescue" narrative as well as chafing at the social expectation for them to display nothing short of eternal gratitude for having been "saved" from circumstances surrounding their birth. Others have argued the best way to help relieve the suffering of children born from crisis or unwanted pregnancies is to create more pathways to help more poor or at-risk birth mothers find the support they need to parent them themselves rather than feel compelled to place them for adoption. To wit, Catholic Relief Services estimates that some eight million children around the world live in orphanages or residential care facilities, but a staggering 80–90% of them have at least one living parent, with poverty being the primary reason they ended up in institutionalized care. See, for example, Dorothy Roberts, *Shattered Bonds: The Color of Child Welfare* (New York: Basic Civitas Books, 2002), Laura Briggs, *Somebody's Children: The Politics of Transracial and Transnational Adoption* (Durham, NC: Duke University Press, 2012), and Catholic Relief Services, *Changing the Way We Care*, https://www.crs.org/our-work-overseas/program-areas/youth/changing-the-way-we-care.

61. Barbara Katz Rothman, "On Markens," *Sociological Forum* 26.1 (2011): 201–205 at 203. The National Organization for Women (NOW), the New York Catholic Conference, and the New York Civil Liberties Union even joined together in an *amicus* brief to oppose surrogacy in the State of New York in the early 1990s. Anemona Hartocollis, "And Surrogacy Makes 3," *New York Times*, Feb 19, 2014, https://www.nytimes.com/2014/02/20/fashion/In-New-York-Some-Couples-Push-for-Legalization-of-Compensated-Surrogacy.html?hpw&rref=fashion&_r=0.

62. "Stop Surrogacy Now Statement," available at https://cbc-network.org/stop-surrogacy-now/. For the quotation about Jennifer Lahl, the president of the CBC, see Chris Lisee, "Conservatives Line Up against Sperm Donors, but Lack the Power to Ban Them," *Religion News Service*, Jun 27, 2012, https://religionnews.com/2012/06/27/conservatives-line-up-against-sperm-donors-but-lack-the-power-to-ban-them/.

63. See, for example, Joan Frawley Desmond, "Unlikely Ally: Feminist Gloria Steinem Joins Fight against Surrogacy," *National Catholic Register*, Jun 19, 2019, https://www.ncregister.com/interview/unlikely-ally-feminist-gloria-steinem-joins-fight-against-surrogacy and "Feminists, Catholics Both Find Reasons to Oppose NY Paid Surrogacy Bill," *Catholic World Report*, Jun 13, 2019, https://www.catholicworldreport.com/2019/06/13/feminists-catholics-both-find-reasons-to-oppose-ny-paid-surrogacy-bill/.

Chapter 4

1. "Melissa" is a pseudonym to protect my friend's privacy.

2. John Keats, "Endymion" (1818).

3. One study of 124 gestational surrogates found that the women incurred more perinatal risks of "preterm birth, low birth weight, hypertension, maternal gestational diabetes, and placenta previa" than they did in their previous non-ART pregnancies of singletons. The researchers concluded that ART procedures might "potentially affect embryo quality and that its negative impact cannot be overcome even with a proven healthy uterine environment" (993). See Irene Woo et al., "Perinatal Outcomes after Natural Conception Versus In Vitro Fertilization (IVF) in Gestational Surrogates: A Model to Evaluate IVF Treatment versus Maternal Effects," *Fertility and Sterility* 108.6 (2017): 993–998 at 993.

4. Practical theologian Duane R. Bidwell describes this last norm in terms of an openness of the covenantal partners to the "care of generations." Margaret Farley's norm of "fruitfulness" for all relationships characterized by "just love" and "just sex" is similar in her requirement they serve more than just the two persons involved. See especially chapter 1 of his *Empowering Couples: A Narrative Approach to Spiritual Care* (Minneapolis, MN: Fortress Press, 2013) and chapter 6 of Margaret A. Farley's *Just Love: A Framework for Christian Sexual Ethics* (New York: Continuum, 2006).

5. For instance, I could imagine one spouse dying in the course of pursuing ART and the widow(er) electing to press on with their childbearing plans. Or siblings living together non-incestuously having reasons for wanting to raise a child together (e.g., to carry on the family name, traditions, or business). These and other exceptions notwithstanding, my account of surrogacy still largely presumes the norm of children

"belonging" to designated parents in families. In this way, my project is not like Sophie Lewis's whose critical reflections on surrogacy led her to endorse utopian socialist ideas of family abolition, where children could be raised instead in a "classless commune" because they would not properly belong to anyone. See her *Full Surrogacy Now: Feminism against the Family* (London: Verso, 2019), 26, 4.

6. Uterine transplantation has emerged as a cutting edge of reproductive technology for women suffering from absolute uterine factor infertility (AUFI). The world's first baby was born to a woman with a transplanted uterus from a live donor in Sweden in 2014, the world's first baby was born to a woman with a transplanted uterus from a deceased donor in Brazil in 2017, and clinical trials of uterine transplantation are taking place in parts of the U.S., Europe, and Asia. See Dani Ejzenberg et al., "Live-birth after Uterus Transplantation from a Deceased Donor in a Recipient with Uterine Infertility," *The Lancet* 392.10165 (2018): 2697–2704.

Should ART advance in such a way where infertile women and others (i.e., transgender persons, cisgender men) could become pregnant with a donor uterus beyond clinical trials or where prospective parents could bear their own child(ren) via an artificial womb our ethical analysis of surrogacy would accordingly be affected. We would then have to consider the appropriateness of the parent hopefuls passing on the physical risks of IVF and gestation to a third party, or if either of the IPs should pursue uterine transplant surgery for pregnancy and childbirth (if either were suitable candidates) and therein incur the medical risks themselves. We would also have to compare a surrogate's willingness to allow the IPs to use her womb to bear their child against another other-regarding, but even riskier and more sacrificial way she could help them realize their family expansion plans: she could donate her uterus to them instead if her own family were complete and concomitantly provide the IPs an additional desideratum: the ability for one of them to experience a pregnancy firsthand. Should ectogenesis in humans someday become possible, we would likewise have to assess its ethics and projected risks and rewards in comparison to the same in surrogacy. See Amel Alghrani, "Uterus Transplantation in and beyond Cisgender Women: Revisiting Procreative Liberty in Light of Emerging Reproductive Technologies," *Journal of Law and the Biosciences* 5.2 (2018): 301–328, Lisa Guntram and Nicola Jane Williams, "Positioning Uterus Transplantation as a 'More Ethical' Alternative to Surrogacy: Exploring Symmetries between Uterus Transplantation and Surrogacy through Analysis of a Swedish Government White Paper," *Bioethics* 32.8 (2018): 509–518, and Seppe Segers, "The Path toward Ectogenesis: Looking beyond the Technical Challenges," *BMC Medical Ethics* 22.59 (2021), https://doi.org/10.1186/s12910-021-00630-6.

7. See David Benatar, *The Human Predicament: A Candid Guide to Life's Biggest Questions* (New York: Oxford University Press, 2017), 76; see also his earlier *Better Never to Have Been: The Harm of Coming into Existence* (New York: Oxford University Press, 2006).

8. In commenting on a rise in belief that "refrain[ing] from having children . . . is the only environmentally sound position they can take in an 'overpopulated,' over-

consuming society," Loretta Ross affirms the reproductive justice framework's commitment to the human right of each individual to determine whether they will (or will not) become a parent: "No one has the responsibility to remain childless based on concern for the 'environmental good.'" See Loretta J. Ross and Rickie Solinger, *Reproductive Justice: An Introduction* (Oakland, CA: University of California Press, 2017), 234.

9. Margaret A. Farley, "Feminist Consciousness and the Interpretation of Scripture," in *Feminist Interpretation of the Bible*, ed. Letty M. Russell, 41–51 (Louisville, KY: Westminster John Knox Press, 1985) at 44, 50.

10. Renita J. Weems, "Re-reading for Liberation: African American Women and the Bible," in *Womanist Theological Ethics: A Reader*, ed. Katie Geneva Cannon, Emilie M. Townes, and Angela D. Sims, 51–63 (Louisville, KY: Westminster John Knox Press, 2011) at 61.

11. Allen Verhey, *Reading the Bible in the Strange World of Medicine* (Grand Rapids, MI: Eerdmans, 2003), 217.

12. Admittedly, others might still bristle at the biblical intimation that (restored) fertility is either a reward for righteousness or God's answer to a fervent prayer and feel even more alone after reading passages such as the Psalmist's praise "He gives the barren woman a home, making her the joyous mother of children" (Ps. 113:9) when God has not "blessed" a person with a child. For these contrasting reactions, see Gina Messina, "Cursing God (Infertility)," in *Encountering the Sacred: Feminist Reflections on Women's Lives*, ed. Rebecca Todd Peters and Grace Y. Kao (London: T&T Clark, 2018) 119–131 at 121–122 and Courtney Reissig, "A Barren Woman's Home Is Not Homeless," *Council on Biblical Manhood and Womanhood*, Mar 11, 2015, https://cbmw.org/topics/barrenness/a-barren-womans-home/.

13. Lisa Cahill, *Family: A Christian Social Perspective* (Minneapolis MN: Augsburg Fortress Press, 2000), 29.

14. Farley, *Just Love*, 187.

15. National Council of Churches in Christ in the U.S.A., "Fearfully and Wonderfully Made: A Policy on Human Biotechnologies," §IIA, adopted Nov 8, 2006, http://nationalcouncilofchurches.us/common-witness/2006/biotech.php.

16. The scholar-activist widely hailed as the mother of feminist Christian ethics, Beverly Wildung Harrison, has shown how Christian defenders of "the institution of normative heterosexuality" are almost always also anti-feminist in their upholding of male superiority and valuing of women primarily as wives and as mothers. See her *Justice in the Making: Feminist Social Ethics*, ed. Elizabeth M. Bounds et al. (Louisville, KY: Westminster John Knox Press, 2004), 62.

17. The revised statement says the following: "Marriage involves a unique commitment between two people, traditionally a man and a woman, to love and support each other for the rest of their lives." See W-4.0601: The Covenant of Marriage in the PCUSA, *Book of Order* 2019–2021: The Constitution of the Presbyterian Church (U.S.A.), Part II, https://www.pcusa.org/site_media/media/uploads/oga/pdf/2019-23-boo-elec_010621.pdf.

18. See Eugene F. Rogers Jr., *Sexuality and the Christian Body: Their Way into the Triune God* (Oxford: Blackwell, 1999) and Deirdre J. Good, Willis J. Jenkins, Cynthia B. Kittredge, Eugene F. Rogers Jr., "A Theology of Marriage Including Same-Sex Couples: A View from the Liberals," *Anglican Theological Review* 93:1 (2011): 51–87 at 51.

19. See Patrick S. Cheng, "Galatians," in *The Queer Bible Commentary*, ed. Deryn Guest et al., 624–629 (London: SCM, 2006).

20. Alice Walker, *In Search of Our Mother's Gardens: Womanist Prose* (New York: Harcourt, 1983), xi.

21. Rather than stop at validating the equal worth of same-sex sexuality, however, Harrison and others have labored to move Christian ethics beyond both the narrow permission versus prohibition question and the disproportionate fixation on marriage to discuss ideal norms (viz., mutuality, bodily integrity, consent and the like) for all mature sexual relationships. Many of these norms can be adapted for and be applied to relationships among members of the surrogacy triad as well, as per the next chapter. Harrison, *Justice in the Making*, 59.

22. My LGBTQIA+-affirming stance admittedly puts me at odds with the evangelical Taiwanese immigrant church of my youth. It is consistent, however, with two Asian American organizations of which I am active: the explicitly feminist and LGBTQIA+ affirming Progressive Asian American Christians (PAAC) group founded in 2016 and the Pacific, Asian, and North American Asian Women in Theological and Ministry (PANAAWTM) network whose foremothers began meeting decades earlier starting in 1984. I hasten to add that the broader (secular) Taiwanese society has undergone a cultural shift in recent decades, as evidenced by Taiwan's becoming the first nation in Asia to have legalized same-sex marriage in 2019.

23. Special Committee on Human Sexuality, "Majority Report: Keeping Body and Soul Together: Sexuality, Spirituality, and Social Justice," Louisville, KY: Office of the General Assembly, Presbyterian Church (U.S.A.), 1991, 82 [hereinafter "Keeping Body and Soul Together"] The 203rd General Assembly, to be clear, did not adopt this report.

24. Special Committee on Human Sexuality, "Keeping Body and Soul Together," 85.

25. The monoethnic Taiwanese American church in which I was raised, Evangelical Formosan Church, has long associated Christianity with the provision of healthcare. This is largely because the first modern missionary to Taiwan also established the first Western medical institution therein (the Canadian Presbyterian George Leslie Mackay (1844–1901)) and Christian healthcare providers in our church have henceforth been hailed as those who especially do "the Lord's work," even as the broader Reformed tradition calls upon *all* Christians to "serve God in the ordinary."

26. PCUSA, "The Covenant of Life and the Caring Community," 195th General Assembly, 1983, 17; https://www.presbyterianmission.org/resource/the-covenant-of -life-and-the-caring-community-biomedical-ethics/.

27. See PCUSA, "Covenant and Creation: Theological Reflections on Contraception and Abortion," 195th General Assembly, 1983, 72, 90, 96, 110; https://www.presby

terianmission.org/wp-content/uploads/8-covenant-of-life-and-covenant-and-crea
tion-1993.pdf and also PCUSA, "The Covenant of Life and the Caring Community,"
16-17.

28. In all of my childhood and precollege years of attending Evangelical Formosan
Church of Orange County in the 1980s and early 1990s, I also cannot recall one sermon
from our senior (woman) pastor, Sunday School lesson, or word from an elder in all
my years of regular attendance excoriating the evils of contraception or pregnancy
termination. I am certain that if I (or anyone else) as a teenager or college student had
gotten pregnant, nearly the entire church community would have counseled me
toward an abortion. My parents who have attended longer can corroborate: abortion
has never been taught as a moral evil as it has in many white evangelical churches, and
contraceptives have always been deemed appropriate for married couples to use to
postpone childbearing or space out their children. My home church was otherwise
conservative in believing that sex was reserved for marriage and that both same-sex
attraction and relationships were deviant.

29. PCUSA, "The Covenant of Life and the Caring Community," 48.

30. In recognition of the possible benefits stem cell research might yield for the
common good, the UMC also permits couples to donate the embryos they will not
ultimately transfer to research so long as they did not originally create them for experimental purposes. See United Methodist Church, "New Developments in Genetic
Science," *The Book of Resolutions of the United Methodist Church—2016* (first adopted
in 1992 and amended and readopted in 2000, 2008, 2016), http://ee.umc.org/what-we
-believe/new-developments-in-genetic-science, VIA1e and the United Methodist
Church, "Ethics of Embryonic Stem Cell Research," *The Book of Resolutions of the
United Methodist Church—2016* (first adopted in 2004 and revised and readopted in
2008 and 2016), http://ee.umc.org/what-we-believe/ethics-of-embryonic-stem-cell
-research.

31. See Kate M. Ott, *A Time to Be Born: A Faith-Based Guide to Assisted Reproductive Technologies* (The Religious Institute, 2009), 34–39 for excerpts from these denominations. While the Taiwanese church community in which I was raised has not
taken a formal position on IVF, I would venture they would not have considered treatments for any diagnosable medical condition (in this case, infertility) inappropriate
for Christians either to use themselves or to administer to others as service providers.
Due to a combination of theological and (Confucian) cultural reasons, we were never
taught that infertile couples who longed for children would only have three licit options available to them: pray fervently for divine intervention to reverse their course,
be resigned about their lack of children as their personal cross to bear, or overcome
the cultural stigma of non-kin adoption to adopt.

32. Resolution Number 1982-A067, "Approve Use of 'In Vitro' Fertilization," 67th
General Convention, *Journal of the General Convention of . . . The Episcopal Church,
New Orleans, 1982* (New York: General Convention, 1983), C-158, https://www.episco
palarchives.org/cgi-bin/acts/acts_resolution.pl?resolution=1982-A067.

33. PCUSA, "The Covenant of Life and the Caring Community." 48.

34. The Board of Pensions of the Presbyterian Church (U.S.A.), "The Benefits Plan 2022 of the Presbyterian Church (U.S.A.)," See Sec. 10.2 Covered Medical Services (i), (t) and Sec. 10.3(a)2: Reimbursement for Medically Necessary Use of Advanced Reproductive Technology, https://www.pensions.org/file/what-we-offer/benefits-guidance/forms-documents/Documents/pln-100.pdf/.

35. Farley, *Just Love*, 189.

36. Of course, the "why" of human rights (what makes every human being qua human being so worthy of respect and esteem) can be articulated in various religious and nonreligious ways. For a small sampling of these writings, see Brian Matz, *Introducing Protestant Social Ethics: Foundations in Scripture, History, and Practice* (Grand Rapids, MI: Baker Academic, 2017), 159, 238n4, John S. Nurser, *For All Peoples and All Nations: The Ecumenical Church and Human Rights* (Washington, D.C.: Georgetown University Press, 2005), and Grace Y. Kao, *Grounding Human Rights in a Pluralist World* (Washington, D.C.: Georgetown University Press, 2011).

37. See the Universal Declaration of Human Rights (UDHR) Art 16.1; the International Covenant on Economic, Social, and Cultural Rights (ICESCR) Art 10.1; the International Covenant on Civil and Political Rights (ICCPR) Art. 7, 23.2 and the Convention on the Rights of the Child (CRC) Art 7.1 The aspirational but legally nonbinding 2005 United Nations Educational, Scientific, and Cultural Organization (UNESCO) Declaration on Bioethics and Human Rights (UDBHR) affirms the "autonomy of persons to make decisions, while taking responsibility for those decisions" in addition to the human right and dignity for the "interests and welfare of the individual . . . [to] have priority over the sole interest of . . . society" (UDBHR, Art. 5, 3).

38. Farley, *Just Love*, 190.

39. As Kwok Pui-lan has observed: "Women's experience has been invoked to challenge the orthodox notions of revelation and dogma by exposing their historical and constructed character. It has also served as the basis to debunk and demystify the androcentric bias of humanism in liberal theology. . . . But women's experience is the most contested source of feminist theology" (54). See her *Postcolonial Imagination & Feminist Theology* (Louisville, KY: Westminster John Knox Press, 2005).

40. L. A. Paul, *Transformative Experiences* (New York: Oxford University Press, 2014). A curiosity about transformative experiences is the challenge they pose for rational choice. Put simply, how can a person ever make an informed choice about *whether* to undergo a transformative experience if, by definition, they need to experience it directly to know what it's like and thus weigh their options in an informed way whether or not to undergo it? To state a different dimension of the puzzle, if a person's point of view and core preferences are projected to change *after* they undergo the experience but it is their pre-changed self who must decide whether or not to have it, the question remains *which* set of preferences should guide their choice: the pre-transformative experience preferences or the post-transformative experience ones?

41. Fiona Woollard, "Mother Knows Best: Pregnancy, Applied Ethics, and Epistemically Transformative Experiences," *Journal of Applied Philosophy* 38.1 (2021): 155–171.

42. SisterSong, "Our History," https://www.sistersong.net/mission.

43. Toni M. Bond Leonard, "Laying the Foundations for a Reproductive Justice Movement," in *Radical Reproductive Justice: Foundations, Theory, Practice, Critique*, ed. Loretta J. Ross et al., 39–49 (New York: The Feminist Press, 2017), 43.

44. Bond Leonard, "Laying the Foundations for a Reproductive Justice Movement," 48. The ACRJ changed its name to Forward Together in 2012.

45. The "New Vision" published in 2005 is available here: https://forwardtogether .org/tools/a-new-vision/.

46. I stress intentions because the extent of bodily sacrifices and medical risks involved, not to mention urgency, may vary dramatically between and among these various practices. The inconveniences, risks, and bodily sacrifices involved in voluntarily donating blood will ordinarily be minimal when compared to donating a different kind of live tissue: bone marrow. The most serious medical risk associated with the latter involves the use of anesthesia during surgery, donors will often experience back pain, fatigue, headaches, or bruising for a few days or few weeks after, and the body will naturally replenish the marrow removed within four to six weeks. In comparison, the inconveniences and medical risks of an IVF pregnancy in surrogacy are arguably greater and will take place over a longer period of time, although bone marrow donors can save the lives of their recipients in ways surrogacy is not commonly understood as doing (with the exception of those who interpret "embryo rescue" in this way).

Of course, donating lifesaving organs such as a kidney or a portion of one's liver involves significantly more immediate and long-term risks than live tissue donation. While a donor's liver function is expected to return to normal within weeks and the liver will naturally regenerate to nearly its full original volume within months, this is not so with live kidney donation, since kidneys are not naturally regenerating and donors should expect 25–35% permanent loss of kidney function post-surgery. While surrogates are not projected to experience a permanent impairment of reproductive function post-childbirth, there are risks associated with every pregnancy, including total loss of reproductive function and even death. For what it is worth, I did not interpret my own surrogacy as more noble or sacrificial as I do lifesaving live tissue or organ donation, especially of kidneys, though all these practices are other-regarding.

47. Private e-mail communication on Jan 26, 2021, with Pauline Everett, PhD, theology graduate of Durham University who is updating her doctoral thesis "A Relational Defence of Surrogate Motherhood" for T&T Clark. There are also Christian critics of surrogacy who otherwise make allowances for surrogacy as "rescue" (see chapter 3).

48. As Wilda C. Gafney notes, "[m]any translations downplay Sarai's abuse of Hagar in verse 6. . . . Yet Sarai's abuse is described with the same verb, '-*n-h*, that led to God's redemption of Israel from Egypt. . . . When Shechem abuses Dinah using the same verb, he rapes her, as does Amnon, Tamar" (35). See her *Womanist Midrash: A Reintroduction to the Women of the Torah and the Throne* (Louisville, KY: Westminster John Knox Press, 2017).

49. In womanist theologian Delores Williams's groundbreaking reading of Hagar,

God's partiality to Sarah and non-liberation of Hagar does more than expose the dangers of surrogacy. The story, together with other biblical texts pertaining to slavery, casts doubt on "black liberation theology's normative claim of God's liberating activity on behalf of *all* the oppressed" and thus raises a "serious question about the biblical witness" (128). See her *Sisters in the Wilderness: The Challenge of Womanist God-Talk* (New York: Orbis, 2013 [1993]).

50. I discuss three different interpretations of Ruth's relationship with Naomi offered by Kwok Pui-Lan, Gale Yee, Sharon Jacob in Grace Y. Kao, "Rethinking Surrogacy from an Asian American Christian Ethical Perspective," in *Theologies of the Multitude for Multitudes: The Legacy of Kwok Pui-Lan*, ed. Rita Nakashima Brock and Tat-siong Benny Liew, 271–292 (Claremont, CA: Claremont Press, 2021). I return to the ways Ruth's story can illuminate our understanding of some commercial and interstate surrogacy arrangements in chapter 6.

51. To be clear, progressive Christians could still affirm the goodness of children in marriage without holding that childrearing is necessary to make that marriage valid or complete by regarding the vocation of parenting as a perspicacious, though not exclusive, way married couples could express the marital norm of fruitfulness and demonstrate care for future generations.

52. Of course, one difference between a same-sex couple's turn to surrogacy and the same by an infertile heterosexual couple is that the former will necessarily require use of a gamete donor as well, while the latter might not.

53. Kristin L. Rooney, "The Relationship between Stress and Infertility," *Dialogues in Clinical Neuroscience* 20.1 (2018): 41–47.

54. Dean A. Murphy, *Gay Men Pursuing Parenthood through Surrogacy: Reconfiguring Kinship* (Sydney: University of New South Wales Press, 2015), 110.

55. Murphy, *Gay Men Pursuing Parenthood through Surrogacy*, 119–120, 122.

56. Gay male couples have developed a reputation of being especially grateful and accommodating clients, which is why some surrogates prefer to partner with them. See Elizabeth F. Schwartz, "LGBT Issues in Surrogacy: Present and Future," *Handbook of Gestational Surrogacy: International Clinical Practice and Policy Issues,* ed. E. Scott Sills, 55–61(Cambridge, UK: Cambridge University Press, 2016).

57. See Maureen Sullivan, "Commentary on Susan Markens's 'Surrogate Motherhood and the Politics of Reproduction,'" in *Sociological Forum* 26.1 (2011): 196–199 at 198. Sullivan is referencing her work *The Family of Women: Lesbian Mothers, Their Children, and the Undoing of Gender* (Berkeley, CA: University of California Press, 2004).

58. Murphy, *Gay Men Pursuing Parenthood through Surrogacy,* 49.

59. Marcia C. Inhorn and Daphna Birenbaum-Carmeli, "Assisted Reproductive Technologies and Culture Change," *Annual Review of Anthropology* 37 (2008): 177–196 at 182.

60. According to Patricia Hill Collins, "othermothering" is the popular practice of African American women "assist[ing] bloodmothers by sharing mothering responsibilities" and therein taking on "child-care responsibilities for one another's children"

in communal networks of care. See her *Black Feminist Thought: Knowledge, Consciousness, and the Politics of Empowerment* (New York: Routledge, 2000), 192–193.

61. Sara Ruddick, *Maternal Thinking: Toward a Politics of Peace* (Boston: Beacon Press, 1989).

62. Alexandra Kimball, *The Seed: Infertility Is a Feminist Issue* (Toronto, Canada: Coach House Books, 2019), 129–130.

63. Kimball, *The Seed*, 126, 130–131. In the next chapter, I will return to the goods of an IP's, especially an IM's, honest grappling with their complex and sometimes ambivalent feelings toward the third parties involved in their child's birth and of the surrogacy triad staying in relationship with one another post-childbirth.

64. Maria Papastavrou et al., "Breastfeeding in the Course of History," *Journal of Pediatrics and Neonatal Care* 2.6 (2015), https://medcraveonline.com/JPNC/JPNC-02-00096.pdf.

65. Lauren Jade Martin, *Reproductive Tourism in the United States: Creating Family in the Mother Country* (New York: Routledge, 2015), 5–6.

66. La Leche League International, "Milk Sharing and Donation," https://www.llli.org/breastfeeding-info/milk-donation/.

67. See, for example, Beatriz M. Reyes-Foster, Shannon K. Carter, and Melanie Sberna Hinojosa, "Milk Sharing in Practice: A Descriptive Analysis of Peer Breastmilk Sharing," *Breastfeeding Medicine* 10.5 (2015): 263–269.

68. When "the supply of maternal milk is insufficient," the AAP does not encourage the use of nonpasteurized milk obtained from "direct, internet-based, or informal human milk sharing," but only donor milk when "appropriate measures" have been taken to "screen donors and collect, store, and pasteurize the milk and then distribute it through established human milk banks." See Committee on Nutrition, Section on Breastfeeding and Committee on Fetus and Newborn, American Academy of Pediatrics, "Donor Human Milk for the High-Risk Infant: Preparation, Safety, and Usage Options in the United States," *Pediatrics* 139.1 (2017): e20163440; DOI: https://doi.org/10.1542/peds.2016-3440.

69. I had hoped to have provided enough breastmilk for my friends' baby to be exclusively fed breastmilk for the first six months of her life, as per WHO and AAP recommendations for optimal infant health. When the inconveniences involved in expressing breastmilk became more than I was willing to manage, I stopped around the four months' mark. Since my supply had exceeded their child's demand, she was able to continue to consume breastmilk for several weeks after. I understood expressing breastmilk as mutually beneficial: it would provide their child with nutrition and it would help me shrink my uterus down to its pre-pregnancy size and lose weight.

70. Ted Peters, *For the Love of Children: Genetic Technology and the Future of the Family* (Louisville, KY: Westminster John Knox Press, 1996), 63–66.

Chapter 5

1. On October 31, 2022, twins Lydia and Timothy Ridgeway were born from embryos that had been frozen for thirty years—what the National Embryo Donation

Center reports may be the longest frozen embryos to result in a live birth. The previous record holder was Molly Gibson who was born from an embryo that had been frozen for close to twenty-seven years in 2020. See Jen Christensen and Nadia Kounang, "Parents Welcome Twins from Embryos Frozen 30 Years Ago," *CNN*, https://www.cnn.com/2022/11/21/health/30-year-old-embryos-twins/index.html.

2. See Eric Scott Sills et al., "Gestational Surrogacy and the Role of Routine Embryo Screening: Current Challenges and Future Direction for Preimplantation Genetic Testing," *Birth Defects Research Part C: Embryo Today* 108.1 (2016): 98–102 and Sung Tae Kim et al., "Decreased Miscarriage Rate and Increased Implantation Rate by Pre-implantation Genetic Screening (PGS) in Advanced Maternal Aged Women," *Fertility and Sterility* 108.3 (2017): e287.

3. PCUSA, "On Providing Just Access to Reproductive Health Care," (Item 21–03) approved by the 220th General Assembly (2012), #2, https://www.presbyterianmission.org/resource/presbyterian-church-us-general-assembly-resolution. Support for developing the moral agency of "women and men . . . to make their own decisions about reproduction, including . . . ARTs, gamete donation and surrogacy" under conditions of informed consent, an "informed conscience," and consultations with their broader "faith, community, and family" can also be found in the Religious Institute's 2008 "Open Letter to Religious Leaders on Assisted Reproductive Technologies," http://religiousinstitute.org/wp-content/uploads/2009/06/olonart000.pdf.

4. Margaret Farley understands the "fruitfulness" norm in her much heralded framework for Christian sexual ethics not necessarily in terms of procreation, but for a couple's love to be "open to a wider community of persons," such as by helping to raise other people's children or nourishing other relationships. See her *Just Love: A Framework for Christian Sexual Ethics* (New York: Continuum, 2006), 226–228.

5. Theologian and ordained PCUSA minister Kendra Hotz provides an insightful account of parenthood as a vocation not suitable for everyone when offering a feminist, Reformed theological reflection on her and her husband's decision to be child-free. In drawing upon John Calvin's notion of calling (*Institutes* 3.10.6), Hotz characterizes marriages with children as ordinarily bringing harmony and coherence—as all callings do—to the lives of those who have them. Those not called to parenting pursue their other callings, which in her case has been to teaching and to theology. Of course, those not called to parenting could still show hospitality to (other people's) children and therein fulfill the marital good of *proles* without themselves bearing offspring, as Hotz does in her role as "Aunt Kendra." Kendra G. Hotz, "Happily Ever After (Voluntary Childlessness)," in *Encountering the Sacred: Feminist Reflections on Women's Lives*, ed. Rebecca Todd Peters and Grace Y. Kao, 149–163 (London: T&T Clark, 2018).

6. Cf. "The desire and ability to parent children are entirely separate from the capacity to conceive and bear them." See Report of the Special Committee on Human Sexuality, "Keeping Body and Soul Together: Sexuality, Spirituality and Social Justice," Louisville, KY: Office of the General Assembly, Presbyterian Church (U.S.A.), 1991, IV, D.4, 85.

7. See Sheryl Gay Stolberg, "For the Infertile, a High-Tech Treadmill" *New York Times*, Dec 14, 1997, https://www.nytimes.com/1997/12/14/us/for-the-infertile-a-high-tech-treadmill.html and Heather Jacobson, *Labor of Love: Gestational Surrogacy and the Work of Making Babies* (New Brunswick, NJ: Rutgers University Press, 2016), 23.

8. Alexandra Kimball, *The Seed: Infertility Is a Feminist Issue* (Toronto: Coach House Books, 2019), 90.

9. For instance, in a sociological study on queer families, a gay white couple (Drew and Nico) were considering both options and ultimately pursued surrogacy because they (1) feared either the birth mother returning and asserting maternal rights in an adoption scenario or receiving possible heterosexist treatment from the courts and (2) believed surrogacy would allow them to "invest affection into their children without concern that they could one day be taken from them" because genetic fatherhood could better secure their rights in their context with the "legal authenticity of a blood-tie." Nico also had a strong urge to have biological children while Drew, who was a known donor to a lesbian couple, did not care personally whether their kids would be biologically his but ultimately wanted to facilitate his partner's yearning. Whether the rights of same-sex couples would actually increase in surrogacy as opposed to adoption as Drew and Nico had calculated it would for them depend upon context and jurisdiction, which is why all same-sex couples contemplating surrogacy or adoption would be wise to attend to the structural biases that might exist against them in both methods of family expansion. See Maura Ryan and Dana Berkowitz, "Constructing Gay and Lesbian Parent Families 'Beyond the Closet,'" *Qualitative Sociology* 32.2 (2009): 153–172 at 161–163.

10. Olga B. A. van den Akker, *Surrogate Motherhood Families* (London: Palgrave MacMillan, 2017), 85–86.

11. Ethics Committee of the American Society for Reproductive Medicine, "Using Family Members as Gamete Donors or Gestational Carriers," *Fertility and Sterility* 107.5 (2017): 1136–1142 at 1139.

12. Katharina Beier and Sabine Wöhlke, "An Ethical Comparison of Living Kidney Donation and Surrogacy: Understanding the Relational Dimension," *Philosophy, Ethics, and Humanities in Medicine* 14. 13 (2019), https://doi.org/10.1186/s13010-019-0080-9; https://peh-med.biomedcentral.com/track/pdf/10.1186/s13010-019-0080-9.pdf.

13. According to the CDC, Black women are three times more likely to die from a pregnancy-related cause than white women. In addition, during 2007–2016, "[B]lack and American Indian/Alaska Native women had significant more pregnancy-related deaths per 100,000 births than did white, Hispanic, and Asian/Pacific Islander women." See CDC, "Working Together to Reduce Black Maternal Mortality," Apr 6, 2022, https://www.cdc.gov/healthequity/features/maternal-mortality/index.html#:~:text=Black%20women%20are%20three%20times,structural%20racism%2C%20and%20%20implicit%20bias and CDC, "Racial/Ethnic Disparities in Pregnancy-Related Deaths—United States, 2007–2016, Morbidity and Mortality Weekly Report, Sep 6, 2019 68.35: 762–765, https://www.cdc.gov/mmwr/volumes/68/wr/mm6835a3.htm.

Other studies have shown that Asian American women have a higher prevalence of gestational diabetes than do women of all other race-ethnicities. When compared to their white counterparts, they also have higher rates of maternal morbidity and mortality despite their overall higher socioeconomic status and tend to wait longer to begin fertility treatments, with this delay impairing prospects for IVF success. See Andrew Kan et al., "Do Asian Women Do as Well as Their Caucasian Counterparts in IVF Treatment: Cohort Study," *Journal of Obstetrics and Gynaecology Research* 41.6 (2015): 946–951, Liwei Chen et al., "Influence of Acculturation on Risk for Gestational Diabetes among Asian Women," *Preventing Chronic Disease*, Dec 5, 2019; DOI: http://dx.doi.org/10.5888/pcd16.190212, and Maryam Siddiqui et al., "Increased Perinatal Morbidity and Mortality among Asian American and Pacific Islander Women in the United States," *Anesthesia & Analgesia* 124.3 (2017): 879–886.

14. Asian Communities for Reproductive Justice, "A New Vision for Advancing Our Movement for Reproductive Health, Reproductive Rights and Reproductive Justice," 5; https://forwardtogether.org/wp-content/uploads/2017/12/ACRJ-A-New-Vision.pdf. ACRJ was a founding member of the SisterSong Women of Color Reproductive Health Collective and changed its name in 2012 to Forward Together to build a multiracial organization. Puerto Rican Catholic feminist Teresa Delgado also encourages moral decision-makers to be informed by the "history of . . . communal accountability and wisdom" in their reproductive decision-making by making room for the wisdom of ancestors. See Teresa Delgado, "Accountable to the Ancestors: A Response to *Trust Women*," *Syndicate*, Apr 17, 2019, https://syndicate.network/symposia/theology/trust-women/.

15. For a discussion of these special considerations, see Ethics Committee of the American Society for Reproductive Medicine, "Using Family Members as Gamete Donors or Gestational Carriers."

16. Jacobson, *Labor of Love*, 89.

17. See Melissa B. Brisman Esq.: Reproductive Lawyer, "Gestational Carrier Contracts," https://www.reproductivelawyer.com/gestational-carrier-contracts/.

18. England's High Court ruled that a transgender man (who was not a surrogate) who is recognized by law as male and who has given birth must still be listed as the child's mother, not father. In the words of Andrew McFarlene, President of the High Court's Family Division: "Whilst that person's gender is 'male,' their parental status, which derives from their biological role in giving birth, is that of 'mother.'" See NBC News, "A Transgender Man Who Gives Birth Is a Mother, U.K. Court Rules," Sep 25, 2019, https://www.nbcnews.com/feature/nbc-out/transgender-man-who-gives-birth-mother-uk-court-rules-n1058556.

19. Ellen Sarasohn Glazer, *The Long Awaited Stork: A Guide to Parenting after Infertility*, revised ed. (San Francisco: Jossey-Bass, 1998), 6.

20. Jacobson, *Labor of Love*, 99.

21. Robin B. Allen and Michelle Hester, "Babies Grow Up," Apr 6, 2021, https://www.shadygrovefertility.com/emotional-support-articles/babies-grow. This article originally appeared in two installments (Win 2007 and Spr 2008) in the RESOLVE Mid-Atlantic Region Newsletter.

22. Elly Teman and Zsuzsa Berend, "Surrogate Non-Motherhood: Israeli and US Surrogates Speak about Kinship and Parenthood," *Anthropology & Medicine* 25.3 (2018): 296–310 at 301.

23. As sociologist Zsuzsa Berend has observed in surrogacy relational dynamics during reproductive loss, "Sharing the emotional intensity over loss is also a way to affirm their commitment to a 'shared journey.' When the couple is less than devastated—because they were not optimistic about the chances, or had other children or another surrogate—about the loss, the value of the life surrogates create, thus the value of their sacrifice, is called into question." See Zsuzsa Berend, "Surrogate Losses: Understandings of Pregnancy Loss and Assisted Reproduction among Surrogate Mothers," *Medical Anthropology Quarterly* 24.2 (2010): 240–262 at 244–245.

24. See §2720.2 A (5) of the Louisiana Surrogacy Bill HB 1102 [MM1], which took effect on Aug 1, 2016, http://www.legis.la.gov/legis/BillInfo.aspx?i=230384. Louisiana also requires the parties to have cleared at least two counseling sessions, separated by at least thirty days, prior to executing the contract with a "licensed clinical social worker, licensed psychologist, medical psychologist, licensed psychiatrist, or licensed counselor" (§2720.2 A (3)).

25. The tragic case of "runaway surrogate" Crystal Kelley and "Baby S" illustrates the difficulties involved where there is no meeting of the minds. In 2013, Kelley made headline news when she refused to abort the fetus she was carrying following the IPs' request that she do after a diagnosis of severe fetal abnormalities (n.b., their arrangement was compensated, not altruistic). She then fled Connecticut for Michigan where surrogacy contracts are null and void and where all birth mothers are recognized as the legal mother and gave birth to Baby S. The IPs were already caring for three children, all three of whom had been born prematurely and two with long-term special needs, and believed it would be more humane for their unborn child and best for their family overall for Kelley to terminate the pregnancy, particularly since doctors were unsure whether Baby S could survive beyond her first birthday. In the end, Baby S was eventually born with a cleft lip and palette, a brain defect and several heart defects, cerebral palsy, and a pituitary gland disorder. She could only speak a few words but learned American Sign Language and used a wheelchair because she couldn't walk. She was raised by her adoptive parents and had multiple surgeries until she died at age eight. See Kevin Dolak, "Surrogate Mother Flees Halfway across US to Save Baby from Intended Parents," *ABC News*, Mar 6, 2013, https://abcnews.go.com/US/surrogate-mother-flees-halfway-us-save-baby-intended/story?id=18668498 and Elizabeth Cohen, "Girl in Famous Surrogacy Case Dies at Age 8," *CNN*, Aug 5, 2020, https://www.cnn.com/2020/08/04/health/seraphina-surrogate-death/index.html.

26. Hyunkyung Choi, Marcia Van Riper, and Suzanne Thoyre, "Decision Making Following a Prenatal Diagnosis of Down Syndrome: An Integrative Review," *Journal of Midwifery and Women's Health* 57.2 (2012): 156–164 at 156. Of the more than 90% of expectant women in Denmark who undergo first trimester screening, more than 95% will terminate their pregnancies if Down syndrome is diagnosed. See Stina Lou et al., "Termination of Pregnancy Following a Prenatal Diagnosis of Down Syndrome: A

Qualitative Study of the Decision-Making Process of Pregnant Couples, *Acta Obstetricia et Gynecologica Scandinavica* 97.10 (2018): 1228–1236 at 1229.

27. Guttmacher Institute, "State Bans on Abortion throughout Pregnancy," Nov 1, 2022, https://www.guttmacher.org/state-policy/explore/state-policies-later-abortions.

28. As the Human Rights Committee clarified after a three-year process when providing General Comment No. 36 (2018) on Article 6 of the International Covenant of Civil and Political Rights (ICCPR) on the right to life, states may regulate the "voluntary termination of pregnancy," but not in ways where any restrictions "jeopardize their [girls' or women's] lives, subject them to physical or mental pain or suffering . . . , discriminate against them or arbitrarily interfere with their privacy" (I.8). State policies leading pregnant persons to resort to "unsafe abortions," such as when the state criminalizes abortion or punishes the medical service providers performing them, may well be regarded as a violation of their right to life. For the text, see CCPR/C/GC/36, https://tbinternet.ohchr.org/_layouts/15/treatybodyexternal/Download.aspx?symbolno=CCPR/C/GC/36&Lang=en.

29. Ruth Walker and Liezl van Zyl, "Surrogate Motherhood and Abortion for Fetal Abnormality," *Bioethics* 29.8 (2015): 529–535 at 532.

30. "Ethical Issues in Surrogate Motherhood: ACOG Committee Opinion No. 88—November 1990," *International Journal of Gynecology & Obstetrics* 37.2 (1992): 139–144. ACOG's more recent statement also affirms the "primacy of the gestational carrier's right to autonomous decision making related to her body and health" (e3). See American College of Obstetricians and Gynecologists (ACOG), "Committee Opinion: Family Building through Gestational Surrogacy," No. 660, Mar 2016 (reaffirmed 2019), https://www.acog.org/Clinical-Guidance-and-Publications/Committee-Opinions/Committee-on-Ethics/Family-Building-Through-Gestational-Surrogacy.

31. Practice Committee of the American Society for Reproductive Medicine and Practice Committee of the Society for Assisted Reproductive Technology, "Recommendations for Practices Using Gestational Carriers: A Committee Opinion," *Fertility and Sterility* 118.1 (2022): 65-74 at 70, https://doi.org/10.1016/j.fertnstert.2022.05.001.

32. ACOG, "Committee Opinion: Family Building through Gestational Surrogacy," 4.

33. See Judith Daar, "Five Signs Your Surrogacy Arrangement Has Gone Awry," *Bill of Health: Examining the Intersection of Health, Law, Biotechnology, and Bioethics*, Harvard Law School, Mar 6, 2013, http://blog.petrieflom.law.harvard.edu/2013/03/06/five-signs-your-surrogacy-arrangement-has-gone-awry/.

34. Lindsey Bever, "'I Am Pro Life': A Surrogate Mother's Stand against 'Reducing' Her Triplets," *Washington Post*, Jan 7, 2016.

35. Walker and Van Zyl, "Surrogate Motherhood and Abortion for Fetal Abnormality," 534.

36. Elizabeth F. Schwartz, "LGBT Issues in Surrogacy: Present and Future Challenges," *Handbook of Gestational Surrogacy: International Clinical Practice and Policy Issues,* ed. E. Scott Sills, 55–61 (Cambridge, UK: Cambridge University Press, 2016), 60.

37. For a sampling of these professed reasons for nondisclosure, see Susan Golombok et al., "Non-Genetic and Non-Gestational Parenthood: Consequences for Parent–Child Relationships and the Psychological Well-Being of Mothers, Fathers and Children at Age 3," *Human Reproduction* 21.7 (2006): 1918–1924 at 1921, 1923 and Jennifer Readings et al., "Secrecy, Disclosure and Everything In-Between: Decisions of Parents of Children Conceived by Donor Insemination, Egg Donation and Surrogacy," *Reproductive Biomedicine* 22.5 (2011): 485–495 at 490-491.

38. Nancy Hass, "To Tell, or Not to Tell, Your Egg Donor Baby? *Elle Magazine*, Aug 20, 2015, https://www.elle.com/life-love/sex-relationships/news/a29904/whose-life-is -it-anyway/.

39. See, for example, Gita Aravamudan, *Baby Makers: A Story of Indian Surrogacy* (Uttar Pradesh: Harper Collins India, 2014) and Jared Yee, "Women Strap on Bellies to Keep Surrogacy Secret," *BioEdge*, May 5, 2012, https://bioedge.org/uncategorized /women-strap-on-bellies-to-keep-surrogacy-secret/.

40. Dani Shapiro, *Inheritance: A Memoir of Genealogy, Paternity, and Love* (New York: Anchor Books, 2019), 200.

41. Readings, "Secrecy, Disclosure, and Everything In-Between," 486.

42. As Shapiro reports, some persons conceived by artificial insemination search their entire lives for their biological fathers, and when it proves unsuccessful, they even have their donor's identification number "tattooed on their bodies [as] a way of marking themselves with their only clue." See her *Inheritance*, 59.

43. Shapiro, *Inheritance*, 200. This shocking discovery led her to explore who we are to one another and "what combination of memory, history, imagination, experience, subjectivity, genetic substance, and that ineffable thing called the soul makes us who we are" (27). She also attempted to reconstruct what her since-deceased parents might have known (n.b., the clinic may have mixed the donor semen with her father's semen to help patients maintain the ruse of intact fertility).

44. See Nancy Freeman-Carroll, "The Possibilities and Pitfalls of Talking about Conception with Donor Egg: Why Parents Struggle and How Clinicians Can Help," *Journal of Infant, Child, and Adolescent Psychotherapy* 15:1 (2016): 40–50 at 41.

45. Negative outcomes for children who found out about their donor conception later in life include shock and confusion, a negative sense of distinctiveness in relation to others, familial distrust, and frustration when searching for information about their genetic parent. A key finding from the 2020 "We Are Donor Conceived Results" covering 481 donor-conceived persons ranging in ages from thirteen to seventy-four from fifteen countries is that "respondents who learned they are donor conceived before age three were significantly more likely to categorize their overall experience of being donor conceived as positive and less likely to say the method of their conception sometimes makes them feel distressed, angry or sad than late discovery respondents." See We Are Donor Conceived, "10 Highlights from the 2020 We Are Donor Conceived Survey," https://www.wearedonorconceived.com/2020-survey-top/10-highlights -from-the-2020-we-are-donor-conceived-survey/.

A recent, first-of-a-kind study in the U.S. about adoption has found those who discovered *after the age of three* they were adopted reported more emotional and lower life satisfaction—even after controlling for the amount of time they knew of their adoption status and their use of coping strategies—than those who had found out earlier. While many previous studies have suggested persons who do not learn the details of their conception until adulthood may feel "mistrust, frustration, and hostility toward their family," this is the first study to have characterized "late discovery" at so young an age as three. See Amanda L. Baden et al., "Delaying Adoption Disclosure: A Survey of Late Discovery Adoptees," *Journal of Family Issues* 40.9 (2019): 1154–1180.

46. As with the case of Dani Shapiro and the tens of thousands of members of the Donor Sibling Registry, these individuals have been left to grapple with unexpected DNA results of previously unknown genetic parents, half-siblings, and other relatives—not all of whom may be delighted to discover they have a new relation. See Joyce C. Harper, Debbie Kennett, and Dan Reisel, "The End of Donor Anonymity: How Genetic Testing Is Likely to Drive Anonymous Gamete Donation out of Business," *Human Reproduction* 31. 6 (2016): 1135–1140.

47. See Nuffield Council on Bioethics, "Donor Conception: Ethical Aspects of Information Sharing," London, Apr 2013, xvi, http://nuffieldbioethics.org/wp-content/uploads/2014/06/Donor_conception_report_2013.pdf; Ethics Committee of the American Society for Reproductive Medicine, "Informing Offspring of Their Conception by Gamete or Embryo Donation: An Ethics Committee Opinion," *Fertility and Sterility* 109.4 (2018): 601–605; UNICEF, *Implementation Handbook for the Convention on the Rights of the Child*, fully revised 3rd ed. (Geneva, Switzerland, 2007), 105–106, https://www.unicef.org/reports/implementation-handbook-convention-rights-child.

48. Ted Peters, *For the Love of Children: Genetic Technology and the Future of the Family* (Louisville, KY: Westminster John Knox Press, 1996), 65. Peters's position is based on his rejection of the "inheritance myth," or the idea that "the biological connection between parents and children is definitive of their relationship" (26). Peters argues to the contrary that Christians have no "theological stake" in prioritizing inherited biology because Jesus displayed "low regard for . . . DNA inheritance or kin altruism" as he "takes our positive experience of intrafamilial love and then expands it beyond genetic kin limits" (27).

49. Peters, *For the Love of Children*, 65.

50. Maggie Kirkman with a concluding section by Alice Kirkman, "Sister-to-Sister Gestational 'Surrogacy' 13 Years On: A Narrative of Parenthood," *Journal of Reproductive and Infant Psychology* 20.3 (2002): 135–147 at 144–145.

51. Susan Golombok et al., "Children Born through Reproductive Donation: A Longitudinal Study of Psychological Adjustment," *Journal of Child Psychology and Psychiatry* 54.6 (2013): 653–660 at 657.

52. Vasanti Jadva et al., "Surrogacy Families 10 Years On: Relationship with the Surrogate, Decisions over Disclosure and Children's Understanding of Their Surrogacy," *Human Reproduction* 27.10 (2012): 3008–3014 at 3011–3012.

53. Dani Shapiro, for example, was eager to meet and get to know her biological

father and ultimately did. She leaves unresolved in *Inheritance* what obligations she believes she would have to other half-siblings who, if discovered in the future from subsequent DNA testing, might also hope to find their (same) biological father, particularly since he and his wife have explicitly told her of their hopes she will maintain their privacy (247–248).

54. van den Akker, *Surrogate Motherhood Families*, 187.

55. The name of the principle itself is inspired by the popular motto and the organizations and books committed to this goal. These include the Trust Women Foundation whose mission is to "open clinics that provide abortion care in underserved communities so that all women can make their own decisions about their health care" (https://trustwomen.org/), signs and posters at protest rallies and marches in support of abortion rights, and Rebecca Todd Peters's book, *Trust Women: A Progressive Christian Argument for Reproductive Justice* published by Beacon Press in 2018.

56. In one British study of families expanded by surrogacy, 77% of surrogate mothers who were relatives or friends of the commissioning couple prior to the start of the arrangement were the ones who initiated the idea of helping them achieve their parenting dreams through surrogacy. Fiona MacCallum et al., "Surrogacy: The Experience of Commissioning Couples," *Human Reproduction* 18.6 (2003): 1334–1342 at 1337.

57. See L. A. Paul, *Transformative Experiences* (New York: Oxford University Press, 2014) and Fiona Woollard, "Mother Knows Best: Pregnancy, Applied Ethics, and Epistemically Transformative Experiences," *Journal of Applied Philosophy* 38:1 (2021): 155–171.

58. Woollard, "Mother Knows Best," 158.

59. Woollard, 164.

60. Kirkman and Kirkman, "Sister-to-Sister Gestational 'Surrogacy' 13 Years On," 137, 142, 160.

61. She concludes in *Surrogate Motherhood Families* from both her own studies and from the findings of others: "Most surrogates report their experience as providing them with an enormous amount of satisfaction at having been instrumental in fulfilling a dream of a most desired baby for their commissioning couple. Some were so happy with their role as surrogate mother that they were willing to do it a second or third time for the same or other couples; others were happy that they met commissioning couples and became their friends" (citations omitted, 89).

62. As some abortion research shows, only a small percentage of women who have had abortions report experiencing "abortion regret" and many others do not find their decision to have terminated an unintentional and unwanted pregnancy to have been difficult. For more on these points, see Rebecca Todd Peters, *Trust Women* and Corinne H. Rocca et al., "Emotions and Decision Rightness over Five Years Following an Abortion: An Examination of Decision Difficulty and Abortion Stigma," *Social Science & Medicine* 248 (2020), https://doi.org/10.1016/j.socscimed.2019.112704.

63. Maura A. Ryan, *Ethics and Economics of Assisted Reproduction: The Cost of Longing* (Washington, D.C.: Georgetown University Press, 2001), 25.

64. See especially chapter 6 of Farley, *Just Love*.

65. Alison Bailey, "Reconceiving Surrogacy: Toward a Reproductive Justice Account of Indian Surrogacy," *Hypatia* 26.4 (2011): 715–741 at 721, 735.

66. Gay male couples in most jurisdictions in Australia who had been precluded from legally adopting children had been turning to surrogacy and other means (e.g., co-parenting with lesbian couples or singles) for decades to expand their families. To be sure, legal discrimination against same-sex couples was finally removed in all Australian states and territories in April 2018. See Dean A. Murphy, *Gay Men Pursuing Parenthood through Surrogacy: Reconfiguring Kinship* (Sydney, Australia: University of New South Wales Press, 2015), 15–16.

67. See, for example, Beth Braverman, "How Much Surrogacy Costs and How to Pay for It," *US News and World Report*, Jun 2, 2022; Genevieve Brown, "How Much Is IVF? Surrogacy? Adoption? Here Are the Financial Costs of Infertility," *Today*, Apr 26, 2022; David Dodge, "What to Know before Your Surrogacy Journey," *New York Times*, Apr 17, 2020.

68. National Council of Churches in Christ in the U.S.A. (NCC), "Fearfully and Wonderfully Made: A Policy on Human Biotechnologies," §IIB, adopted Nov 8, 2006, http://nationalcouncilofchurches.us/common-witness/2006/biotech.php.

69. See World Health Organization, "Infertility," Sep 14, 2020, https://www.who.int/news-room/fact-sheets/detail/infertility and World Health Organization, "Infertility: Who Response," https://www.who.int/health-topics/infertility#tab=tab_3.

70. van den Akker, *Surrogate Motherhood Families*, 22, 76.

71. Toni Bond, "Faithful Voices: Creating a Womanist Theo-Ethic of Reproductive Justice," PhD diss., Claremont School of Theology, 2020, 178–179. Of course, Black people not being well-represented as either IPs or as surrogates may be connected to reasons other than lack of access to IVF. There may also be greater wariness and distrust of invasive medical interventions owing in part to histories of medical abuse and distrust, cultural stigma surrounding surrogacy as a social practice, and other ways to respond to infertility.

72. For supporting evidence for these claims, Alexandra Kimball cites the failed attempts to attract adequate funding for programs in sub-Saharan Africa to diagnose and treat women for infertility (where contagious diseases lead many women to suffer from secondary infertility) due to the "perception that the area is already overpopulated." She also observes that many of the free or low-cost women's health clinics in North Africa that serve large numbers of women of color provide "birth control, early pregnancy care, and abortion-referral services, but not workups or treatment for infertility" (Kimball, *The Seed*, 49). To be sure, networks such as Fertility for Colored Girls (https://www.fertilityforcoloredgirls.org/) help community members "pool human and narrative resources to help African American women cope with issues related to infertility" as they discuss topics such as "fibroid complications, miscarriages, and biological unknowns that may serve as medical roadblocks to motherhood." See Stephanie Buckhanon Crowder, *When Momma Speaks: The Bible and Motherhood from a Womanist Perspective* (Louisville, KY: Westminster John Knox Press, 2016), 49.

73. Abha Khetarpal and Satendra Singh, "Infertility: Why Can't We Classify This Inability as Disability," *Australasian Medical Journal* 5.6 (2012): 334–339 at 337–338.

74. To illustrate, Massachusetts state law requires health insurance companies that provide pregnancy-related benefits to also cover infertility diagnosis and treatment. The law defines infertility as "the condition of a presumably healthy individual who is unable to conceive or produce conception during a one-year period." Insurance is not offered for gay men because "the fact that medical help is needed is not based on infertility, but rather attempting pregnancy with a male partner." Insurance help is, however, available for women (even in same-sex couples). But to be eligible for coverage, most plans will require women thirty-five years old or younger to pay out-of-pocket for twelve cycles of IUI or IVC without conceiving (to demonstrate infertility) or if over thirty-five, paying out-of-pocket for six cycles of IUI or IVF without conceiving before becoming eligible for (covered) infertility diagnosis and treatment. See American Society for Reproductive Medicine, State Infertility Laws: Massachusetts, https://www.reproductivefacts.org/resources/state-infertility-insurance-laws/states/massachussetts/ and "Insurance Coverage for LGBTQ Patients," BostonIVF, http://www.gayivf.com/affording-treatment/insurance.cfm.

75. See "How Starbucks Covers Pricey In Vitro Fertilization for Even Its Part Time Employees," Sep 5, 2017, https://www.cbsnews.com/news/starbucks-offers-in-vitro-fertilization-employees/ and Heidi Peiper, "Timeline: Starbucks History of LGBTQIA2+ Inclusion," May 16, 2022, https://stories.starbucks.com/stories/2019/starbucks-pride-a-long-legacy-of-lgbtq-inclusion/.

76. Margaret P. Battin, "Bioethics," in *A Companion to Applied Ethics*, ed. R. G. Frey and Christopher Heath Wellman (Malden, MA: Wiley-Blackwell, 2005), 306.

Chapter 6

1. The one exception to pregnancy being easy for me was the undiagnosed postpartum mild depression I felt for a few weeks some ten months after I bore my first son.

2. As noted in previous chapters, these difficulties include the tension my surrogacy created between my parents and me, the awkward contract stage with Katie and Steven, my longer than anticipated postpartum recovery due to my emergency C-section, and the stress and uncertainty I endured about possible abortion scenarios and the IPs' plans for their daughter's nutrition involving continued use of my body.

3. Ethics and Religious Liberty Commission (ERLC), "Issue Analysis: Surrogacy," Southern Baptist Convention, Jul 10, 2014, https://erlc.com/resource-library/articles/issue-analysis-surrogacy. Heather Jacobson who interviewed sixty-three persons during 2009–2012 and frequented online surrogacy boards from 2009 to 2015 estimates that first-time surrogates usually earn between $20,000 and $35,000 for successfully completing a surrogacy journey. See her *Labor of Love: Gestational Surrogacy and the Work of Making Babies* (New Brunswick, NJ: Rutgers University Press, 2016), 2–3.

A 2018 study of 204 U.S. gestational surrogates conducted by two women's health researchers also found their mean base compensation to be $27,162.80—a figure matching the base pay of $20,000–$35,000 gestational surrogates commonly self-report in online discussion forums, with repeat surrogates and those working in hot spots like California reporting higher amounts. See Erika L. Fuchs and Abbey B. Berenson, "Outcomes for Gestational Carriers versus Traditional Surrogates in the United States," *Journal of Women's Health* 27.5 (2018): 640–645 at 641.

4. Delores Williams, *Sisters in the Wilderness: The Challenge of Womanist God-Talk* (New York: Orbis, 2013 [1993]), 73–74.

5. This letter is reproduced in Vivian Wang, "Surrogate Pregnancy Battle Pits Progressives against Feminists," *New York Times*, Jun 12, 2019, https://www.nytimes.com /2019/06/12/nyregion/surrogate-pregnancy-law-ny.html.

6. Allen Verhey also argues persons who put their sperm, eggs, or wombs on the market have reduced themselves to the "status of the animated tools of reproductive technologies," with "animated tool" being "Aristotle's definition of a slave." See his *Reading the Bible in the Strange World of Medicine* (Grand Rapids, MI: Eerdmans, 2003), 266-267.

7. Allen Verhey, *Reading the Bible in the Strange World of Medicine*, 266, 279.

8. See §114 of the European Parliament, "Annual Report on Human Rights and Democracy in the World 2014 and the European Union's Policy on the Matter (2015/2229(INI))," Nov 30, 2015, A8–0344/2015, https://www.europarl.europa.eu/do ceo/document/A-8-2015-0344_EN.html. They reaffirmed in their 2021 EU Strategy for Gender Equality that "sexual exploitation for surrogacy and reproductive purposes . . . is unacceptable and a violation of human dignity and human rights." European Parliament, "EU Strategy for Gender Equality 2019/2169(INI)," Jan 21, 2021, A9–0234 /2020, §32, https://www.europarl.europa.eu/doceo/document/TA-9-2021-0025_EN .pdf.

9. European Parliament, "The Impact of the War against Ukraine on Women (2022/2633(RSP))," May 5, 2022; P9_TA(2022)0206, §V, §13–§14, https://www.europarl .europa.eu/doceo/document/TA-9-2022-0206_EN.html.

10. See §286 of Louisiana Surrogacy Bill HB 1102 [MM1], which has been in effect since August 1, 2016, http://www.legis.la.gov/legis/BillInfo.aspx?i=230384.

11. For the Special Rapporteur Maud de Boer-Buquicchio's statement and thematic report (A/74/162), see https://www.ohchr.org/EN/Issues/Children/Pages/Surrogacy .aspx.

12. Jacobson, *Labor of Love*, 37. Cf. "These three explanations for the rule against welfare recipients—impact on the surrogate's welfare benefits, impact on the surrogate's body, and impact on the IP-surrogate relationship—focus on the internal dynamics of ensuring successful journeys."

13. See Grace Y. Kao, "Toward a Feminist Christian Vision of Gestational Surrogacy," *Journal of the Society of Christian Ethics* 39.1 (2019): 161–179 at 178. As I have noted elsewhere, "[S]tudies show Asian American/Pacific Islander women in comparison to all other races may have a higher socioeconomic status, a greater likelihood of carrying private insurance, and be more apt to enter pregnancy free of serious comorbidities, [but] they still statistically experience higher rates of maternal morbidity and mortal-

ity than their white counterparts do. Other studies reveal that Asian/Pacific Islander women also have the highest rates of ART utilization in comparison to other racial-ethnic groups. But Asian American women tend to wait longer than their other counterparts do to begin IVF after struggling with infertility and this 'delay' can impede their success at achieving a clinical pregnancy or live birth since older age is correlated with fertility decline and reproductive loss." See Grace Y. Kao, "Rethinking Surrogacy from an Asian American Christian Ethical Perspective," in *Theologies of the Multitude for the Multitudes: The Legacy of Kwok Pui-lan*, ed. Rita Nakashima Brock and Tatsiong Benny Liew (Claremont, CA: Claremont Press, 2021), 271–292 at 278.

14. Kao, "Rethinking Surrogacy from an Asian American Christian Ethical Perspective," 280, 278.

15. Following Valerie Saiving Goldstein's groundbreaking article, "The Human Situation: A Feminine View," *Journal of Religion* 40.2 (1960): 100–112, feminist theologians and ethicists have been interrogating white male theologians' valorization of self-sacrifice and denigration of self-love.

16. Jacobson, *Labor of Love*, 51-56. See also Janice C. Ciccarelli and Linda J. Beckman, "Navigating Rough Waters: An Overview of Psychological Aspects of Surrogacy," *Journal of Social Issues* 61.1 (2005): 21–43 at 29–31.

17. Zsuzsa Berend, "The Social Context for Surrogates' Motivations and Satisfaction," *Reproductive Biomedicine Online* 29 (2014): 399–401 at 400.

18. Jacobsen, *Labor of Love*, 59.

19. Helena Ragoné, "Chasing the Blood Tie: Surrogate Mothers, Adoptive Mothers and Fathers," *American Anthropological Association* 23.2 (1996): 352–365 at 357, 355. Her book-length ethnography is *Surrogate Motherhood: Conception in the Heart* (Boulder, CO: Westview Press, 1994).

20. Ragoné, "Chasing the Blood Tie," 455.

21. Jacobson, *Labor of Love*, 67.

22. Whenever I read about American surrogates who tend to downplay their economic motives, I cannot help but think of the many undergraduate pre-med majors I have taught over the course of my professional career, who—particularly if they are middle class—have likewise found it more palatable to state altruistic than self-interested motives for their career path. That is, they have consistently emphasized how they have wanted to become doctors to "help people," with very few acknowledging they have also been drawn to the profession for its prestige, status, and pay.

23. Yuri Hibino, "Becoming a Surrogate Online: 'Message Board' Surrogacy in Thailand," *Asian Bioethics Review* 5.1 (2013): 56–72 at 59–64.

24. Amrita Pande, "Commercial Surrogacy in India: Manufacturing a Perfect Mother-Worker," *Signs: Journal of Women in Culture and Society* 35.4 (2010): 969–992 at 987–988.

25. See Amrita Pande, "Not an 'Angel', Not a 'Whore': Surrogates as 'Dirty' Workers in India," *Indian Journal of Gender Studies* 16.2 (2009): 141–173 at 168.

26. Elly Teman, *Birthing a Mother: The Surrogate Body and the Pregnant Self* (Berkeley: University of California Press, 2010), 23; see also Part III of her book.

27. In advocating for regulating surrogacy under fair trade principles as opposed to banning it, Casey Humbyrd has drawn a similar conclusion: "[H]ow is payment for surrogacy different from financial inducement for other types of work? Our will might not consent to being a house cleaner, but our poverty might. Does it follow that offering payment for house cleaning is exploitative? To quote the judicial opinion in a commercial surrogacy case, there is no evidence that surrogacy will: 'exploit poor women to any greater degree than economic necessity in general exploits them by inducing them to accept lower-paid or otherwise undesirable employment.' See her "Fair Trade International Surrogacy," *Developing World Bioethics* 9.3 (2009): 111–118 at 115, quoting the Supreme Court of California. Anna Johnson, Plaintiff and Appellant v. Mark Calvert et al., Defendants and Respondents. No. S023721, 20 May 1993.

28. See Lori B. Andrews, "Surrogate Motherhood: The Challenge for Feminists," in *The Ethics of Reproductive Technology*, ed. Kenneth D. Alpern (New York: Oxford University Press, 1992), 205–219 at 212.

29. As Lori Andrews has argued in "Surrogate Motherhood," one need not worry about a "slippery slope" when moving from compensating surrogacies to putting organs on the market because there is a key disanalogy with organ donation: "An organ is not meant to be removed from the body; it [can] endange[r] the life of the donor to live without the organ. In contrast, babies are conceived to leave the body and the life of the surrogate is not endangered by living without the child" (212).

30. Renée C. Fox and Judith P. Swazey, *Spare Parts: Organ Replacement in American Society* (New York: Oxford University Press, 2002 [1992]), 40, quoted in note 14 of N. Scheper-Hughes, "The Tyranny of the Gift: Sacrificial Violence in Living Donor Transplants," *American Journal of Transplantation* 7.3 (2007): 507–511.

31. Gary Chapman, *The Five Love Languages* (Chicago: Northfield Publishing, 1992).

32. As one intended mother who used both an egg donor and gestational surrogate recounts: "We wanted to pay, because it made the relationship feel more reciprocal. There was one woman who responded to my surrogacy listing who said she didn't want any financial compensation. Although it sounded as if she really didn't need money—she was an affluent divorcée in Sonoma County—I felt that we would need to pay her. 'That's our contribution,' I said, flummoxed—'one of the things we can give back.' Turning the lengthy labor of surrogacy into volunteer work felt as if it put tremendous pressure on the experience to be fulfilling at every moment. I worried she would back out or resent or regret it." See Melanie Therstrom, "Meet the Twiblings," *New York Times*, Dec 29, 2010; https://www.nytimes.com/2011/01/02/magazine/02 babymaking-t.html.

33. I recognize, of course, that my ability to have freely given this gift to my friends is connected to my class privilege that not all women who become pregnant for others have, meaning that whatever money I might have earned as a surrogate in California if I had charged the market rate for my services would not have made a qualitative difference in our lives, such as by paying off debts or funding my children's education in ways we wouldn't otherwise have been able to do so.

34. See John Berkman, "Gestating the Embryos of Others: Surrogacy? Adoption? Rescue?" *National Catholic Bioethics Quarterly* 3.2 (2003): 309–329 and Susan L. Bender and Phyllis Chesler, "Handmaids for Hire: Should Commercial Surrogacy Be Legalized in NYS?" *New York Law Journal*, Feb 22, 2019, https://www.law.com/new yorklawjournal/2019/02/22/handmaids-for-hire-should-commercial-surrogacy-be -legalized-in-nys/?slreturn=20190220230639. Lori B. Andrews reaches a similar con- clusion about the oddness of tolerating uncompensated, but not compensated, surro- gacies in her "Surrogate Motherhood: The Challenge for Feminists," 212.

35. Ethics Committee of the American Society for Reproductive Medicine, "Con- sideration of the Gestational Carrier: An Ethics Committee Opinion," *Fertility and Sterility* 110.6 (2018): 1017–1021 at 1020.

36. Amrita Pande has cautioned against payment schemes that involve paying in installments when the majority is paid upon delivery of the baby since such schemes would "clearly disadvantage[e] surrogates . . . in the event of a late miscarriage." See her "Cross-Body Reproductive Surrogacy in India," in *Handbook of Gestational Sur- rogacy*, ed. E. Scott Sills, 143–148 (New York: Cambridge University Press, 2016), 146. The ASRM encourages single-embryo transfer while acknowledging that there is "additional risk, burden, and costs associated with a possible multiple pregnancy" that should be "addressed in the . . . contract." Multiple gestation does involve in- creased risks, and increasing compensation when there are increased risks is common in other scenarios, but care should be taken not to create financial incen- tives for the surrogate to accept multiple embryo transfer or endure multiple gesta- tion given these increased risks of doing so. See American Society for Reproductive Medicine, "Consideration of the Gestational Carrier: An Ethics Committee Opin- ion," 1020.

37. United Nations, "Surrogacy: Special Rapporteur on the Sale and Sexual Ex- ploitation of Children," https://www.ohchr.org/en/special-procedures/sr-sale-of -children/surrogacy.

38. One area of disagreement I have with the Special Rapporteur's recommenda- tions is that the surro-mom would always retain parentage and parenting responsibil- ities at the time of birth. But my framework permits reasonable pluralism on this score, with only some following the British model (even though it is likely premised upon the idea that women would "naturally" bond with the life she has nurtured in her womb and thus might well change her mind about relinquishment), and others following the Californian model of permitting pre-birth parentage orders to take effect on the day of the child's birth.

39. Jacobson, *Labor of Love*, 81.

40. Jacobson, *Labor of Love*, 106 and Zsuzsa Berend, "The Romance of Surrogacy," *Sociological Forum* 27.4 (2012): 913–936 at 914, 928. Ragoné has argued similarly: the gift language surrogates use even while accepting compensation for their services im- plies their belief that no amount of money would ever "be sufficient to repay the debt incurred" ("Chasing the Blood Tie," 356).

41. Elly Teman and Zsuzsa Berend, "Surrogate Non-Motherhood: Israeli and US

Surrogates Speak about Kinship and Parenthood," *Anthropology & Medicine* 25.3 (2018): 296–310 at 307–308.

42. Hibino and Shimazono, "Becoming a Surrogate Online: 'Message Board' Surrogacy in Thailand," 67.

43. Pande, "Cross Border Reproductive Surrogacy in India," 147; for more about the interpersonal connections forged between surrogate and IPs, see also her "Commercial Surrogacy in India: Manufacturing a Perfect Mother-Worker," *986-988*.

44. Kalee Thompson, "Whoa, Baby! Why American Surrogates Are in Demand for Chinese Families," *Hollywood Reporter,* Nov 4, 2016, https://www.hollywoodreporter .com/news/general-news/whoa-baby-why-american-surrogates-are-demand-chinese -families-942832/. For comparable media coverage, see also Alexandra Harney, "Wealthy Chinese Seek U.S. Surrogates for Second Child, Green Card," *Reuters,* Sep 22, 2013, https://www.reuters.com/article/us-china-surrogates/wealthy-chinese-seek -u-s-surrogates-for-second-child-green-card-idUSBRE98L0JD20130922; and Ivan Watson and Connie Young, "California Mom, Chinese Dads: The Story of an American Surrogate," *CNN Money,* Aug 24, 2015, https://money.cnn.com/2015/08/24/news /surrogacy-china-american-mom/index.html.

45. In a National Science Foundation (NSF)–funded qualitative study of reproductive travel where more than 125 couples from nearly fifty countries were interviewed, the researchers found their subjects bristling at the concept: "Their own travel, they explain, is undertaken out of the desperate need for a child and is highly stressful and costly. Because reproductive tourism implies fun, leisure, and holidays under the sun, it is a term that is cavalier and insensitive. . . . In virtually every case, infertile couples describe their preferences *not* to travel if only legal, trustworthy, and economical services were made available closer to home" (905). See Marcia C. Inhorn and Pasquale Patrizio, "Rethinking Reproductive 'Tourism' as Reproductive 'Exile,'" *Fertility and Sterility* 92.3 (2009): 904–906 at 905.

46. It is worth noting that the second portion of this catastrophe is impossible when the U.S. is the destination country given the U.S. policy of birthright citizenship, which is one of the many reasons accounting for the U.S.'s popularity as a global surrogacy spot for foreign intended parents.

47. These disaster examples include a controversial case in 2010 when married Spanish men had a child through a California-based surrogate (the surrogate was the child's legal mother and surrogacy contracts are considered null and void in Spain), and the men could only keep the child after department of the Ministry of Justice issued an Instrucción and an Italian court ordering a surrogate-born child born abroad of a Russian women to be removed from his Italian parents and placed in a foster home until the European Court of Human Rights ruling that the decision violated Article 8 of the European Convention on Human Rights in 2015. See Alex Finkelstein et al., "Surrogacy Law and Policy in the U.S.: National Conversation Informed by Global Lawmaking," Columbia Law School Sexuality and Gender Law Clinic (2016), 12–13.

48. Owen Bowcott, "Unregistered Surrogate-born Children Creating 'Legal Time-

bomb,' Judge Warns," *The Guardian*, May 18, 2015, https://www.theguardian.com /lifeandstyle/2015/may/18/unregistered-surrogate-born-children-creating-legal-time bomb-judge-warns.

49. See especially Art 7.1 and 24.3 of the Convention of the Rights of the Child (CRC), Art 15 of the Universal Declaration of Human Rights, and Art 24.2-33 of the International Covenant on Civil and Political Rights.

50. As Amrita Pande has argued, because the "desire for genetic babies is unlikely to diminish in the near future" and reproductive technologies already exist to potentially fulfill them, any attempts to ban surrogacy through prohibitive national laws will "just push it underground" or to greener pastures. See Pande, "Cross-Border Reproductive Surrogacy in India," 145.

51. Viveca Söderström-Anttila et al., "Surrogacy: Outcomes for Surrogate Mothers, Children and the Resulting Families—A Systematic Review," *Human Reproduction Update* 22.2 (2016): 260–276 at 262.

52. See, for example, Council of Europe, "*Mennesson v. France* (2014)," https://www .coe.int/en/web/impact-convention-human-rights/-/france-recognises-family-ties-of -parents-of-surrogate-children, Mulon Associés, "What About the Legal Status of the Parents of a Child Born out of Surrogacy?" Feb 5, 2021, https://www.mulon-associes. com/en/our-news/admin-user/what-about-the-legal-status-of-the-parents-of-a-child -born-out-of-surrogacy/ and Jérôme Courduriès, "At the Nation's Doorstep: The Fate of Children in France Born via Surrogacy," *Reproductive Biomedicine and Society Online* 7 (2018): 47–54.

53. United Nations, "Surrogacy: Special Rapporteur on the Sale and Sexual Exploitation of Children," https://www.ohchr.org/en/special-procedures/sr-sale-of-chil dren/surrogacy. See her thematic report presented at the 37th session of the Human Rights Council in March 2018 for details (A/HRC/37/60).

54. See the various documents and reports in the Hauge Conference on Private International Law, "The Parentage/Surrogacy Project," https://www.hcch.net/en/proj ects/legislative-projects/parentage-surrogacy. The Hague's "Preliminary Report on International Surrogacy Arrangements" was issued in 2012 and a final report is expected to be submitted to the Council on General Affairs and policy (CGAP) of the Hague in 2023.

55. Humbyrd, "Fair Trade International Surrogacy," 116–117.

56. See "Up to 1,000 Babies Born to Surrogate Mothers Stranded in Russia " *The Guardian*, Jul 29, 2020; https://www.theguardian.com/lifeandstyle/2020/jul/29/up-to -1000-babies-born-to-surrogate-mothers-stranded-in-russia and Margaret E. Swain and Colin James Rogerson, "Addressing Legal Issues in Cross-Border Gestational Surrogacy: Current Topics and Trends," *Fertility and Sterility* 115.2 (2021): 268–273.

57. Swain and Rogerson, "Addressing Legal Issues in Cross-Border Gestational Surrogacy," 269–270.

58. See "Up to 1,000 Babies Born to Surrogate Mothers Stranded in Russia and Swain and Rogerson, "Addressing Legal Issues in Cross-Border Gestational Surrogacy.

59. See, for example, Drew Weisholtz, "They're in the U.S., Their Babies Were Born

in the Ukraine. Now They're Working to Get Them Out," *Today Show*, Mar 1, 2022, https://www.today.com/parents/babies/us-parents-working-save-preemie-twins -born-surrogate-ukraine-rcna18079 and Kim Bellware, "They Found a Surrogate in Ukraine. Now a U.S. Couple Must Get Their Preemie Twins out of a War Zone," *Washington Post*, Mar 1, 2022, https://www.washingtonpost.com/nation/2022/02/27 /ukraine-russia-babies-surrogates/.

60. Ido Ziv and Yael Freund-Eschar, "The Pregnancy Experience of Gay Couples Expecting a Child through Overseas Surrogacy," *Family Journal* 23.2 (2015): 158–166. This study highlighted the importance of the intended parents establishing a close relationship with their surrogate which is "customary in the United States but generally not in countries such as India" (158).

61. Nicola Carone, Roberto Baiocco, and Vittorio Lingiardi, "Italian Gay Fathers' Experiences of Transnational Surrogacy and Their Relationships with the Surrogate Pre- and Post-Birth," *Reproductive Biomedicine Online* 34 (2017):181–190 at 185, 186.

62. Teman and Berend, "Surrogate Non-Motherhood," 301, 307.

63. Miranda Davis, ed. *Babies for Sale: Transnational Surrogacy, Human Rights, and the Politics of Reproduction* (London: Zed Books, 2017), 26, 58, 63, 86, 239.

64. Daisy Deomampo, "Transnational Surrogacy in India: Interrogating Power and Women's Agency," *Frontiers: A Journal of Women Studies* 34.3 (2013): 167–188 at 173.

65. Virginia Rozée, Sayeed Unisa, and Elise de La Rochebrochard, "The Social Paradoxers of Commercial Surrogacy in Developing Countries: India before the New Law of 2018," *BMC Women's Health* 20.234 (2020), 7, 10, https://doi.org/10.1186/s12905-020 -01087-2.

66. Deomampo, "Transnational Surrogacy in India," 176, 184, 172.

67. Deomampo, 177, 18.

68. Sharon Jacob, *Reading Mary Alongside Indian Surrogate Mothers: Violent Love, Oppressive Liberation, and Infancy Narratives* (New York: Palgrave Macmillan, 2015), xviii, 45, 47; cf. Matt 1:17. For a comparison of Jacob's reading with two other feminist scholars of religion of Asian heritage, see Kao, "Rethinking Surrogacy from an Asian American Christian Ethical Perspective."

69. Jacob, *Reading Mary Alongside Indian Surrogate Mothers*, 61.

70. Amrita Pande, "Transnational Commercial Surrogacy in India: To Ban or Not to Ban," in *Babies for Sale*, 328–343 at 332.

71. See Amrita Pande, *Wombs in Labor: Transnational Commercial Surrogacy in India* (New York: Columbia University Press, 2014) 122.

72. Pande, *Wombs in Labor*, 172. Pande in "Transnational Commercial Surrogacy in India: To Ban or Not to Ban" argues that countries that permit (only) altruistic surrogacy are "naïve," since prohibiting compensated arrangements does nothing to "reduce the exploitative potential of this industry or empower its workers" (338).

73. See Elizabeth F. Schwartz, "LGBT Issues in Surrogacy: Present and Future," *Handbook of Gestational Surrogacy: International Clinical Practice and Policy Issues*, ed. E. Scott Sills, 55–61 (Cambridge, UK: Cambridge University Press, 2016), 59.

74. There is some evidence some intended parents are traveling abroad for "non-medical sex selection of embryos" (2). See Carmel Shalev et al., "Ethics and Regulation of Inter-Country Medically Assisted Reproduction: A Call for Action," *Israel Journal of Health Policy Research* 5:59 (2016), https://doi.org/10.1186/s13584-016-0117-0.

75. Helena Ragoné, "Surrogate Motherhood and American Kinship," in *Kinship and Family: An Anthropological Reader*, ed. Robert Parkin and Linda Stone, 342–361 (Malden, MA: Blackwell, 2004) at 349. In a different context, sociologist Amrita Pande who has conducted ethnographic studies on surrogates in Anand, India, for over a decade has acknowledged how the social stigma surrounding surrogacy is partly tied to "lack of information—people are not aware of the reproductive technology which separates pregnancy from sexual intercourse" and the popular media, where the portrayal of commercial surrogacy often "equate[s] surrogacy with sex—an infertile wife agrees to bring a sex worker home who is then impregnated by her husband through normal intercourse." See her "Not an 'Angel', Not a 'Whore': Surrogates as 'Dirty' Workers in India," *Indian Journal of Gender Studies* 16.2 (2009): 141–173 at 154–155.

76. As anthropologist Helena Ragoné correctly observes in her groundbreaking ethnography, the link between sexual intercourse and reproduction may have been severed by ART, but the two are still symbolically connected through the birth of a child. She recounts one intended father, James, really empathizing with their surrogate's husband (Mark), noting that he doesn't "understand how he [Mark] could let his wife have another man's child" because James himself couldn't if their roles were reversed. See her *Surrogate Motherhood*, 122.

77. For Nevada, see Nev. Rev. Stat. NRS 126.500–126.810 and Creative Family Connections, "Gestational Surrogacy in Nevada," https://www.creativefamilyconnections.com/us-surrogacy-law-map/nevada/. For Maine, see Title 19-A: Domestic Relations, Chapter 61: Maine Parentage Act, Subchapter 8: Gestational Carrier Agreement, §1931 Eligibility to Enter Gestational Carrier Agreement, E; https://legislature.maine.gov/statutes/19-A/title19-Asec1931.html.

78. See Pip Trowse, "Surrogacy: Is it Harder to Relinquish Genes?" *Journal of Law and Medicine* 18.3 (2011): 614–633.

79. Vasanti Jadva et al., "Surrogacy: The Experiences of Surrogate Mothers," *Human Reproduction* 18.10 (2003): 2196–2204 at 2197, 2200. Psychologist Olga B. A. van den Akker estimates that two-thirds of Britain's pre-millennium surrogate-born children were conceived through traditional surrogacy. See her *Surrogate Motherhood Families* (London: Palgrave Macmillan, 2017), 8.

80. This same study found that traditional surrogates maintained less frequent contact with the newly expanded families than gestational surrogates did, though no differences were found in how satisfied each group were about the amount of contact maintained. See Susan Imrie and Vasanti Jadva, "The Long-Term Experiences of Surrogates: Relationships and Contact with Surrogacy Families in Genetic and Gestational Surrogacy Arrangements," *Reproductive Biomedicine Online* 29 (2014): 425–335 at 430–431.

81. Traditional surrogates should meet all standard eligibility requirements set by

reputable fertility clinics, including having had at least one successful childbirth before without incident since it is unknown whether someone with no prior experience can even become pregnant and safely carry to term and also cannot give truly informed consent about undergoing all that pregnancy involves for someone else. Because traditional surrogacy is more frowned upon and involves fewer steps to achieve a pregnancy, there might be greater temptations for parties to "go indy" by not involving a fertility clinic or surrogacy agency/charity.

In a popular magazine, Lindsay Curtis provides a first-person account of becoming a traditional surrogate at twenty-three and again fifteen months later. She writes of "throw[ing] convention to the wayside" and agreeing to become pregnant for others in an independent arrangement without ever having had children herself. She recounts it was "impossible to stay detached," and while she "do[esn't] regret the two lives [she] helped create" and finds "joy knowing that there are two families raising beloved daughters" through her actions, she admits she would not have done it had she had been a mother first (as she is now). In her words, "As a young woman without children, I had no way of knowing exactly what I was giving up. Now that I'm a parent and truly enjoy motherhood, I'm certain I couldn't carry a baby and part with her or her ever again." See Lindsay Curtis, "I Was a Traditional Surrogate and This Is What It Was Like," *Parents,* May 8, 2019, https://www.parents.com/pregnancy/giving-birth /stories/i-was-a-traditional-surrogate-and-this-is-what-it-was-like/.

82. Jacobson, *Labor of Love:,* 57–58.

83. Teman and Berend, "Surrogate Non-Motherhood," 296–310 at 302. Teman is referencing her earlier, first-of-its-kind ethnography of Jewish-Israeli gestational surrogates in *Birthing a Mother.*

84. Teman and Berend, "Surrogate Non-Motherhood," 300, 304.

85. Olga van den Akker, "Genetic and Gestational Surrogate Mothers' Experience of Surrogacy," *Journal of Reproductive and Infant Psychology* 21.2 (2003): 145–161 at 156. See also her *Surrogate Motherhood Families,* 100.

86. See Jennifer Readings et al., "Secrecy, Disclosure and Everything In-Between: Decisions of Parents of Children Conceived by Donor Insemination, Egg Donation and Surrogacy," *Reproductive Biomedicine* 22.5 (2011): 485–495 at 491, 493 and Vasanti Jadva et al. "Surrogacy Families 10 Years On: Relationship with the Surrogate, Decisions over Disclosure and Children's Understanding of Their Surrogacy Origins," *Human Reproduction* 27.10 (2012): 3008–3014 at 3013.

87. Readings et al., "Disclosure Decisions of Donor Insemination, Egg Donation, and Surrogacy Parents," 492–493.

88. As Olga B. A. van den Akker notes in *Surrogate Motherhood Families,* some couples begin with gestational surrogacy and only turn to traditional surrogacy after repeated failures of their preferred method (9). That said, there is a greater possibility of the surrogate contracting an infectious disease through insemination, especially if it takes place outside of a clinical setting.

89. Linda Layne, "Gay Fatherhood via Surrogacy: A Feminist-Health-Informed Reading of Five Memoirs," *Reproductive Biomedicine and Society Online* 7 (2018): 76–79 at 78.

90. In a study of gay men who became fathers through surrogacy, one couple (Russell and Anthony) successfully entered into an "informal traditional surrogacy" arrangement with a mutual friend (Wendy) without involving clinical intervention. See Deborah Dempsey, "Surrogacy, Gay Male Couples and the Significance of Biogenetic Paternity," *New Genetics and Society* 32.1 (2013): 37–53 at 45.

91. See Dempsey, "Surrogacy, Gay Male Couples and the Significance of Biogenetic Paternity," 49–50. In a separate study, one couple open about biogenetic paternity (Kevin and Rick) described themselves as having a direct biological connection with their daughter because Rick's sister had been their egg donor. See Dean A. Murphy, *Gay Men Pursuing Parenthood via Surrogacy: Reconfiguring Kinship* (Sydney, Australia: University of North South Wales Press, 2015), 141.

Conclusion

1. See Andrew Marszal, "Indian Woman Gives Birth at 72 With Help of IVF," *The Telegraph*, May 10, 2016, https://www.telegraph.co.uk/news/2016/05/10/indian-woman -gives-birth-at-70-with-help-of-ivf/; Courtney Hutchison, "Labor of Love: Woman Carries Her Daughter's Baby," *ABC News*, Feb 14, 2011; Sam Cabal, "Twins Born from Embryos Frozen 30 Years Ago," *BBC New*, https://www.bbc.com/news/world-us -canada-63718914; Alyssa Schnell, "Breastfeeding without Giving Birth," *La Leche League*, Mar 23, 2020, https://www.llli.org/breastfeeding-without-giving-birth-2/.

2. Neha Dahiya and Suneela Garg, "Three-Parent Baby: Is It Ethical?" *Indian Journal of Medical Ethics* 3.2 (2018): 169 and B. P. Jones et al., "Uterine Transplantation in Transgender Women," *BJOG: An International Journal of Obstetrics and Gynaecology* 126.2 (2018): 152–156; Eleanor Robertson, "Feminists, Get Ready: Pregnancy and Abortion Are about to Be Disrupted," *The Guardian*, Oct 12, 2015, https://www.theguardian .com/commentisfree/2015/oct/12/feminists-get-ready-pregnancy-and-abortion-are -about-to-be-disrupted.

3. After successfully gestating lamb fetuses in artificial wombs, the team at Children's Hospital of Philadelphia (CHOP) is hoping to make "biobags" to save extremely premature babies (e.g., 20–24 weeks). See Emily A. Partridge et al., "An Extra-Uterine System to Physiologically Support the Extreme Premature Lamb," *Nature Communications*, Apr 25, 2017; https://doi.org/10.1038/ncomms15112 and Jenny Kleeman, "Parents Can Look at Their Foetus in 'Real Time': Are Artificial Wombs the Future?" *The Guardian*, Jun 27, 2020, https://www.theguardian.com/lifeandstyle/2020/jun/27 /parents-can-look-foetus-real-time-artificial-wombs-future.

INDEX

AAP (American Academy of Pediatricians), 108, 219n68, 219n69
abnormalities. See congenital anomalies; disabilities
 chromosomal, 18, 110
 congenital, 166
 fetal, 110, 118, 134, 135, 223n25
 uterine, 19
abortion. See pregnancy termination
abortion rights, 60, 63, 75, 111, 132, 227n55
Abraham/Abram (biblical), 13, 24, 101
 See also Bible
access to surrogacy/fertility services, 72, 87, 96, 184, 228n71
 bans on, 29, 31
 global inequities in, 147
 for same-sex couples, 103, 149, 178
ACOG (American College of Obstetricians and Gynecologists), 22, 95, 132, 134, 200n17, 224n30
activists, 5, 64, 92, 156, 157, 213n16
 reproductive justice, 99, 176, 179
adolescents, 51, 52, 137, 138, 140, 141, 202n47, 215n28
adoptees, 44, 51, 70, 104, 137, 138, 210n60, 226n45

international, 52
 from Thailand, 71
adoption, 207n37, 210n56, 210n59, 210n60, 215n31, 225–226n45, 228n66
 advocates, 71, 81, 83, 191n2
 closed, 188
 domestic, 207n38
 embryo/prenatal, 68, 69, 70, 206n31, 207n34, 209n50
 laws, 31, 33
 ministries, 206n32
 of "needy" children, 80–83
 open, 207n38
 perceived benefits of, 72, 79–80
 proceedings, 27, 150, 196n28
 from Russia, 196n30
 scenario, 6, 33, 103, 108, 221n9
adoption agencies, 33, 71, 138
advanced maternal age (AMA), 16, 34, 100
Africa, 228n72
African Americans. See Blacks
Allen, Robin, 140
altruistic surrogacy, 13, 44, 76, 154, 179, 207n37, 236n72
 compensated vs., 158, 160, 161, 165, 185

Van den Akker, Olga B. A., 46, 115, 144,
    182, 237n79, 238n88
Van Zyl, Liezl, 131–132
Verhey, Allen, 67, 157, 206n32, 230n6
Virginia, 27, 30, 123, 195n23
vocation, 4, 5, 77, 88, 103, 149, 218n51,
    220n5
    See also call to parenthood
vulnerabilities, 93, 118, 123, 124, 157, 174,
    189
    to discrimination, 185
    as objection to surrogacy, 8
    of surrogacy triad, 171
    of surrogate-born children, 96

WADRJ (Women of African Descent for
    Reproductive Justice), 98
Walker, Alice, 92
Walker, Ruth, 131–132
Washington State, 30
Weaver, Darlene Fozard, 82, 207n34,
    210n56
Weems, Renita J., 89
welfare (public assistance), 21, 148, 159,
    230n12
well-being, 5, 76, 87, 113, 115, 169, 185
    children's, 43, 51, 52, 57, 141, 189,
    203n57
    psychological, 37, 40, 43, 48, 52, 180
    sexual and reproductive, 93
    surrogates,' 116
    of surrogates of color, 99
    women's, 176
Western countries, 29, 93, 155, 159, 168,
    214n25

Western Europe, 28
wet-nursing, 107
Whitehead, Mary Beth, 25, 38, 61, 166,
    195n19
    See also Baby M
whites, 97, 215n28, 221n9, 231n15
    among parent hopefuls, 147, 155, 168
    in cross-border surrogacy, 170
    hiring women of color, 8
    in race relations, 156
    rates of maternal morbidity, 221–
    222n13, 230–231n13
    stereotypes, 159
    in structural inequities, 146
    values of, 162
Williams, Delores, 156, 217–218n49
womanists, 92, 189
    Delores Williams, 156, 217–218n49
    Renita Weems, 89
    Toni M. Bond, 99, 147
    Wilda Gafney, 101, 217n48
Women of African Descent for Repro-
    ductive Justice (WADRJ), 98
women of color, 5, 8, 98–99, 146, 147, 158,
    221n13, 228n72
    See also Asian/Pacific Islanders;
    Blacks; SisterSong Women of Color
    Reproductive Justice Collective
women's experience, 97, 156, 216n39
women's rights, 62, 64, 73, 134, 189
Woollard, Fiona, 97, 142, 143
World Health Organization (WHO), 147,
    172, 219n69
worst-case scenarios, 22, 118, 120, 122,
    170, 171, 173

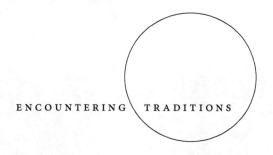

ENCOUNTERING TRADITIONS

CPSIA information can be obtained
at www.ICGtesting.com
Printed in the USA
JSHW082303060623
42800JS00002B/3